How to Pas

C000185245

Accounting

Third Level

LONDON CHAMBER of COMMERCE & INDUSTRY COMMERCIAL EDUCATION TRUST EXAMINATIONS BOARD

Maurice Sholl
FCA, FLCC, ARCM, ATCL, ALCM

M&E

Macdonald & Evans Ltd
128 Long Acre, London WC2E 9AN

A Division of Pearson Professional Limited

First published in 1996

© London Chamber of Commerce and Industry Examinations Board 1996

ISBN 0 7121 0867 X

British Library Cataloguing in Publication Data
A CIP catalogue record for this book can be obtained from the British Library

All rights reserved; no part of this publication may be reproduced, stored
in a retrieval system, or transmitted in any form or by any means, electronic,
mechanical, photocopying, recording, or otherwise without either the prior
written permission of the Publishers or a licence permitting restricted copying
in the United Kingdom issued by the Copyright Licensing Agency Ltd,
90 Tottenham Court Road, London W1P 9HE. This book may not be lent,
resold, hired out or otherwise disposed of by way of trade in any form
of binding or cover other than that in which it is published, without the
prior consent of the Publishers.

10 9 8 7 6 5 4 3 2 1

Typeset by Land & Unwin (Data Sciences) Limited
Printed and bound in Great Britain by Clays Ltd, St Ives plc

The Publishers' policy is to use paper manufactured from sustainable forests.

Contents

Introduction

This book follows the syllabus of the Third Level Accounting examination of the London Chamber of Commerce and Industry Examinations Board.

Organisation

The text is divided into 11 chapters and 4 appendices:

- Chapters 1 to 8 use the same subject headings as those in the syllabus.
- Chapters 9 to 11 refer to aims of the syllabus not specifically discussed elsewhere, namely disclosure of accounting policies, stocks and long-term contracts, and depreciation.
- Appendices 1 and 2 relate to examination technique.
- Appendix 3 summarises Statements of Standard Accounting Practice (SSAP) and Financial Reporting Standards (FRS).
- Appendix 4 gives skeleton answers to practice questions.

Format within the chapters

Chapter 1 revises some topics already covered in the Second Level text. Chapters 2 to 11 contain the following headings:

1 *Objectives* Why are the accounting entries necessary?

2 *Scenario* In what circumstances do the accounting entries arise?

3 *Methods* How are the accounting entries done?

4 *Problems* What difficulties may arise?

5 *Examples*

6 *Practice questions*

How to use this book

1 Study the text which covers the part of the chapter you are working on; if it deals with a subject covered in the First or Second Level, make sure you understand the relevant sections in the appropriate textbooks as this book assumes prior knowledge of items appearing in the earlier books.

2 Check all the examples that relate to the part of the chapter you are studying and tick off all entries as you agree the reason and the method for them. Do not leave an entry until you are quite certain why it is being made and what effect it will have.

3 Work the relevant practice questions to the part of the chapter and then check your answers with the skeleton answers given in Appendix 4. Do not look up the answers before you have worked the question as it is vital to

get practice in actually doing the question. Look back in the text to clarify any differences between your answer and the skeleton answer given. Most of the examples and practice questions have been selected from past Third Level Accounting examination papers.

4 Work the complete examination papers in Appendix 2 and as many past papers as possible. Try to work within the time limit allowed in the actual examination.

It is essential to practise your examination technique.

About the author

Maurice Sholl has a wide teaching experience in Universities and (former) Polytechnics in London and the East Midlands. His commercial activities have included practising as a Chartered Accountant, auditing in Latin America and industrial accounting in Brazil and Ireland.

He has examined in auditing and accountancy and related subjects for the LCCIEB for well over twenty years.

1

Income statements and balance sheets for sole traders, partnerships, companies and non-trading organisations

After carefully studying this chapter you should be able to:

1 *prepare Trading and Profit & Loss Accounts for sole traders, partnerships and companies;*

2 *prepare Income & Expenditure Accounts and Receipts & Payments Accounts for non-trading organisations;*

3 *prepare Balance Sheets for sole traders, partnerships, companies and non-trading organisations.*

This book is the third volume in a series of textbooks on financial accounting. The author assumes that readers have access to and have worked through the previous volumes.

Income statements and balance sheets for sole traders, partnerships, companies and non-trading organisations have been considered in the first and second volumes.

In addition to meeting the requirements at First and Second Level, the Third Level Accounting candidate must be able to:

1 *understand accounting information derived from all sources;*

2 *use, appreciate and analytically interpret accounting statements and data;*

3 *prepare accounting statements and data following established concepts and conventions, including the Companies Acts, Statements of Standard Accounting Practice (SSAPs), Financial Reporting Standards (FRSs) and up-to-date presentations.*

Understand accounting information derived from all sources

The sources from which accounting information is derived are manual, mechanical and electronic. An understanding of these sources comes from careful reading and analysis of examples in textbooks, examination questions and published accounts.

In examination conditions, candidates are required to demonstrate this understanding in their use of information presented by the examiner in formats derived from various sources.

The following examples illustrate different formats: the first uses a computer printout and the second uses a columnar bank statement.

EXAMPLE 1

Computer printout

Quango Ltd trades from its head office and three branches. All purchases are made by head office and sales at all 4 outlets earn the same gross profit percentage on *cost to head office*. Quango Ltd adopts a different policy for each branch when pricing transfers between head office and branches. Transfers between branches are priced at the original price for those goods which was charged by the head office to the branch. Transfers between branches are only made to satisfy customer orders at the receiving branches and do not occur near the end of a quarterly accounting period.

Due to a fault in a computer disk, the printout for stock control for the quarter ended 31 March Year 21 had some missing figures. The printout, with the missing figures marked with an asterisk(*), was as follows:

	Head office £'000	Branch 1 £'000	Branch 2 £'000	Branch 3 £'000
Stock 1 January	1,210	200	66	NIL
Purchases	4,000	NIL	NIL	NIL
Goods from head office	NIL	2,080	737	500
Goods from Branch 3	NIL	NIL	*	NIL
Total of above	*	*	*	*
Goods to Branch 1	−1,040	NIL	NIL	NIL
Goods to Branch 2	−670	NIL	NIL	−10
Goods to Branch 3	−500	NIL	NIL	NIL
Stock 31 March	−1,300	−*	−*	−40
Cost of goods sold	*	*	*	*
Gross profit	*	*	*	*
Sales	3,400	2,060	812	*

Required

(a) Copy out the above printout and starting with the head office column, fill in the spaces marked with an asterisk★. Note: make all calculations to the nearest £.   (11 marks)

(b) Identify the three bases used by the head office of Quango Ltd for charging goods to its branches. Show calculations.   (3 marks)

(c) State one benefit to Quango Ltd of using each of the three bases identified in **(b)** above.   (3 marks)

Total (17 marks)

Solution

(a)

	Head office £'000	Branch 1 £'000	Branch 2 £'000	Branch 3 £'000
Stock 1 January	1,210	200	66	NIL
Purchases	4,000	NIL	NIL	NIL
Goods from head office	NIL	2,080	737	500
Goods from Branch 3	NIL	NIL	10	NIL
Total of above	5,210	2,280	813	500
Less goods at cost				
Sent to Branch 1	−1,040	NIL	NIL	NIL
Sent to Branch 2	−670	NIL	NIL	−10
Sent to Branch 3	−500	NIL	NIL	NIL
Stock 31 March	−1,300	−220	−367	−40
Cost of goods sold	1,700	2,060	446	450
Gross profit	1,700	0	366*	450
Sales	3,400	2,060	812	900

Note to the solution

★The gross profit of Branch 2 is calculated as follows:

	Invoice price to Branch 2 £'000	Gross profit £'000		Selling price £'000
Gross profit at branch on:				
Goods from head office	720	396	(792 × 50%)	792
Gross profit at head office		40	(396 × 10%)	
Gross profit at branch		356	(792 × 50% × 90%)	
Goods from Branch 3	10	10	(at CP)	20
	730	366		812

(b) Goods were invoiced by head office to branches on the following bases:

- Branch 1: at selling price as head office itself has gross profit of 50% and goods invoiced to Branch 1 for £2,080 cost £1,040

- Branch 2: at cost price + 10% because goods invoiced to Branch 2 for £737 originally cost £670

- Branch 3: at cost price because goods invoiced to Branch 3 for £500 cost £500

(c) The selling price controls branch stock debtors and cash, but involves much recording.

The cost price + 10% might reflect costs and expenses incurred by head office in sending goods to a branch.

The cost price is the easiest method but gives limited control and discloses gross profit to branch staff.

EXAMPLE 2

Columnar bank statement

B Fuddle began trading on 1 January when he opened a business bank account with Elduff Bank plc. He did not keep books of account. His business bank statements for January showed:

Elduff Bank plc Current account with Mr B Fuddle

Jan	(notes added by B Fuddle)	Cheque number	Withdrawals £'000	Deposits £'000	Balance £'000
1	B Fuddle (transfer from private account)			10.0	10.0
2	X Supplier of Goods plc	1	4.0		6.0
3	Office Furniture Ltd	4	7.0		1.0 DR
13	Y Goods for Resale Ltd	2	3.9		4.9 DR
13	Cash (from sales)			4.0	0.9 DR
16	Cash (from sales)			9.8	8.9
31	Bank charges and expenses		0.1		8.8
31	B Fuddle (transfer to private account)	6	1.7		7.1

Inspection of B Fuddle's cheque book showed:

1   Cheque number 3 was destroyed on 4 January.

2   Cheque number 5, for £8,940, drawn on 25 January, payable to Z Wholesale Goods plc for goods bought for resale, was presented in Feburary.

3   Cheque number 7 for £1,100, drawn on 31 January, was a refund in respect of sales returns for January.

The bank statements for B Fuddle's private bank account show that the bank had credited in error his private bank account instead of his business bank account with £3,000 from cash sales which he paid into the bank on 30 January. The bank had also debited in error his private bank account instead of his business account with the standing order for £2,400 in respect of the business rent for the period 1 January to 31 March. B Fuddle states he paid all cash received from sales into his business bank account *after* paying business expenses of £3,100 and private expenses of £1,000. All suppliers were paid by cheque on the date of purchase of goods; all sales were for cash at a fixed mark-up of 25%. There was no stock difference at 31 January. The office furniture delivered on 1 January will have a residual value of 10% of cost after 7 years working life; B Fuddle agrees to write off depreciation on a monthly basis using the straight line method from the date of acquisition.

Required

Prepare, *in vertical layout*, B Fuddle's:

(a) Trading and profit and loss account for the month of January   (10 marks)

(b) Balance sheet at 31 January   (7 marks)

Total (17 marks)

Solution

(a)   **B Fuddle Trading and Profit & Loss Account for the month of January**

		£	£
Sales	(3,000 + 9,800 − 1,100 + 4,000 + 3,100 + 1,000)		19,800
Purchases	(4,000 + 3,900 + 8,940)	16,840	
Stock	(Residual)	1,000	
Cost of goods sold	(Residual)		15,840
Gross profit	(19,800 × 25 ÷ 125)		3,960
Bank charges		100	
Rent	(2,400 ÷ 3)	800	
Business expenses		3,100	
Depreciation	(7,000 × 90% ÷ 7 ÷ 12)	75	
			4,075
Net loss			115

(b)   **B Fuddle Balance Sheet at 31 March**

	£	£	£
Fixed Asset	Cost	Depn	
Office furniture	7,000	75	6,925
Current Assets			
Stock	1,000		
Prepaid rent (2,400 − 800)	1,600		
		2,600	
Liability due within one year			
Bank (7,100 + 3,000 − 8,940 − 1,100 − 2,400)		2,340	
			260
			7,185
Financed by:			
Capital introduced	10,000		
Less net loss	115	9,885	
Less drawings (1,700 + 1,000)		2,700	
			7,185

EXAMPLE 3

The following is an example of how a subject from Second Level Book-keeping and Accounts might be asked in Third Level Accounting.

X says, 'I am very annoyed because my accountant states I have made a loss. This is impossible as I paid my £12,000 savings to Y to buy a business on 1 January Year 8 and now have *more* cash in the bank than I paid for the business.'

Required

(a) Give one brief comment on X's concept of profit. (3 marks)

X continues, 'The £12,000 I paid was made up of: £3,000 for a 10-year lease of my shop from 1 January Year 8; £2,000 for fixtures which should last 8 years and then be worth £400; £4,000 for stock; and £3,000 for debtors. At 31 December Year 8 the value of my debtors is ⅓ of the value of debts I acquired and my stock is ½ of the value of stock I acquired and I owe £6,000 for goods supplied. I have kept to the trade recommendation of turning over my average stock 8 times in the year. I have paid interest at 30% pa to 30 September Year 8 on the loan of £7,000 I received from Z Finance Ltd, on 1 April Year 8. My accountant says my business expenses of £8,000 are too high as, before charging any depreciation or loan interest, they are 80% of my gross profit, but I have only paid for half of them so far. I have only drawn £1,000 from the business in the year.

Required

(b) Prepare for X for Year 8:

    (i)   Trading and profit and loss account (9 marks)

    (ii) Summarised bank account (5 marks)

Total (17 marks)

Solution

(a) Cash is not the same as profit, because we must consider the amount of all assets and liabilities. Some expenses are not paid in cash (such as depreciation) and other expenses may be paid in advance or in arrears (such as rent or electricity).

(b) (i)   **Trading and Profit & Loss Account for Year 8**

		£	£	£
Sales				34,000
Cost of goods sold				
Stock acquired		4,000		
Purchases		22,000	26,000	
Closing stock	(4,000 × ½)		2,000	
Cost of goods sold	(3,000 × 8)			24,000
Gross profit	(8,000 ÷ 80%)			10,000
Depreciation lease	(3,000 ÷ 10)		300	
Depreciation fixtures	((2,000 − 400) ÷ 8)		200	
Loan interest	(7,000 × 30% × 9/12)		1,575	
General business expenses			8,000	
				10,075
Net loss				75

(b) (ii)   **Bank Account**

	£
Cash introduced	12,000
Loan Z Finance Ltd	7,000
Debtors (3,000 + 34,000 − 1,000)	36,000
	55,000
Purchase of business	12,000
Loan interest (1,575 × 2/3)	1,050
Business expenses (8,000 ÷ 2)	4,000
Drawings	1,000
Creditors (22,000 − 6,000)	16,000
	34,050
Balance at year end	20,950
	55,000

Use, appreciate and analytically interpret accounting statements and data

In examination conditions, candidates are required to demonstrate their understanding of accounting statements and data by their comments on the accounts prepared as part of the answer or given by the examiner. The following examples from later pages of this book illustrate the type of comment required:

1. *Example of commentary on ratios*   In Cinco (Chapter 8) the candidate is presented with a set of ratios that a certain type of business is expected to achieve; the candidate must (by use of incomplete records) calculate the ratios that the business has achieved and then compare the actual ratios with the expected ones.

2. *Example of commentary on utilisation of profits earned*   In Nosetok plc (Chapter 3) the candidate has prepared final accounts for a company. The directors propose a dividend and the candidate is asked to comment on the amount: a shareholder considers the dividend inadequate. To answer this question it is necessary to consider the availability of both reserves and cash resources with which to pay the dividend.

3. *Example of intepreting comments in a directors' report*   In Quizi plc (Appendix 2) an extract from a typical directors' report is given. The candidate is required to analyse the comments and find the basis for them.

Prepare accounting statements and data, following established concepts and conventions

This heading includes:

1. Statements of Standard Accounting Practice (SSAP) and Financial Reporting Standards (FRS). Relevant extracts from the SSAPs and FRSs are in Appendix 3. Their application appears throughout the volume.

2 Up-to-date presentations. In order to keep up-to-date, it is essential for Third Level candidates to study accounts of public companies published in the financial press and the questions in Third Level Accounting examination papers.

3 Companies Acts. The book, *How to Pass Book-keeping and Accounts*, Second Level, gives examples of Profit & Loss Accounts and Balance Sheets of limited companies for internal use. Candidates for the Third Level examination must learn and apply the formats of Profit & Loss Accounts and Balance Sheets of limited companies for publication.

These formats are as follows:

Profit & Loss Account

		£'000	£'000
1	Turnover		x
2	Cost of sales		x
3	Gross profit (loss)		x
4	Distribution costs	x	
5	Administrative expenses	x	
			x
6	Other operating income		x
			x
7	Income from shares in group companies	x	
8	Income from shares in related companies	x	
9	Income from other fixed asset investments	x	
10	Other interest receivable and similar income	x	
			x
			x
11	Amounts written off investments	x	
12	Interest payable and similar charges	x	
			x
	Profit (loss) on ordinary activities before taxation		x
13	Tax on profit (loss) on ordinary activities*		x
14	Profit (loss) on ordinary activities after taxation*		x
15	Extraordinary income*	x	
16	Extraordinary charges*	x	
17	Extraordinary profit (loss)*	x	
18	Tax on extraordinary profit (loss)*	x	x
			x
19	Other taxes not shown under the above items*		x
20	Profit (loss) for the financial year		x
21	Dividends proposed for the year		x
22	Retained profit for the year		x

Comments on individual items in the Profit & Loss Account

1 Turnover is another word for total sales less total returns in the financial year.

2 Cost of sales here means cost of goods sold or services rendered. In the case of a merchanting company, it will be the cost of opening stock plus purchases less closing stock of goods for resale.

3 Gross profit (loss) is the difference between turnover and cost of sales.

4 Distribution costs are those costs incurred in selling and delivering goods to customers and will include running costs of and depreciation on delivery vehicles, salesmen's expenses, salaries and commissions, advertisements.

5 Administrative expenses are the expenses that are incurred in running the business, such as office expenses, depreciation of office equipment, cash discounts allowed, administrative remuneration, audit fees and expenses.

6 Other operating income includes discounts received and rents receivable.

7 Income from shares in group companies means dividends received on shares the company owns in other companies in which it has a controlling interest.

8 Income from shares in related companies means dividends received on shares the company owns in other companies in which it has a strong influence that does not amount to full control.

9 Income from other fixed asset investments includes dividends arising from investments in companies that are not in the group or related to the company.

10 Other interest receivable and similar income includes interest and income not included above.

11 Amounts written off investments means losses in value of investments.

12 Interest payable and similar charges includes interest on amounts borrowed by the company in the form of bank and other loans.

22 Retained profit for the year will be added to the retained profits brought forward at the beginning of the year to give the retained profits carried forward at the end of the year.

Items 13, 14, 15, 16, 17, 18 and 19 are included in the Profit & Loss Account format above in order to give the complete layout, but are not included in the Third Level Accounting syllabus.

Balance Sheet

		£'000	£'000	£'000
1	Called up share capital not paid			X
2	*Fixed assets*			
	(a) Intangible assets		X	
	(b) Tangible assets		X	
	(c) Investments		X	
				X
3	*Current assets*			
	(a) Stock	X		
	(b) Debtors, prepayments and accrued income	X		
	(c) Investments	X		
	(d) Cash at bank and in hand	X		
			X	
4	Creditors: amounts falling due within one year		X	
5	Net current assets			X
6	Total assets less amounts falling due within one year			X
7	Creditors: amounts falling due after more than one year		X	
8	Provisions for liabilities and charges		X	
				X
9	Capital and Reserves			X

Comments on individual items in the Balance Sheet

1   *Called up share capital not paid*   This is the amount that shareholders have not paid the company for allotment and calls.

2   *Fixed assets*   These are assets which a company owns (usually for a long time) in order to carry on its business. They are divided into:

   (a)   intangible assets: these may include goodwill (as far as it is not written off), patents, trade marks and similar items;

   (b)   tangible assets: these usually include land and buildings, plant and machinery, fixtures and fittings and motor vehicles;

   (c)   investments: these are investments the company intends retaining for a long time, such as shares in and loans to subsidiary and related companies.

3   *Current assets*   These are assets which a company holds (usually for a short time) intended to be realised in cash as soon as possible. They are divided into:

   (a)   stock: this may include raw materials, work in progress, finished goods, prepayments;

   (b)   debtors, prepayments and accrued income;

   (c)   investments: these are investments the company does not intend holding for a long time;

(d) cash at bank and in hand: this may include amounts on current and deposit accounts at the bank and cash.

4 *Creditors* Amounts falling due within one year may include trade creditors, short-term bank overdrafts and loans and debentures repayable within one year of the balance sheet date.

5 *Net current assets* This is a subtotal that shows the working capital of the company.

6 *Total assets less amounts falling due within one year* This is a subtotal.

7 *Creditors* Amounts falling due after more than one year; this may include any long-term debentures and bank loans due more than one year after the balance sheet date.

8 *Provisions for liabilities and charges* These include amounts the company owes for pensions.

9 *Capital and reserves* These include the issued shares of the company, reserves the company cannot distribute by way of cash dividend such as share premium and profit and loss account.

The following is an example of up-to-date presentation layout of company accounts:

EXAMPLE

For the first time the accountant of Window plc is using computer software to produce the company's final accounts for publication for Year 24. The manual prints the following:

Profit & Loss Account

Code		£	£
A	Turnover		
B	Cost of goods sold		_____
	Gross profit		
C	Distribution costs		
D	Administration cost	_____	_____
E	Income from investments		_____
	Profit on ordinary activities		
F	Proposed dividends		_____
	Retained profits for the financial year		_____

Balance Sheet

Code		£	£	£
	Fixed assets			
G	Intangible			
H	Tangible			
I	Investments	___	___	
	Current assets			
J	Stocks			
K	Debtors			
L	Investments			
M	Bank	___		
N	Liabilities falling due within one year		___	
	Net current assets			
O	Liabilities falling due after one year			___
	Financed by:			
P	Capital and reserves			___

The accountant must code all the items in the trial balance at the year end before feeding them into the computer. The accountant is considering the following items at 31 December Year 24:

1 Debenture interest for Year 24

2 Debenture interest accrued at end of Year 24

3 Debentures repayable in 5 equal instalments starting on 1 May Year 25

4 Redeemable preference shares Year 36 to Year 38

5 Interim preference dividend paid in respect of Year 24

6 Work in progress at 31 December Year 24

7 Share premium

8 Cost of machinery at 31 December Year 24

9 Patents

10 Provision for depreciation of machinery at 31 December Year 24

11 Depreciation of delivery vehicles in respect of Year 24

12 Provision for doubtful debts at 31 December Year 24

13 Shares held as temporary substitute for cash

14 Salesmen's salaries for Year 24

15 Delivery charges on goods purchased for resale in Year 24

16 Cost of computer stationery used in Year 24

Required

Code each of the entries in the trial balance. Note that some entries may require more than one code. (17 marks)

Solution

1 D	5 F	9 G	13 L
2 N	6 J	10 H	14 C
3 N & O	7 P	11 C	15 B
4 P	8 H	12 K	16 D

PRACTICE QUESTIONS

There are practice questions at the end of each chapter; candidates should work each one through without reference to the answer and then to compare their answer with that given in Appendix 4. The questions in this chapter are intended to revise the work done in the first two books and to illustrate how the topics covered in them are examined in Third Level Accounting examination questions.

1.1 The following definitions refer to terms which appear in the annual reports of limited companies:

(i) consists of stocks, debtors, short-term investments, cash at bank and cash in hand

(ii) consists of share capital, distributable and non-distributable reserves

(iii) the profits for the year due to the ordinary shareholders divided by the average number of ordinary shares in issue during the year

(iv) the total of debtors, short-term investments, cash at bank and cash in hand divided by the total of liabilities due within one year of the balance sheet date

(v) a statement showing the financial position of a company at a certain date

Required

(a) State *in no more than three words* what each of the above definitions refers to.

(5 marks)

The following is the trial balance of a limited company at 31 December Year 18.

	£'000	£'000
Work in progress	150	
Land and buildings	100	
Profit for Year 18 before appropriations		35
Creditors payable within 3 months		140
Cash	55	
Ordinary shares of £0.50 each fully paid		300
Share premium		120
Raw materials	80	
Debtors	160	
Profit & Loss Account balance at 1 January Year 18		80
Plant and machinery	170	
10% debentures Years 18/19		60
Motor vehicles	120	
Finished goods	100	
12% debentures Years 48/49		200
	935	935

The directors propose an ordinary dividend of £0.025 per share for Year 18.

Required

  (b) Calculate each of the four items you have defined in **(a) (i)**, **(ii)**, **(iii)** and **(iv)** above to the nearest decimal place.   (5 marks)

  (c) Prepare in good style the statement defined in **(a)(v)** above.   (7 marks)

                                                                            Total (17 marks)

1.2 Albal's published Profit & Loss Account for Year 20 included the following headings:

  - Administrative expenses
  - Cost of sales
  - Distributive expenses
  - Extraordinary charges
  - Gross profit
  - Interest payable
  - Profit on ordinary activities
  - Turnover

Albal plc's trial balance at 31 December Year 20 included the following items:

  1   Depreciation of lorries used to collect raw materials

  2   Depreciation of motor vehicles used to distribute goods to customers

  3   Depreciation of motor vehicles used by salesmen

  4   Depreciation of motor vehicles used by non-executive directors

  5   Remuneration of company's auditors

  6   Remuneration of production staff

  7   Remuneration of office staff

  8   Remuneration of non-executive directors

  9   Remuneration of sales staff

  10 Legal costs of collecting debts

  11 Interest on bank overdraft

  12 Interest on loan repayable in Year 28

  13 Manufacturing overhead expenses

  14 Returns inwards

  15 Provision for bad debts after adjustment at 31 December Year 20

  16 Cost of raw materials

  17 Investment in subsidiary company

  18 Uninsured fire loss of Albal plc's fourth largest building

Required

Draft Albal's profit and loss account for Year 20 in *vertical* layout showing *each* of the listed headings and under which heading, if any, each of the above 18 items will appear.   (17 marks)

1.3 Solis, Isi and Taurus are in partnership sharing residual profits and losses in the ratio of 3 : 2 : 1 respectively. Solis is entitled to a commission of 0.075% of the total gross fees received and Taurus to a commission of 0.5% of gross fees received in excess of £400,000 per annum. Isi is entitled to a salary of £4,000 per annum. All partners receive interest on their fixed capital of 5% per annum and are charged 10% on their total drawings in the year. If Taurus's share of the residual profits in any single year is less than £25,000, it is to be made up to that amount by Solis.

The following balances appeared in their books at 31 December Year 27:

	Solis £	Isi £	Taurus £
Fixed capital (unchanged for 15 years)	200,000	150,000	50,000
Current accounts at 1 January Year 27	18,375 Dr	16,600 Dr	800 Cr
Drawings for Year 27	20,000	19,000	18,000
Commission for Year 27	375	NIL	?

Staff salaries were 75% of the total fees received in the year and other expenses for the year were £9,825.

Required

Prepare for Solis, Isi and Taurus for Year 27:

   (a) the profit and loss and appropriation account;   (11 marks)

   (b) the partners' current accounts (in columnar form).   (3 marks)

After preparation of the accounts for Year 27 it was agreed that:

1   Profits and losses would be divided equally between the partners from 1 January Year 28.

2   Goodwill previously valued at £120,000 and now revalued at £210,000 should continue to be excluded from the partnership accounts.

3   The value of the partnership land and buildings should be increased in the partnership accounts by £60,000.

Required

   (c) Prepare the fixed capital accounts for Year 28 showing the necessary adjustments.   (3 marks)

                                                      Total (17 marks)

1.4 The Weer Club had 2,358 members in Year 31; 25 members owed subscriptions for Year 30 at the beginning of Year 31 but they had all paid these arrears by the end of Year 31; 29 members owed subscriptions for Year 31 at the end of Year 31; the Weer Club was certain that these arrears would all be paid eventually. No subscriptions are ever received in advance of the year to which they relate. The subscription rate was 25% higher in Year 31 than in Year 30. In Year 31, the Weer Club received £117,450 in respect of all subscriptions.

Required

   (a) Calculate the subscription rate for Year 31 and then prepare the Weer Club's subscriptions account for Year 31.   (7 marks)

In Year 31 the Weer Club had fixed expenses of £100,000 and variable expenses of £10 per member.

Required

(b) Prepare the Weer Club's income and expenditure account for Year 31.   (3 marks)

(c) Calculate how many members the Weer Club needed in Year 31 for the subscriptions income to equal the total expenses.   (3 marks)

In Year 32:

1   the subscriptions rate was increased by 20%;

2   the number of members fell by ⅑th;

3   fixed expenses remained at £100,000;

4   variable expenses remained at £10 per member.

Required

(d) Prepare the Weer Club's income and expenditure account for Year 32.

(4 marks)

Total (17 marks)

POINTS TO REMEMBER

- At Third Level, accounting information may be presented to candidates in formats derived from manual and non-manual sources.

- Candidates must be able to prepare accounts in accordance with current up-to-date accounting practice.

2

Accounting for specific partnership circumstances

After carefully studying this chapter you should be able to:

1 *account for changes in partnership interests;*

2 *account for dissolution of partnerships;*

3 *account for admission or retirement of partners;*

4 *account for conversion of a partnership into a company.*

The specific accounting circumstances dealt with in this chapter are:

1   *changes in partnership interests;*

2   *dissolution;*

3   *admission or retirement of partners;*

4   *conversion of partnership into a company.*

As each of the above topics relates to a different aspect of partnership accounting, they will be considered individually in the following pages, in the order listed. However there is a similarity in the treatment of varying profit/loss sharing ratios and movements of capital in all four circumstances.

Changes in partnership interests

Objectives

There are two objectives here:

1   to divide the profits/losses arising on a profit and loss account during the year between the partners in accordance with the changes of partnership ratios

2   to make any adjustments necessary to compensate partners for their interests in 'hidden assets' upon any change in their interests

Scenario

The partnership changes as some partners assume different levels of activity within their business. For example, a senior partner may decide to undertake less work as he gets older, and some of his duties are assumed by a younger junior partner. As a result:

1   The junior partner would expect a greater share of the profits arising after the date of the change.

2   The senior partner would expect to receive some compensation for his share of any undervaluation of assets in the books at the time of the change. This is because a revaluation would be effected at the new profit/loss sharing ratio whereas the senior partner contributed to such assets at the old ratio.

Methods

As there are two objectives there will be two methods.

1   Assume A, B and C decided to change their profit/loss sharing ratio on 1 July Year 34 and their next profit and loss account is for the year to 31 December Year 34. The format of the profit and loss account must allow the partners to find out the profits arising in the first half year so that these can be divided in the old ratio and then the profits arising in the second half year so that these can be divided in the new ratio.

Their profit and loss account must be prepared in the following format:

	Half year to 30 June	Half year to 31 December	Total for year to 31 December
Gross profit*	x	x	x
Expenses**			
Apportioned on a time basis	x	x	x
Apportioned on a turnover basis	x	x	x
Specific to either period	x	x	x
Net profit (loss)	x	x	x

Notes to the accounts

The total column may not always be necessary.

★ As the gross profit is the result of all the individual entries in the trading account it is usually only possible to apportion it on the basis of when the sales took place and what the gross profit ratio was in that period. Do not attempt to apportion each individual item appearing in the Trading Account.

★★ As it is not normally required and as it would also be time consuming to apportion each expense individually to the periods, list the expenses that are apportioned on a time basis. Then apportion the total between the periods. Similarly list and apportion the expenses that are apportioned on a turnover basis. The items that are specific to either period must be apportioned individually according to their nature.

2   There are various ways to adjust for items that are not recorded (or are undervalued) in the Balance Sheet when ratios are changed. They all give the same result: the partners whose share of the profits is reduced will be

credited with their proportion of the unrecorded or undervalued items and those whose share of the profits is increased will be debited with their proportion of the same items.

Assume the unrecorded items are valued at £60,000 and that A, B and C shared profits/losses up to 30 June in the ratio of 3 : 2 : 1 respectively but decided to share them equally from 1 July. Two such methods of compensating A for his reduction of profits are:

(a) **Gross method**

		£'000	£'000
Unrecorded items		60	
A capital	(³⁄₆) (old ratio)		30
B capital	(²⁄₆)		20
C capital	(¹⁄₆)		10
A capital	(²⁄₆) (new ratio)	20	
B capital	(²⁄₆)	20	
C capital	(²⁄₆)	20	
Unrecorded items			60

(b) **Net method**

		£'000	£'000
C capital	((³⁄₆ – ²⁄₆) × 60)	10	
A capital	((³⁄₆ – ²⁄₆) × 60)		10

Note how B is unaffected by the adjustments, whereas in both **(a)** and **(b)**, C is debited with £10,000 and A is credited with £10,000.

Problems

It is necessary to take great care to ensure that:

(a) the correct apportionment between periods is applied;

(b) expenses are correctly classified as those apportioned on
- a time basis
- a turnover basis or
- a specific basis.

It is also essential to:

(a) read the question to see if items being revalued are in the books or not before the change in ratio takes place and if they are to be brought into the books or not;

(b) apply the correct ratio to the adjustments – namely old before the change and new after the change.

EXAMPLE

Al, Ben and Carl have been in business sharing profits/losses equally for many years. They decide to share profits in the ratio of Al, Ben and Carl 1 : 1 : 3 from 1 September Year 59. The following information has been extracted from their books for Year 59:

Sales	£750,000
Cost of goods sold	52% of sales value
Expenses varying on a sales basis	15% of sales value
Expenses varying on a time basis	16% of sales value
An exceptional expense that was incurred on 3 April Year 59	£17,500
An exceptional expense that was incurred on 5 November Year 59	£11,000

The average monthly sales for the 6 months to 30 June Year 59 was 150% times the average monthly sales for the 6 months to 31 December Year 59.

Required

(a) Prepare a summarised profit and loss account in columnar form to show separately the profits for the period to 31 August Year 59 and the period from 1 September Year 59.

(b) Prepare a profit and loss appropriation account to show the division of the profit/loss between the partners for Year 59.

(c) Assuming that goodwill, which has never been included in the partnership accounts, was valued at £42,000 at 1 September Year 59, prepare a journal entry to adjust for this item on the change of profit/loss sharing ratio. The partners decide to continue to exclude goodwill from the partnership books.

The candidate must first make some calculations to enable the necessary accounts to be prepared. These are:

	£
Gross profit (750,000 × (100 − 52)%)	360,000
Proportion of sales for 8-month period to 31 August Year 59 to 4-month period to 31 December Year 59: Before = ((6 × 1.5) + 2) = 11. After = 4.	
Gross profit for 8-month period to 31 August Year 59 ($^{11}/15$ × 360,000)	264,000
Gross profit for 4-month period to 31 December ($^{4}/15$ × 360,000)	96,000
Expenses varying on a sales basis (15% × 750,000)	112,500
Sales basis expenses for 8-month period to 31 August ($^{11}/15$ × 112,500)	82,500
Sales basis expenses for 4-month period to 31 December ($^{4}/15$ × 112,500)	30,000
Expenses varying on a time basis (16% × 750,000)	120,000
Time basis expenses for 8-month period to 31 August ($^{8}/12$ × 120,000)	80,000
Time basis expenses for 4-month period to 31 December ($^{4}/12$ × 120,000)	40,000

(a) Summarised Profit & Loss Account for the year ended 31 December Year 59

	8 months to 31 August £	4 months to 31 December £	Year to 31 December £
Gross profit	264,000	96,000	360,000
Expenses:			
Sales basis	82,500	30,000	112,500
Time basis	80,000	40,000	120,000
Specific	17,500	11,000	28,500
	180,000	81,000	261,000
Net profit	84,000	15,000	99,000

(b)   **Profit & Loss Appropriation Account for Year 59**

	£	£	£
Al	28,000	3,000	31,000
Ben	28,000	3,000	31,000
Carl	28,000	9,000	37,000
	84,000	15,000	99,000

(c)   **Journal Entry to adjust for goodwill**

	Old	New	Diffce	£	£
Carl	33.3% – 60.0%		– 26.6% × £42,000	11,200	
Al	33.3% – 20.0%		+13.3% × £42,000		5,600
Ben	33.3% – 20.0%		+13.3% × £42,000		5,600

Partnership dissolution

Objectives

The objectives are:

1   to dissolve the partnership;

2   settle the creditors; and

3   distribute the remaining assets between the partners.

The accountant's objective is to record all transactions relating to the dissolution.

Scenario

The partners decide to dissolve their partnership. There are various possible reasons for this decision, such as losses arising in the business or retirement of the partners or lack of finance.

Method

Open a dissolution (of partnership) account and transfer to it either:

(a) profits and losses arising on realisation of assets and settlement of liabilities; or

(b) net book value of all sundry net assets and the total amount realised on dissolution.

The final profit/loss on dissolution is divided between the partners in their profit/loss sharing ratio by transfer from the Dissolution Account to their capital accounts. It is also necessary to prepare a cash account reflecting the cash element of the dissolution transactions. The final balance/overdraft will be paid to or received from the partners; the amount for each partner will equal the balance on his/her capital account and when transferred will close that account and the cash account.

Problems

The problems that will be met vary, as they depend on the circumstances of each case. Examples include:

(a) deducting provisions for depreciation or doubtful debts from the asset to which they relate so that the net value of the asset is compared with its realisation price;

(b) dividing profit/loss on distribution between the partners in profit/loss-sharing ratio; *but*

(c) distributing the final balance on the asset accounts (usually cash only) so as to close the partners' capital accounts;

(d) transferring to each partner the agreed valuation of assets taken over by him and the agreed valuation of each liability assumed by him.

EXAMPLE 1

George, Han and Ng have been in partnership for many years sharing profits/losses in the ratio of 2 : 3 : 1 respectively. They agree to dissolve the partnership on 31 December. George and Han will retire from business but Ng will continue in business by himself. They prepare the following balance sheet at 31 December:

George, Han and Ng Balance Sheet at 31 December

	Cost	Depreciation		
Fixed assets	£	£		£
Land and buildings	40,000			40,000
Plant and machinery	35,000	15,000		20,000
	75,000	15,000		60,000
Current assets				
Stock	36,000			
Debtors (after deducting provision for doubtful debts £1,000)	37,000	73,000		
Liabilities due within one year				
Trade creditors	15,000			
Bank overdraft	13,000	28,000		
				45,000
				105,000
Represented by				
Loan account from George				30,000
Capital George		25,000		
Capital Han		25,000		
Capital Ng		25,000		75,000
				105,000

They ceased trading on 31 December and, the day after, the following transactions took place:

1   They received £34,000 for the sale of some of their land and buildings; Ng took over the rest at an agreed valuation of £12,000.

2   They sold some plant and machinery for £14,000 cash and Ng took over the rest at an agreed valuation of £5,500.

3   Ng took over all the stock at the Balance Sheet value.

4   They wrote off bad debts of £3,000; half of the debtors paid the amount they owed after deducting a discount of 2%. Ng took over all the rest at an agreed valuation of 96% of their gross amount.

5   They paid the creditors in full after receiving a discount of 3%.

6   George's loan account was transferred to his capital account and cash was paid to and/or received from the partners to balance their capital accounts.

Required

Prepare a dissolution account, a cash account and, in columnar layout, the partners' capital accounts, to close the books.

Solution

(a) Open the three accounts required.

(b) Record in them each of the transactions numbered 1 to 6 above.

(c) Transfer, in the profit/loss sharing ratio, the profit/loss on dissolution to the partners' capital accounts.

(d) Balance off the partners' capital accounts by transfers to the cash account, which will also be closed.

Dissolution Account

	£		£
Plant and machinery		Land and buildings	
(35,000 − 15,000 − 14,000 − 5,500)	500	(34,000 + 12,000 − 40,000)	6,000
Debtors		Creditors	
((½(37,000 + 1,000 − 3,000) = 17,500))		(15,000 × 3%)	450
((17,500 × 98%) +			
(17,500 × 96%) − 37,000)	3,050		
Profit divided in profit/loss ratio £			
⅔ George 967			
⅜ Han 1,450			
⅙ Ng 483			
	2,900		
	6,450		6,450

Cash Account

	£		£
Land and buildings	34,000	Bank overdraft	13,000
Plant and machinery	14,000	Creditors (15,000 − 450)	14,550
Debtors (17,500 × 98%)	17,150	Partners: George	25,967
Partner: Ng	14,817	Han	26,450
	79,967		79,967

Partners' Capital Accounts

	George £	Han £	Ng £		George £	Han £	Ng £
Land and buildings			12,000	Balance 31 Dec	25,000	25,000	25,000
Plant and machinery			5,500	Profit	967	1,450	483
Stock			36,000	Loan account			30,000
Debtors							
(17,500 × 96%)			16,800				
Cash to balance	25,967	26,450		Cash to balance			14,817
	25,967	26,450	70,300		25,967	26,450	70,300

EXAMPLE 2

Denise and Mickey were partners in a farm. Their partnership agreement stated that:

1   The fixed capital of Denise (£18,000) and Mickey (£19,000) would bear interest at 10% per annum.

2   Any loans made by the partners to the partnership would bear interest at 8% per annum.

3   The partners' annual salaries would be Denise £4,000 and Mickey £7,000.

4   The residual profits/losses would be shared between Denise and Mickey in the ratio of 3 : 2 respectively.

5   The partners' current accounts would be closed at the end of each financial year by each partner drawing cash out or paying cash into the partnership.

The partnership's net profit for the year ended 31 December Year 8 was £26,000 *before* charging any interest on capital or loans or any partnership salaries.

The partners' loans to the partnership were:

(a) Denise lent £5,000 on 1 April Year 8;

(b) Mickey lent £20,000 on 1 January Year 6, but was repaid £7,500 on 31 December Year 7;

(c) no other loans and no repayments were made in Year 8.

Required

(a) Prepare for Denise and Mickey a profit and loss appropriation account for Year 8.   (5 marks)

As they could not renew the lease of their farm, they decided to dissolve the partnership on 1 January Year 9. They agreed to take over the farm vehicles themselves at the following valuations: Denise £5,000 and Mickey £4,000. All remaining assets (except cash £2,000) were sold for £71,500; trade creditors allowed them discounts for immediate payment, amounting to 3% of the £14,000 they owed at the end of Year 8 and they paid their farm workers £4,000 compensation.

Required

(b) Assuming all dissolution transactions took place on 1 January Year 9, prepare for Denise and Mickey the:

    (i)   dissolution cash account;

    (ii)   realisation account;

    (iii) capital accounts in columnar form.   (12 marks)

                                     Total (17 marks)

Solution

(a) Profit & Loss Account

		£	£
Profit			26,000
Salaries	(4,000 + 7,000)	11,000	
Loan interest	(5,000 × 8% × 9 ÷ 12)	300	
	(20,000 − 7,500) × 8%)	1,000	
Capital interest	(18,000 + 19,000) × 10%)	3,700	16,000
			10,000
Residue	Denise 3/5	6,000	
	Mickey 2/5	4,000	10,000

(b) (i) Dissolution Cash Account

	£
Balance	2,000
Sale of assets	71,500
	73,500
Compensation	4,000
Creditors (14,000 × 97%)	13,580
Capital Denise	24,252
Capital Mickey	31,668
	73,500

(ii) Realisation Account

		£
Vehicles taken over (5,000 + 4,000)		9,000
Discounts received (14,000 × 3%)		420
Sale of assets		71,500
		80,920
Less Sundry assets	(18,000 + 19,000 + 5,000 + 12,500 + 14,000 − 2,000)	−66,500
Compensation		−4,000
Residue	Denise	−6,252
	Mickey	−4,168
		80,920

(iii)   **Capital**

	Denise £	Mickey £
Balance 1 January	18,000	19,000
Loans	5,000	12,500
Dissolution profit	6,252	4,168
Vehicles	−5,000	−4,000
Cash	−24,252	−31,668

Admission or retirement of partners

Objectives

When new partners are admitted into the partnership or old ones retire, the three objectives are:

1 to divide the profits/losses arising on the profit and loss account during the year between the partners in accordance with changes in the partnership ratios

2 to make any adjustments necessary to compensate partners for their interests in 'hidden assets' upon any change in their ratio of sharing profits/losses

3 to record any capital in the form of cash or assets introduced into the partnership by partners or withdrawn by partners

Scenario

New partners (with or without capital) are admitted to the firm and/or old partners retire but the firm continues in business using the same books of account. The reasons for these changes include:

- changes in trading conditions
- ageing of partners
- need for additional capital
- variation of partners' activities within the firm

Methods

The methods used in dividing the profits/losses in accordance with changes in the partnership ratios and in making adjustments to compensate partners have been discussed above.

Capital introduced into the partnership is recorded by debiting the asset(s) brought in and crediting the capital account of the partner concerned. Capital withdrawn from the partnership is recorded by debiting the capital account of the partner withdrawing it and crediting the asset(s). This may produce a profit/loss for the partnership.

Problems

Problems arising in the first two scenarios have been discussed above.

It is necessary to take great care in calculating the total value of any assets brought into the partnership by new partners as these may be brought in from a different business and may already have been depreciated. They will be brought in at an agreed valuation. Also take care with assets taken out of the partnership: bear in mind any profit or loss arising.

The following example illustrates the adjustments necessary to compensate partners for their interests in 'hidden assets' and to record capital introduced and withdrawn by the partners.

EXAMPLE

Aber, Bar and Chee were in partnership sharing profits and losses in the ratio 5 : 3 : 2 respectively. Their summarised balance sheet at 31 December Year 24 was as follows:

	$		$
Capital Aber	135,000	Land and buildings	90,000
Capital Bar	63,000	Office equipment	36,000
Capital Chee	45,000	Motor vehicles	14,400
Loan from Aber	27,000	Stock at cost	61,200
Sundry creditors	45,000	Debtors *less* provision	62,100
		Bank	51,300
	315,000		315,000

On 31 December Year 24, Aber decided to retire from the partnership and Bar and Chee decided to continue in partnership sharing profits and losses in the ratio of 3 : 2 respectively. The partners agreed in relation both to the retirement and to the continuing partnership to adjust the above book values as follows:

1   Increase the value of land and buildings to $112,500.

2   Decrease the value of office equipment to $32,400.

3   Write off obsolete stock which had cost $4,500.

4   Increase the provision for doubtful debts by $1,300.

5   A provision for legal damages of $2,700 included in sundry creditors was no longer necessary.

6   Goodwill, at present unrecorded, was valued at $169,200.

Aber also agreed to take over a motor vehicle with a book value of $5,800 and office equipment revalued under **2** above at $9,900. Aber was also to be charged $34,200 for goodwill relating to the business that he would take with him.

Bar and Chee agreed to introduce in total $100,000 cash in their new profit sharing ratio. This sum would be paid to Aber who agreed to transfer any balance left on his capital account to his loan account. Finally it was decided that the remaining goodwill should not appear in the balance sheet of the new partnership.

Required

Assume that all the above matters were dealt with immediately after 31 December Year 24 and prepare:

(a) the partnership revaluation account

(b) the partners' capital accounts in columnar form relating both to the old and the new partnership

(c) the opening balance sheet of the partnership

Solution

(a)   **Partnership Revaluation Account**

	$		$
Office equipment (36,000 – 32,400)	3,600	Land and buildings (112,500 – 90,000)	22,500
Stock	4,500	Sundry creditors (provision)	2,700
Debtors (provision)	1,300	Goodwill	169,200
Capital A (50%) 92,500			
Capital B (30%) 55,500			
Capital C (20%) 37,000	185,000		
	194,400		194,400

(b)   **Capital Accounts**

	Aber	Bar	Chee		Aber	Bar	Chee
	$	$	$		$	$	$
Motor vehicles	5,800			Opening balances	135,000	63,000	45,000
Office equip	9,900			Revaluation account	92,500	55,500	37,000
Goodwill	34,200			Bank 3 : 2	–	60,000	40,000
3 : 2 × (169,200 – 34,200)		81,000	54,000				
Bank	100,000						
Loan	77,600						
Closing bal	–	97,500	68,000				
	227,500	178,500	122,000		227,500	178,500	122,000

(c)   **Balance Sheet**

	$	$		$	$
Capital			*Fixed assets*		
Bar	97,500		Land and buildings		112,500
Chee	68,000	165,500	Office equipment (32,400 – 9,900)		22,500
Loan			Motor vehicles (14,400 – 5,800)		8,600
Aber (77,600 + 27,000)		104,600			143,600
			Current assets		
Liabilities due within			Stock (61,200 – 4,500)	56,700	
one year			Debtors (62,100 – 1,300)	60,800	
Sundry creditors			Bank	51,300	168,800
(45,000 – 2,700)		42,300			
		312,400			312,400

Conversion of a partnership into a company

Objectives

To record in the books:

1 of the partnership the transfer of its business to the limited company and the subsequent dissolution of the partnership

2 of the limited company the formation of the company and its acquisition of the partnership business

Scenario

The partners of a partnership may decide to convert the partnership business into a limited company to gain the benefits of limited liability, or to obtain greater sources of finance. The partnership business is sold to the company that is formed specifically to acquire the business and the partnership is dissolved. The company usually pays for the partnership business in the form of its own shares (and sometimes by debentures) or the cash proceeds from the sale of its own shares to third parties. The actual dates of formation of the company and its acquisition of the business may result in the company earning 'profits prior to incorporation'. This topic is discussed in Chapter 3. Also see Chapter 3 for discussion of the issue of shares or debentures.

Method

The accounting aspects must be considered in the books:

- of the partnership and
- of the new limited company.

In some cases the company will continue to use the partnership books.

Record the transfer in the books of the partnership

In order to record the transfer of the business to the new limited company in the books of the partnership it is necessary to open the accounts which are already required for the dissolution of a partnership (*see* page 22) and the following special accounts will be opened (in addition to the usual accounts):

	Additional account	*Objective of account*
1	Sale of business or realisation	To ascertain the profit/loss on sale of the business by comparing the book value of the sundry net assets sold against the sale price obtained for them (called the purchase consideration).
2	New limited company	To record the actual sale of the business to the new limited company and to show how the company pays for the business.
3	Shares and/or debentures in new company	To record the actual shares and/or debentures received by the partnership and their distribution to the partners.

The accounting entries recording the transfer of the business in these accounts and the others required will be illustrated by the following journal entries:

Journal Entries

Transaction	*Debit*	*Credit*
(a) Charge company with purchase consideration	New company	Sale of business
(b) Transfer assets to company	Sale of business	Individual asset accounts (such as stock)
(c) Liabilities assumed by company	Individual liability accounts	Sale of business
(d) Settlement of the purchase consideration	New company shares and/or debentures and cash (if any)	New company
(e) Transfer of profit/loss on sale of business to the partners	Sale of business	Partners' capital accounts in profit/loss ratio
(f) Transfer of shares and/or debentures to partners	Partners' capital accounts	New company shares and/or debentures

Record the formation of the company

In order to record the formation of the new limited company and its acquisition of the partnership business the following special accounts will be opened (in addition to the usual accounts):

	Additional account	*Objective of account*
1	Purchase of business	To ascertain the goodwill or the reserve not free for distribution arising on the purchase of the partnership business by comparing the company's valuation of the sundry net assets purchased with the purchase consideration
2	Vendors of business (ie partnership)	To record the actual purchase of the sundry net assets and to show how the vendors are paid for the business
3	Shares and/or debentures	To record the issuing of the shares or debentures in settlement of the purchase consideration

If the shares or debentures are issued at more than their nominal value there will also be a share premium account to record the excess.

The accounting entries recording the purchase of the business in these accounts and the others required will be illustrated by the following journal entries:

Journal Entries

Transaction	*Debit*	*Credit*
(a) Credit partnership with purchase consideration	Purchase of business	Vendors
(b) Transfer assets to company	Individual asset accounts (such as stock) Goodwill (if any)	Purchase of business account
(c) Liabilities assumed by company	Purchase of business account	Individual liabilities accounts
(d) Settlement of the purchase consideration	Vendors	Shares and/or debentures Share and/or debenture premium

Problems

The problems must be considered in relation to the partnership and also in relation to the new limited company.

With regard to the accounting treatment of the purchase consideration, if the valuation of the purchase consideration is not given in the question it must be calculated.

It is important to remember the following:

In the partnership books

Purchase consideration less book value of sundry net assets gives us the profit/loss on sale of business.

In the company books

Purchase consideration less the company's valuation of the sundry net assets acquired gives us the goodwill or the non-distributable reserve. Purchase consideration less the nominal value of shares (and/or debentures) issued in settlement of the purchase of the business gives us the premium on shares (and/or debentures).

Other problems may arise:

In the partnership books

1   *When transferring fixed assets to the sale of business account*   If the fixed assets are kept at cost in the books and a separate provision is made for accumulated depreciation, it is necessary to transfer:

   (a)   the cost of the asset to the sale of business (debit sale of business and credit cost of fixed asset); *and*

   (b)   the accumulated depreciation on the asset (debit the provision for depreciation and credit the sale of business).

2   The profit/loss on the sale of the business is distributed in the partners' profit/loss ratio.

3   The distribution of any balance on cash and of shares and/or debentures received from the new limited company must be made in accordance with the partnership agreement. Usually:

   (a)   ordinary shares are divided in profit/loss sharing ratio;

   (b)   debentures and preference shares are divided in relation to the balances on the partners' capital accounts;

   (c)   cash is distributed to balance off each partner's capital.

4   If any partners have a debit balance on their capital accounts these must be repaid. As a result the amount remaining on the cash account should equal the total of the credit balances on the other partners' capital accounts.

In the company books

1   The opening book value of fixed assets in the company is the value placed upon those assets by the company. The cost and the provision for depreciation in the partnership books will not appear in the books of the company.

2   Goodwill is written off to the profit and loss account as soon as there are available profits.

3   Reserves arising on acquisition of the business and premiums on issue of shares are not free for distribution.

EXAMPLE

This has been split into two parts showing:

(a) the partnership dissolution and

(b) the company formation

(a) Partnership dissolution

Lion and Monkey carried on business in partnership, sharing profits/losses in the ratio of 3 : 2 respectively. Their summarised balance sheet on 31 December Year 18 was as follows:

Balance Sheet

	£'000		£'000
Fixed capital accounts		Buildings and machinery	73
Lion	70	Two cars	17
Monkey	50		
Current accounts		Stock	48
Lion	30	Sundry debtors	84
Monkey	–12	Bank	16
Loan from Monkey	40		
Sundry creditors	60		
	238		238

Both partners decided to retire on 1 January Year 19 and accepted an offer from Warthog Ltd to take over the buildings, machinery, stock and goodwill of the partnership for a purchase consideration of £240,000. This consideration was to be satisfied by the company making an allotment to the partners of 60,000 12% £1 preference shares at a premium of 20%, a payment of £75,000 in cash and the balance by making an allotment to the partners of 300,000 ordinary shares with a nominal value of £0.20 each.

The partnership received £78,000 from sundry debtors in full settlement and paid £55,000 to sundry creditors in full settlement. On dissolution the partners agreed:

1   to transfer current and loan account balances to fixed capital accounts;

2   to value the car taken over by Lion at £14,000 and the car taken over by Monkey at £10,000;

3   to distribute to Monkey preference shares equal in value to his loan and to distribute the remaining preference shares to Lion;

4   to distribute the ordinary shares to Lion and Monkey in their profit/loss sharing ratio at 31 December Year 18;

5   to take cash in settlement of the balances remaining.

Required

(a) Calculate the total value of the ordinary shares allotted by Warthog Ltd to Lion and Monkey

(b) Prepare the realisation account, bank account and fixed capital accounts of the partnership in columnar form including the final cash settlement.

Solution

(a)

	£'000	£'000
Purchase consideration		240
Less Preference shares (60,000 × 1.2)	72	
Cash	75	147
Value of ordinary shares		93

(b)

Realisation Account

	£'000		£'000
Sundry fixed assets	90	Warthog Ltd	240
Stock	48	Cash (Debtors)	78
Debtors	84	Creditors (discounts received)	5
Capital Lion (3/5 × 125) = 75		Capital (motor cars (14 + 10))	24
Capital Monkey (2/5 × 25) = 50	125		
	347		347

Bank Account

	£'000			£'000
Opening balance	16	Sundry creditors		55
Warthog Ltd	75	Capital Lion	73.20	
Sundry Debtors	78	Capital Monkey	40.80	114
	169			169

Capital Accounts

	Lion £'000	Monkey £'000		Lion £'000	Monkey £'000
Current account		12	Opening balance	70	50
Motor vehicles	14	10	Current account	30	
Warthog Ltd			Loan		40
Preference shares	32	40	Profit on realisation	75	50
Ordinary shares					
(93 × 3/5)	55.80				
(93 × 2/5)		37.20			
Bank	73.20	40.80			
	175.00	140.00		175.00	140.00

(b) Illustrating company formation

This is a continuation of the example given in part **(a)** above. The following transactions took place on 1 January Year 19:

1   In order to raise sufficient cash to pay the £75,000 to Lion and Monkey and to provide £15,000 cash to pay for current trading expenditure Warthog Ltd sold on 1 January Year 19 more ordinary shares of £0.20 each at £0.30 each cash.

2   Warthog Ltd valued the tangible fixed assets and stock acquired from Lion and Monkey as follows:

	£'000
Buildings and machinery	152
Stock	48

It may be assumed that Warthog Ltd valued goodwill as the difference between the total of the tangible fixed assets and stock and the purchase consideration.

Required

(a)   Prepare journal entries

   (i)   to record in the company's books all the transactions outlined in Example part **(a)** above that are relevant to the company

   (ii) to record the issue of shares detailed above and

   (iii) to record the company's acquisition of the partnership's tangible and intangible fixed assets and stock

(b)   Prepare, in vertical form, the balance sheet of Warthog Ltd on 1 January Year 19 assuming there were no further transactions.

Solution

Journal Entries

	£'000	£'000
Purchase of business	240	
Lion and Monkey		240
Buildings and machinery	152	
Stock	48	
Goodwill (residual)	40	
Purchase of business		240
Lion and Monkey	240	
Preference share capital		60
Share premium (60,000 × 0.20)		12
Ordinary share capital (300,000 × 0.20)		60
Share premium (residual)		33
Cash		75
Cash (75,000 + 15,000)	90	
Ordinary share capital (90,000 × 0.20 ÷ 0.30)		60
Share premium (90,000 × 0.10 ÷ 0.30)		30

(b)   Warthog Ltd Balance Sheet at 1 January Year 19

	£'000	£'000
Fixed assets		
Intangible: goodwill	40	
Tangible: buildings and machinery	152	
		192
Current assets		
Stock	48	
Cash (90,000 – 75,000)	15	
		63
		255
Financed by:		
Capital and reserves		
Ordinary shares of £0.20 each (60,000 + 60,000)		120
Preference shares of £1.00 each		60
		180
Share premium (12,000 + 33,000 + 30,000)		75
		255

PRACTICE QUESTIONS

2.1 The accountant of Albert, Bill and Cyril used the wrong computer program to prepare the final accounts of the partnership for Year 42. The computer program used by the accountant resulted in the following:

1   Albert was given a commission of 1% of sales in excess of £300,000.

2   Bill was given a partnership salary of £6,000 per annum.

3   5% interest per annum was allowed on each partner's fixed capital.

4   10% interest per annum was charged on each partner's total of drawings for the year.

5   12% interest per annum was allowed on each partner's loans to the partnership.

6   Residual profits were divided between Albert, Bill and Cyril in the ratio of 3 : 2 : 1 respectively.

7   Cyril's minimum net share of partnership profits was guaranteed by Albert at not less than £6,000.

The following items were in the year-end accounts for Year 42 of Albert, Bill and Cyril:

	Albert £'000	Bill £'000	Cyril £'000	£'000
Fixed capital 1 January Year 42	60	50	40	
Drawings for Year 42	9.5	9	2.5	
Loan to partnership made on 1 July Year 42		60		
Profits for Year 42 before any debits or credits for items in the partnership agreement				36
Sales for Year 42				480

Required

(a) Prepare the profit and loss appropriation account of Albert, Bill and Cyril based on the computer program used in error by the accountant. Use columnar layout and show the total credited or debited to each partner's capital account after any transfer between the partners required as a result of Cyril's total minimum share of profits as guaranteed by Albert.

Albert, Bill and Cyril actually had no formal partnership agreement.

(b) Prepare the profit and loss appropriation account of Albert, Bill and Cyril as it should have been prepared using the same columnar layout as in (a).

(c) Prepare one composite journal entry to correct the books for the error made by the accountant.

2.2 Mouse will become a junior partner in the existing partnership of Eli and Funt as from 1 January Year 21 on the following terms:

1   Goodwill will be revalued at six years' purchase of the weighted average net profits/losses of the five years to 31 December Year 20; the weightings will be 1, 2, 3, 4 and 5 for Years 16, 17, 18, 19 and 20 respectively. The profits/losses for this period were:

		£
Year 16	Loss	32,000
Year 17	Profit	6,000
Year 18	Profit	15,000
Year 19	Profit	20,000
Year 20	Profit	9,000

2   Mouse will invest £20,000 in the partnership, 40% as capital and 60% as his share of the goodwill.

3   Mouse's share of the profits/losses of the firm will be based upon his share of the goodwill; Eli and Funt will continue to share profits/losses between themselves in the ratio of 60% : 40%.

Required

(a) Value the goodwill at 31 December Year 20.

(b) Calculate the proposed profit/loss sharing ratio of Eli, Funt and Mouse.

The summarised balance sheet of Eli and Funt at 31 December Year 20 was as follows:

Balance Sheet

	£'000	£'000	£'000
Goodwill	10		
Tangible fixed assets	100		
		110	
Current assets	150		
Liabilities due within one year	20		
		130	
			240
Financed by capital: Eli	180		
Funt	60		240

Subsequently on 1 January Year 21, the 3 partners agreed to exclude goodwill from their balance sheet and to make the following revaluations in their balance sheet:

- stock at £5,000 *less* than its present balance sheet value
- fixed assets at £30,000 *more* than their present balance sheet value

Required

(c) Prepare a balance sheet at 1 January Year 21 for Eli, Funt and Mouse assuming that no transactions other than those outlined above had taken place.

POINTS TO REMEMBER

Changes in profit (loss) sharing ratio

- If the profit sharing ratio of the partners changes during an accounting period, use a format for the profit and loss account with the following three columns:

  1 period before the change

  2 period after the change

  3 total for the accounting period

- Apportion gross profit (loss) between the two periods on a turnover basis; do not apportion each individual item in the trading account.

- Do not apportion each item individually

- Classify the items into:

  (a) items apportioned on a turnover basis

  (b) items apportioned on a time basis

  (c) items apportioned on a different basis

  Charge all items in (a) in one total in the two periods in the profit and loss account. Charge all items in (b) in one total in the two periods in the profit and loss account. Charge other items individually in the profit and loss account.

- Compensate partners whose share of the profits (losses) goes down due to the change in ratio, by crediting their capital accounts in the old profit (loss) sharing basis with the value of the net 'hidden' assets to bring those assets into the books. If such assets are to be excluded from the books, debit all partners with those assets in the new profit (loss) sharing basis.

Partnership dissolution

- Use the dissolution account for dissolving a partnership.

- Debit assets to the dissolution account individually or in total; credit liabilities to the dissolution account individually or in total.

- Credit the dissolution account with the proceeds from the sale of any individual assets or of the business as a whole.

- Remember to deduct provisions for doubtful debts and depreciation in arriving at the net value of assets transferred to the dissolution account.

- Divide the profit (loss) on dissolution between the partners in the profit (loss) sharing ratio.

- Distribute cash and any other assets remaining to the partners, so as to balance off their capital accounts; this will not be in the profit (loss) sharing ratio.

Admission/retirement of partners

- Debit assets brought into the partnership to asset accounts and credit the partner bringing that asset into the partnership.

- Credit liabilities brought into the partnership to liability accounts and debit the partner bringing that liability into the partnership.

- Reverse entries to above, in respect of assets and liabilities taken out of the partnership by partners.

Conversion of partnership into a company

- In the books of the partnership write up the accounts as for dissolution, the company being the buyer of the business.

- In the books of the company write up the accounts as for company formation, the partnership being the vendor of the business.

- Unless the partners agree otherwise, distribute ordinary shares in the company to partners in profit (loss) sharing ratio.

- Unless the partners agree otherwise, distribute other assets apart from cash in the ratio of the balances of capital.

- Unless the partners agree otherwise, distribute any cash remaining in order to balance of the capital accounts; this will not be in the profit (loss) sharing ratio.

- In the books of the company, the fixed assets will appear at cost price to the company, not at the original cost to the partnership.

- The company will write off the cost of goodwill against available reserves.

3

Accounting for specific company circumstances

> After carefully studying this chapter you should be able to:
>
> 1 *account for issue of shares, and issue and redemption of debentures;*
>
> 2 *account for distributable profits;*
>
> 3 *account for profits prior to incorporation;*
>
> 4 *account for amalgamations of companies;*
>
> 5 *account for reconstructions and capital reductions of companies.*

The specific accounting circumstances included in this chapter are:

1 *issue of shares or debentures;*

2 *distributable profits;*

3 *profits prior to incorporation;*

4 *amalgamations;*

5 *reconstructions and capital reductions.*

As each of the above topics relates to a different aspect of company accounting, they will be considered individually in the following pages, in the order listed.

Issue of shares or debentures

Shares may be offered for sale at par or at a premium: debentures may be offered at par, or at a premium, or at a discount.

Objective

To account for cash received and issue of shares or debentures in date order of the actual transactions.

Scenario

Information available will include the terms of issue and the details of actual transactions resulting from the issue of shares (debentures). Forfeiture and reissue of shares (debentures) may be included.

Method

Arrange the transactions in chronological order and prepare the following journal entries to record them:

Transaction	Journal entry
(a) Offer published for sale of shares	No journal entry required
(b) Receipt of application monies	Cash debit Application and allotment credit
(c) Acceptance of applications	Application and allotment debit Shares credit Premium (if any) credit
(d) Refund of excess application monies	Application and allotment debit Cash credit
(e) Call made on shares	Call account debit Shares credit
(f) Receipt of call monies	Cash debit Call account credit
(g) Forfeiture of shares	Debit shares (called-up amount) Debit premium (called-up amount) Call credit (amount unpaid) Forfeited shares credit (amount paid)
(h) Reissue of shares	Forfeited shares debit (amount paid by 1st shareholder) Cash (amount paid by 2nd shareholder) Shares (capital amount called) Share premium (premium called) Profit on reissue (profit)

Problem

It is essential to keep the journal entries in date order. The first event is the receipt of application money (ie cash first). But on the allotment the calls precede the receipt of cash (ie cash second).

EXAMPLE

On 31 October Year 22 Tegdub plc had offered for sale $75,000 12% debentures at $98. $50 was payable on application on 1 January Year 23 and $48 on allotment on 1 February Year 23. Applications were received in respect of $90,000 debentures and the company returned excess application money on 26 January Year 23. All money due on allotment was received before the end of February

Year 23. In accordance with the terms of the debenture issue, interest was payable from 1 March Year 23.

Required

Prepare journal entries without narratives to record the issue of and payment for debentures.

Solution

(a)   **Journal Entries**

			$'000	$'000
1 Jan	Cash (90,000 × 50%)		45.0	
	Debenture application and allotment A/C			45.0
26 Feb	Debenture application and allotment A/C		7.5	
	Cash			7.5
	Debenture application and allotment A/C		73.5	
	Debenture discount		1.5	
	Debentures			75.0
31 Mar	Cash		36.0	
	Debenture application and allotment A/C			36.0

EXAMPLE

The directors of Quonk plc offered for sale to:

(a) its existing ordinary shareholders 2,000,000 ordinary shares of £1.00 each at par; and

(b) the general public 3,000,000 ordinary shares of £1.00 each at £1.10 each.

The amounts payable were:

Year 41		Existing shareholders	General public
1 April	Application	£0.50 per share	£0.60 per share
1 May	Allotment	£0.50 per share	£0.30 per share*
1 November	Call		£0.20 per share
* including the premium			

Applications were received for 2,000,000 ordinary shares from existing shareholders and for 4,000,000 from the general public; the excess money received was carried forward and offset against the amounts due on allotment.

All monies due upon application, allotment and call were fully paid when due, *except* for the call due from a new shareholder, Mr Outrage, who applied for and was allocated 1,000 shares. His shares were forfeited and then reissued as fully paid to Mr Meek for £950.00 cash.

Required

Prepare journal entries without narratives to record the transactions (including those for cash) given above.

Solution

Journal Entries

	£	£
Cash (2,000,000 × 0.50) + (4,000,000 × 0.60)	3,400,000	
Application and allotment		3,400,000
Application and allotment (2,000,000 × 1.00) + (3,000,000 × 0.90)	4,700,000	
Share capital (2,000,000 × 1.00) + (3,000,000 × 0.80)		4,400,000
Share premium (3,000,000 × 0.10)		300,000
Cash (2,000,000 × 0.5) + (3,000,000 × 0.3) – (1,000,000 × 0.6)	1,300,000	
Application and allotment		1,300,000
Call (3,000,000 × 0.20)	600,000	
Share capital		600,000
Cash (3,000,000 × 0.2) – (1,000 × 0.2)	599,800	
Call		599,800
Share capital	1,000	
Share premium	100	
Call (1,000 × 0.20)		200
Forfeited shares		900
Forfeited shares	900	
Cash	950	
Share capital		1,000
Share premium		100
Profit on reissue of forfeited shares		750

Distributable profits

Some profits are free for distribution in the form of a cash dividend: others are not free for distribution in that form.

Objective

Find out which profits are free for cash distribution and which are not, to enable the directors of the company to determine the maximum dividend they may propose to the shareholders for declaration.

Scenario

The candidate will be presented with information relating to the profits and reserves of a company and/or the information needed to calculate the profits. This could take the form of a trial balance and notes, or simply a list of figures. It could appear as part of a large question or as an individual question.

Method

If the balance on the profit and loss account is not given, prepare a profit and loss account to find out the balance. Classify the balances relating to the company's profits and reserves into those that are free for distribution in the form of a cash dividend and those that are not free for distribution in the form of a cash dividend.

Problems

It is essential for the candidate to know how to distinguish between the two categories of profits and reserves; the definitions of the items in each category must be carefully learnt and then applied. These definitions are:

(a) Profits free for distribution in the form of a cash dividend are the accumulated realised profits less any accumulated losses.

(b) Profits not free for distribution in the form of a cash dividend include share premium account; revaluation reserve; capital redemption reserve and profits prior to incorporation. (These reserves are discussed elsewhere in this book or in previous books in this series.)

In applying the definitions the candidate must:

1 Give the headings of each category. These are:

(a) 'Profits free for distribution in the form of a cash dividend';

(b) 'Profits not free for distribution in the form of a cash dividend'.

2 List and name under each heading each reserve.

3 Finally add up the total for each category.

EXAMPLE I

This question reviews the legality of cash distributions. Blangorse plc was formed on 15 April Year 3 to take over the business of Esrog from 1 January Year 3. The budgeted balance sheet of Blangorse plc at the end of Year 17 included the following:

	£'000
Excess of issue price of shares over their nominal value	12
Credit balance on Profit & Loss Account	98
Professional revaluation of land	15
Transfer to reserve from Profit & Loss Account arising when the company redeemed some preference shares at par	70
Amounts transferred from Profit & Loss Account to a reserve to enable the company to continue paying dividends on its shares in the future	17
Profits arising between 1 January Year 3 and 15 April Year 3	8

At the end of Year 17 Blangorse plc had on issue 500,000 ordinary shares of £1.00 each fully paid and 100,000 8% preference shares of £0.50 each fully paid.

Required

Determine the maximum dividend per ordinary share that Blangorse plc may declare for Year 17.

Solution

The question is answered in three stages:

(a) list and total the reserves free for each distribution;

(b) deduct the dividends payable to the preference shareholders;

(c) divide the balance by the number of ordinary shares on issue.

(a) Reserves free for cash distribution	£'000
Reserve for dividends in future years	17
Credit balance on Profit & Loss Account	98
	115

(b) *Less* dividends payable to the preference shareholders	
(100,000 × 0.50 × 8%)	4
	111

(c) Divide by number of ordinary shares on issue
£111,000 ÷ 5,000,000 = £0.222 per share.

EXAMPLE 2

This arises at the end of a large question. It reviews the financial aspects of cash distributions. The candidate should have prepared the following balance sheet in earlier parts of the answer to this question.

Nosetok plc Balance Sheet at 31 December Year 37

	Cost	Depreciation	
Fixed assets	£'000	£'000	£'000
Shop buildings	48		48
Shop fittings	51	19	32
	99	19	80
Current assets			
Stock	150		
Debtors	34		
Bank	2	186	
Liabilities due within one year			
Trade creditors	27		
Bank overdraft	3		
Proposed dividend	16	46	
			140
			220
Financed by capital and reserves			
Ordinary share capital in shares of £1.00 each			80
Profit & Loss Account			140
			220

Required

Comment on the amount of the dividend proposed as a shareholder considers it inadequate.

Solution

Answer this section by referring to the contradictory facts that:

(a) the reserves would allow a larger dividend; hence it is legally permissible to pay a larger dividend;

(b) there is insufficient liquidity to pay a larger dividend; hence it is not financially plausible to pay a larger dividend.

Fact **(b)** determines the possibility of a larger dividend as the company cannot make itself insolvent. Therefore fact **(b)** must override **(a)**.

Profits prior to incorporation

A company is frequently formed to take over an existing business. In such cases the company may take over the business from a date before the company itself was incorporated.

Objective

As a company cannot earn any profits (losses) before it has come into existence, any profits arising in the period between the date of take-over and the date of incorporation are not free for distribution in the form of a cash dividend (*see* above). The objective is to find out the amount of such profits so that they can be retained in the correct reserve account in the company's records.

Scenario

This topic is more likely to appear as a small question but it could appear as part of a larger one if, for example, the examiner gives details of a company formation and then continues to develop the trading history of the company thereafter.

The candidate is presented with:

(a) A trading and profit and loss account for the period from the date of the take-over of the business to the end of the company's first trading period. In between these two dates is the date of incorporation of the company. If there is no trading and profit and loss account prepared, the candidate will be given the information necessary to compile one.

(b) The various bases upon which to apportion items appearing in the trading and profit and loss account.

Method

The method depends on the information supplied. If there is no trading and profit and loss account given, it will first be necessary to compile one. After this, the candidate must apportion each item between 'prior to incorporation' and 'post-incorporation'. The following is a suggested layout for an apportioned trading and profit and loss account:

	Profits prior to incorporation £	Profits post incorporation £	Total £
Gross profit*	X	X	X
Expenses **			
Apportioned on a time basis	X	X	X
Apportioned on a turnover basis	X	X	X
Specific to either period	X	X	X
Net profit (loss)	X	X	X

Notes to the accounts

* It is not usually necessary to apportion each item in the trading account as the gross profit is always apportioned on the basis of sales.

** Expenses of each category would be listed and then the totals apportioned; it is not necessary to apportion each item individually.

Problems

The main problems are:

(a) the difficulty in deciding to which category to allocate certain items;

(b) if the candidate is confronted with incomplete records he/she must apply the methods of incomplete records such as control accounts to find out sales or purchases or some of the expenses;

(c) uncertainty on the use that may be made of the two types of profit when they are calculated.

EXAMPLE 1

Osiac plc was incorporated 1 April Year 33 to take over an existing business from 1 January Year 33. The following is the draft trading and profit and loss account for Osiac plc for year ended 31 December Year 33:

Notes		£'000	£'000
(a)	Sales		100
	Cost of goods sold:		
	Purchases	77	
	Stock 31 December Year 33	16	61
(b)	Gross profit		39
(c)	Legal expenses	2	
(d)	Commission on goods sold	5	
(e)	Directors' fees	3	
(f)	Office expenses	11	
(g)	Rent on buildings	4	
(h)	Motor expenses	6	
(i)	Interest payable	3	
			34
	Net profit		5

Notes

(a) The business is seasonal; the monthly average sales in March, April and May were at twice the monthly average rate for the rest of the year.

(b) Gross profit remained at the same average proportion to sales throughout the year.

(c) Analysis of legal expenses:

 • company formation expenses   70%
 • debt collection, which is to be apportioned on a sales basis   30%

(d) Commission on goods sold is fixed at 5% of sales value.

(e) Directors' fees were only payable after company formation.

(f) Office expenses are to be apportioned on a time basis.

(g) Rent on buildings is to be apportioned on a time basis.

(h) Analysis of motor expenses:

 • sales staff motoring expenses   90%
 • administrative expenses   10%

(i) Before the company was formed, the business borrowed money; the interest payable on the loan was £1,000. The rest of the interest payable was on the company's debentures.

Required

Redraft the given account in columnar form to show the profit/loss prior to incorporation and the profit/loss post incorporation.

Solution

The method of answering the question will include the following steps:

1 Apportion the gross profit on a sales basis between the two periods. Do *not* attempt to apportion the individual entries in the trading account; this is impossible without knowing the stock at the end of the period prior to incorporation.

2 Divide the profit and loss account items into the 3 categories:

(a) those that vary in accordance with sales

(b) those that vary on a time basis

(c) those that relate specifically to either period

Preliminary calculation

The sales basis will be Prior (1 + 1 + 2) to Post (2 + 2 + 1 + 1 + 1 + 1 + 1 + 1 + 1)

Giving   Prior 4/15 to Post 11/15

The draft account will be:

Osiac plc
Columnar Profit & Loss Account for year ending 31 December Year 33

		Profits prior to incorporation £	Profits post incorporation £	Total £
Gross Profit 4 : 11		10,400	28,600	39,000
Less expenses:				
Sales basis: Debt collect	600			
Commission	5,000			
Motor 90%	5,400			
Apportion 4 : 11	11,000	2,933	8,067	11,000
Time basis: Office	11,000			
Rent	4,000			
Motor 10%	600			
Apportion 3 : 9	15,600	3,900	11,700	15,600
Specific Co. formation (2,000 × 70%)			1,400	
Directors			3,000	
Interest		1,000	2,000	7,400
		7,833	26,167	34,000
Net profit		2,567	2,433	5,000

EXAMPLE 2

X Ltd was formed on 1 April Year 10 to take over the business of Tincan from 1 January Year 10, on which date the business had moved to new premises. The net assets other than goodwill, which was unrecorded, were taken over at book value. The company issued 260,000 ordinary shares of £1 each fully paid to the public for £1.10 each in cash; the whole of the proceeds were paid to Tincan as the agreed purchase consideration. X Ltd continued to use the same books of account.

The following is the company's trial balance at 31 December Year 10:

	£'000	£'000
Tincan capital account at 1 January Year 10		245
Rent, total cost of a 2-year lease from 1 January year 10*	4	
Salaries*	20	
Lighting and heating*	18	
Suspense account, cash paid to Tincan	286	
Wages§	50	
Suspense account, cash received from applicants for shares		286
Purchase/sales	570	870
Stock 1 January Year 10	140	
Debtors/creditors	90	100
Delivery vehicle expenses§	109	
Office equipment/provision for depreciation	60	45
Company formation expenses	1	
Expenses of moving to new premises	3	
Payment on account of directors' fees	3	
Bank	110	
Delivery vehicles/provision for depreciation	190	110
Bad debt written off, 1 February Year 10	2	
	1,656	1,656

Notes to the trial balance

1   Average monthly sales for January, February and March Year 10 were twice the average monthly sales for the rest of Year 10.

2   At 31 December X Ltd had stock valued at £155,000; had paid £200 for lighting and heating in advance; owed £400 for wages; owed £4,000 for directors' fees.

3   X Ltd decided to write off the cost of goodwill, company formation expenses and removal expenses, so as to leave the maximum amount of distributable profits.

4   It was decided not to propose a dividend for Year 10.

5   At 31 December Year 10 X Ltd also decided:

   (a)   to create a provision for doubtful debts of 2% of the debtors at the year end;§

   (b)   to provide for depreciation at 10% of the original cost to Tincan of the office equipment;★

   (c)   to provide for depreciation at 20% of the original cost to Tincan of the delivery vehicles.§

   ★ These expenses accrue on a time basis.
   § These expenses accrue on a sales basis.

Required

(a) Prepare journal entries (without narratives) to record the allotment of shares, the acquisition of goodwill and the settlement of the amount owing to the vendor. (6 marks)

(b) Prepare for X Ltd the trading and profit and loss account for Year 10 in columnar form showing the gross profit and the net profit for the period before and for the period after the company's formation. (21 marks)

(c) Prepare, *in good style*, the vertical balance sheet of X Ltd at 31 December Year 10. (16 marks)

(d) Prepare, to one decimal place, one ratio relating to X Ltd's performance for Year 10 and one ratio relating to X Ltd's financial position at 31 December Year 10. (6 marks)

Total (49 marks)

Solution

(a) **Journal Entries**

	£	£
Suspense account – cash received from applicants for shares	286,000	
Share capital		260,000
Share premium		26,000
Tincan capital	245,000	
Goodwill	41,000	
Suspense Account – cash paid to Tincan		286,000

(b) **X Ltd Trading and Profit & Loss Account Year 10**

	£	£	Before formation £	After formation £	Total £
Sales					870,000
Cost of goods sold					
Stock 1 January	140,000				
Purchases	570,000	710,000			
Stock 31 December		155,000			555,000
Gross profit					
Sales basis 6 : 9			126,000	189,000	315,000
Time basis					
Rent (4,000 × ½)		2,000			
Lighting and heating (18,000 – 200)		17,800			
Salaries		20,000			
Depreciation					
Office equipment (60,000 × 10%)		6,000			
Time basis 3 : 9		45,800	11,450	34,350	45,800

	£	£	Before formation £	After formation £	Total £
Sales basis					
Wages (50,000 + 400)		50,400			
Delivery expenses		109,000			
Depreciation:					
Delivery vehicles (190,000 × 20%)		38,000			
Provision					
doubtful debts (90,000 × 2%)		1,800			
Sales basis 6 : 9		199,200	79,680	119,520	199,200
Specific expenses					
Bad debts written off			2,000		2,000
Moving			3,000		3,000
Directors' fees				7,000	7,000
			96,130	160,870	257,000
Net profit			29,870	28,130	58,000
Less goodwill			29,870	11,130	41,000
Carried forward				17,000	17,000

(c) **X Ltd Balance Sheet at 31 December Year 10**

	Cost £	Depreciation £	£
Tangible fixed assets			
Office equipment (60,000 − 45,000)	15,000	6,000	9,000
Delivery vehicles (190,000 − 110,000)	80,000	38,000	42,000
	95,000	44,000	51,000
Current assets			
Stock	155,000		
Debtors (90,000 − 1,800)	88,200		
Prepaid expenses (2,000 + 200)	2,200		
Bank	110,000	355,400	
Liabilities due within one year			
Creditors	100,000		
Accrued expenses (4,000 + 400)	4,400	104,400	
Working capital			251,000
			302,000
Financed by:			
Capital and reserves			
Ordinary shares			260,000
Share premium (26,000 − 1,000)			25,000
Profit & Loss Account			17,000
			302,000

(d)

Performance: gross profit to sales ratio	315 ÷ 870%	36.2%
Financial position: working capital	355,400 ÷ 103,400	3.4 : 1

Amalgamations

There are various ways in which companies may be amalgamated. It will be seen that there is some similarity between amalgamations of companies and those of other organisations.

Objective

The objective of amalgamation is to achieve the benefits of economy of size by making one larger organisation instead of two or more smaller ones. The intention is to obtain a cheaper method of running a business through

- a reduction in overhead expenses
- greater purchasing power
- greater freedom from hostile take-over bids.

Scenario

There are various ways of amalgamating companies; these include:

- companies exchanging shares
- formation of a group of companies by one company buying all or a majority of shares in the other company
- one company acquiring the sundry net assets of the other company which is then liquidated

Method

The candidate may be asked to prepare journal entries and/or accounts to record the amalgamation in the books; or to prepare a balance sheet to show the result of the amalgamation.

Problems

The problems include:

- calculation of the number of shares to be allocated
- calculation of some assets, particularly goodwill
- valuation of shares on a profit and/or a sundry net asset basis

EXAMPLES

Three examples are given, based on the same circumstances, in order to contast the different ways in which companies may be amalgamated.

Basic circumstances

Ex Ltd and Wy Ltd decided to amalgamate at 31 December Year 42. The summarised balance sheets of the companies at 31 December Year 42 were:

	Ex Ltd			Wy Ltd		
	£'000	£'000	£'000	£'000	£'000	£'000
Fixed assets						
Land and buildings	50			36		
Motor vehicles	30		80	24		60
Current assets						
Stock	35			18		
Debtors	15			10		
Account at Green Bank plc	18	68		–	28	
Liabilities due within one year						
Trade creditors	20			12		
Overdraft at Blue Bank plc	–	20	48	10	22	6
			128			66
Represented by capital and reserves						
Ordinary share capital, in shares of						
£1.00 each fully paid			100			50
Profit & Loss Account			28			16
			128			66

The directors of both companies agree to revalue the assets and liabilities of their companies in all calculations and in any subsequent accounts:

	Ex Ltd	Wy Ltd
	£'000	£'000
Goodwill	4	nil
Land and buildings	70	38
Motor vehicles	32	21
Debtors[1]	13	9
Creditors[2]	20	14
Stock	33	16

Notes

1   Debtors of Ex Ltd include £1,500 owing by Wy Ltd.

2   Creditors of Wy Ltd include £1,000 owing to Ex Ltd.

3   The difference between the amount owing by Wy Ltd in the books of Ex Ltd and the amount owing to Ex Ltd in the books of Wy Ltd at 31 December is due cash sent by Wy Ltd to Ex Ltd on 30 December Year 42, which was received by Wy Ltd on 2 January Year 43.

EXAMPLE I

The members of both companies agree the following scheme of amalgamation:

1   The shareholders of Wy Ltd will exchange all their shares in Wy Ltd for new ordinary shares in Ex Ltd.

2   The number of shares to be allocated will be based on the value per share of the sundry net assets of each company.

3   Wy Ltd will then be liquidated and Ex Ltd will assume all its assets and liabilities with the consent of the debtors and the creditors of both companies.

Required

(a) Calculate the value of one share in Ex Ltd and the value of one share in Wy Ltd and then calculate how many shares in Ex Ltd should be allocated in exchange for each share in Wy Ltd.

(b) Prepare the balance sheet of Ex Ltd after the amalgamation.

Solution

(a) Calculation of the sundry net assets of each company can be done either by:

- redrafting the draft balance sheets given with the new values or
- adjusting the values of sundry net assets given by the net differences arising on revaluation

The method adopted depends on the circumstances of the question.

In the following workings the original balance sheets are redrafted:

Redrafted Balance Sheets

	Ex Ltd			Wy Ltd		
	£'000	£'000	£'000	£'000	£'000	£'000
Fixed assets						
Intangible goodwill	4			–		
Tangible Land and buildings	70			38		
Motor vehicles	32		106	21		59
Current assets						
Stock	33			16		
Debtors	13			9		
Account at Green Bank plc	18	64		–	25	
Liabilities due within one year						
Trade creditors	20			14		
Overdraft at Blue Bank plc	–	20	44	10	24	1
			150			60
Number of ordinary shares		÷	100		÷	50
Value per share		£1.50 each			£1.20 each	

Therefore each share in Wy Ltd would be exchanged for 0.80 of a share in Ex Ltd (1.20 ÷ 1.50); or one share in Ex Ltd would cost 1.25 shares in Wy Ltd.

Note to the balance sheet

The differences outlined above in Notes 1, 2 and 3 to the balance sheet of the basic circumstances do not affect this part of the answer, because adjustment for them made in the books of Ex Ltd would decrease the amount of debtors and bring into the balance sheet cash in transit of the same amount; the sundry net assets would remain the same.

(b) **Balance Sheet of Ex Ltd (after the amalgamation)**

	£'000	£'000	£'000
Fixed assets			
Intangible goodwill	4		
Tangible: Land and buildings (70 + 38)	108		
Motor vehicles (32 + 21)	53		165
Current assets			
Stock and stock in transit (133 + 16)	49.0		
Debtors (13 + 9 – 1.5)	20.5		
Cash in transit (1.5 – 1.0)	0.5		
Account at Green Bank plc	18.0	88	
Liabilities due within one year			
Trade creditors (20 + 14 – 1)	33.0		
Overdraft at Blue Bank plc	10.0	43	45
			210
Represented by capital and reserves			
Ordinary share capital in shares of £1.00 each fully paid (100 + (50 × 0.8))			140
Share premium (60 – 40)			20
Reserve on revaluation of assets of Ex Ltd (150 – 128)			22
Profit & Loss Account			28
			210

EXAMPLE 2

The basic circumstances are the same as in Example 1. The members of both companies agree the following scheme of amalgamation:

1   Ex Ltd will purchase all the shares of Wy Ltd valued on the same basis.

2   Ex Ltd will become a holding company and Wy Ltd will become a subsidiary company.

3   The purchase of shares will be financed entirely by the issue of 11% debentures (repayable in 10 years) to a finance company at par for cash.

Required
Prepare:

(a) Journal entry(ies) with no narratives in the books of Ex Ltd to record the purchase of the shares and its financing.

(b) The balance sheet of Ex Ltd after the transactions are completed.

The candidate should observe that a consolidated balance sheet is *not* required as part of this example. Consolidated accounts are considered in Chapter 4.

Solution

(a)   **Journal of Ex Ltd**

	£'000	£'000
Shares in Ex Ltd (50,000 × 1.20)	60	
11% debentures		60

Alternatively, there could be two journal entries as follows:

	£'000	£'000
Shares in Ex Ltd (50,000 × 1.20)	60	
Cash or shareholders of Wy Ltd		60
Cash or shareholders in Wy Ltd	60	
11% debentures		60

(b)   **Ex Ltd Balance Sheet (after the amalgamation)**

	£'000	£'000	£'000
Fixed assets			
Intangible goodwill	4		
Tangible: Land and buildings	70		
Motor vehicles	32		
Investments Shares in Wy Ltd at cost	60		166
Current assets			
Stock	33		
Debtors	13		
Account at Green Bank plc	18	64	
Liabilities due within one year			
Trade creditors		20	44
			210
Liabilities due more than one year			
11% debentures			60
			150
Represented by capital and reserves			
Ordinary shares of £1.00 each fully paid			100
Reserve on revaluation of assets (150 – 128)			22
Profit & Loss Account			28
			150

Note to the balance sheet

The above balance sheet is the same as the redraft of Ex Ltd's balance sheet, subject to the £60,000 debentures and £60,000 investment in Wy Ltd.

EXAMPLE 3

The basic circumstances are the same as in Examples 1 and 2. The members of both companies agree the following scheme of amalgamation:

1   Ex Ltd will take over all the assets and assume all the liabilities of Wy Ltd.

2   Ex Ltd will pay for the sundry net assets in cash.

3   The scheme will be financed entirely by the issue of 11% debentures (repayable in 10 years) to a finance company at par for cash.

4   Wy Ltd will be liquidated.

Required

Prepare the account for the liquidator of Wy Ltd as it might appear in the books of Ex Ltd. Note that:

1   Wy Ltd will be liquidated and its assets and liabilities will be brought into the books of Ex Ltd.

2   No journal entries or balance sheets are required and only the books of Ex Ltd are required.

Solution

Liquidator of Wy Ltd Account

	£		£
Trade creditors (14 – 1)	13,000	Land and buildings	38,000
Overdraft at Blue Bank plc	10,000	Motor vehicles	21,000
Cash	60,000	Stock	16,000
		Cash in transit	500
		Debtors (9 – 1.5)	7,500
	83,000		83,000

Capital reconstructions and reductions

Objective

The objective is to account for a reorganisation of the capital and the financing of a company carried out in order to enable the company to continue trading.

Scenario

The scenario is that of a company which has problems in capital and cash flow. Such problems are usually caused by

- big losses accumulating on trading operations and
- high interest charges particularly for short-term finance

The balance sheet includes accumulated losses and overvalued assets.

Method

The directors of the company submit a scheme of reorganisation to members and to the High Court for approval. The scheme might include all or any of the following:

- writing down assets to realistic values
- bringing into the accounts liabilities not presently there
- writing down capital to realistic amounts
- obtaining additional working capital and long-term financing to enable the company to continue trading

The accounting entries will centre around the preparation of a 'capital reconstruction and reduction account'; this is similar to a profit and loss account, but it is charged with any losses and credited with any gains arising on the capital reconstruction or reduction.

Problems

The problems may include the treatment and calculation of contingent liabilities; intangible assets; treatment of any balance on the capital reduction account.

EXAMPLE

The summarised balance sheet of Camel Ltd at 15 December Year 28 is as follows:

	£'000		£'000
8% cumulative preference		Goodwill, patents and	
shares, £1 each	500	trade marks	175
Ordinary shares of £1 each	1,000	Land and buildings	440
Profit & Loss Account (Dr)	−550	Plant and machinery	430
10% debentures	250	Shares in subsidary	150
Accrued debenture interest	25	Stock	365
Creditors	412	Debtors	492
Bank overdraft	300		
Loan from director	115		
	2,052		2,052

Notes

1 Dividends on preference shares are three years in arrears. There is a contingent liability for £50,000 damages in a court case.

2 A capital reduction scheme, agreed and approved by the court, to take place on the date of the above balance sheet, is as follows:

   (a) the ordinary shares will be reduced to £0.25 each;

   (b) the cumulative preference shares will be reduced to £0.80 each. The cumulative preference shareholders also agreed to waive ⅔ of the arrears of the preference dividend and to accept new ordinary shares to be issued in satisfaction of the remaining arrears;

(c) all intangible fixed assets and the debit balance on the profit and loss account will be written off;

(d) the debenture holder agreed to take over, in part satisfaction of the debt, a building (book value £90,000) at a valuation of £125,000. The accrued debenture interest will be paid in cash;

(e) Camel Ltd will issue £110,000 12% debentures for cash;

(f) the remaining land and buildings will be revalued at £380,000. The obsolete stock of £128,000 and bad debts of £87,000 will be written off;

(g) the shares in the subsidiary will be sold for £270,000 cash;

(h) £50,000 cash will be paid in settlement of the court case. The director's loan account will be debited with £10,000 of these damages;

(i) £15,000 of the loan from the director will be repaid in cash, the remainder being settled by issuing new ordinary shares.

Required

Prepare:

(a) The capital reduction account and bank account of Camel Ltd in relation to the scheme.

(b) The summarised balance sheet of Camel Ltd immediately after completing the capital reduction scheme and assuming that no other transactions have taken place.

Solution

(a)

Capital Reduction Account

	£'000		£'000
Ordinary shares (500 × 0.08)	40	Ordinary shares (1000 × 0.75)	750
Goodwill etc	175	Preference shares (500 × 0.2)	100
Profit and loss	550	Sales of property (125 – 90)	35
Stock and debtors (128 + 87)	215	Gain on revaluation (380 – 440 + 90)	30
Damages	50	Sale of shares profit (270 – 150)	120
Balance non-distributable	15	Director's loan (damages)	10
	1,045		1,045

Bank Account

	£'000		£'000
12% debentures	110	Opening balance	300
Shares in subsidiary	270	Debentures interest	25
Closing balance	10	Damages	50
		Director's loan	15
	390		390

(b)   **Summarised Balance Sheet**

	£'000		£'000
8% cumulative preference		Land and buildings	380
shares, £1 each (500 × 0.8)	400	Plant and machinery	430
Ordinary shares			
((1,000 × 0.25) + 40 + 115 – 10 – 15)	380	Stock (365 – 128)	237
Non-distributable reserve	15	Debtors (492 – 87)	405
10% debentures (250 – 125)	125		
12% debentures	110		
Creditors	412		
Bank overdraft	10		
	1,452		1,452

PRACTICE QUESTIONS

3.1 These are the relevant facts concerning Newton plc.

1   On 31 December Year 44 Newton plc's capital consisted of:

- £10,000,000 in ordinary shares of £0.50 each fully paid
- 50,000 8% debentures of £100 each, £50 paid

2   Debenture interest is payable in two equal instalments on 1 January and 1 July.

3   The directors had proposed a final dividend of £0.10 per ordinary share for Year 44.

4   On 1 January Year 45, the members confirmed the final dividend for Year 44. It was paid 15 days later.

5   On 1 April Year 45, the directors called up and received in full the previously uncalled amount on the 8% debentures.

6   On 1 July Year 45, the directors paid an interim dividend of £0.07 per ordinary share.

7   On 31 December the directors proposed a final dividend of £0.09 per ordinary share.

Required

(a) Prepare journal entries to record all the transactions relating to shares and debentures during Year 45. Narratives are *not* required.   (13 marks)

(b) Show how the relevant information given above or derived from your journal entries would appear in the published balance sheet of Newton plc at 31 December Year 45. Indicate the heading under which each entry would appear.
                                                                      (4 marks)

Notes

1   Comparative figures are *not* required.

2   Make all calculations to the nearest £.   Total (17 marks)

3.2 The following trial balance was extracted from the books of Trojan plc at 31 December Year 41:

	£'000	£'000
Bank overdraft		60
Vehicles cost/provision for depreciation at 1 January	135	20
Machinery cost/provision for depreciation at 1 January	170	40
Cost of goods sold/sales	560	800
Ordinary shares of £1.00 each fully paid		250
10% cumulative preference shares of £1.00 each fully paid		150
8% debentures repayable 1 April Year 42		100
Profit & Loss Account at 1 January	100	
Administration expenses, salaries, wages, etc	170	
Debtors/Creditors	160	130
Stock at 31 December Year 41	55	
Land and buildings at cost	110	
Temporary investment 30,000 ordinary shares of £1.00 each, £0.80 paid held in Horse Ltd at cost	90	
	1,550	1,550

In preparing the accounts for publication, the following must be taken into consideration:

1 Depreciation for Year 41:

- vehicles 20% on cost
- machinery 10% on reducing balance

Depreciation of vehicles is a distribution cost and depreciation of machinery is an administration cost.

2 No debenture interest for Year 41 has been paid or brought into the books of Trojan plc.

3 No preference dividends have been paid or declared for Years 39, 40 and 41.

4 The company's only salesman sued the company for wrongful dismissal. The dispute was settled in March Year 42; the salesman was awarded damages of £10,000 in addition to the unpaid sales commission for Year 41 of 0.5% of sales in excess of £600,000 per annum. Neither the damages nor the commission have been entered in the books of Trojan plc.

5 The amount of £160,000 for debtors includes £100,000 from White plc which is now in liquidation; Trojan plc expects to receive no payment at all. Provision must be made for bad debts of 0.5% after deduction of the amount owing by White plc. Provision must also be made for discounts allowable of 3%. The provisions for bad debts suffered and discounts allowable at 1 January Year 41 have been offset against the expenses for these items incurred in Year 41, and the net amounts are included in the administration expenses in the given trial balance.

6 Horse Ltd has made a call of £0.20 per share payable on 31 December Year 41 on all ordinary shareholders; the directors of Trojan plc decided to pay the call. The cheque was drawn on 30 December Year 41, but was not entered in the books of Trojan plc in Year 41.

Required

Prepare for Trojan plc in good style, showing the *minimum* information required for publication:

(a) The profit and loss account for the year ended 31 December Year 41.

Note

The workings showing the profit or loss on ordinary trading activities must be clearly distinguished from the profit and loss account for publication.

(b) The balance sheet at 31 December Year 41.

On 1 January Year 41 the company, its creditors and shareholders agree upon the following scheme of capital reconstruction:

1 Sell part of the company's land and buildings for £58,000 and revalue the remainder at £60,000.

2 Revalue machinery at £100,000 and vehicles at £48,000.

3 Revalue stock at £47,404.

4 Increase the provision for bad debts from 0.5% to 5%.

5 Sell the shares in Horse Ltd for £115,806.

6 Repay the debentures with accrued interest in full.

7 Pay the preference shareholders one year's dividend only in full settlement of their claims for arrears.

8 In lieu of each £1.00 ordinary share presently held, issue to the ordinary shareholders one new ordinary share of £0.50 each, £0.10 paid and call up the remaining £0.40.

9 Write off the balance on the profit and loss account.

10 Pay 50% of the amounts owed in full settlement of their claims to all creditors other than the debenture holders and the bank.

Required

(c) Prepare journal entries for all transactions outlined in the scheme of reconstruction including cash. Assume the scheme is carried through exactly as agreed and the call was fully paid.

Note

No narrations are required.

POINTS TO REMEMBER

Issue of shares or debentures

- If question asks for journal entries, the answer must be presented in that method. This is the usual method.

- Show all workings to support journal entries. Give narratives only if required. Include cash element of transactions, unless question instructs otherwise.

- Journal entries must be in date order:

  1 receipt of cash upon application

  2 allotment of shares or debentures

  3 receipt of allotment cash and refund of excess application cash

  4 call made on shares or debentures

  5 receipt of cash from call

  6 forfeiture of shares or debentures for non-payment of allotment money or call

  7 reissue of forfeited shares or debentures

Distributable profits

- Profits not free for distribution in the form of a cash dividend include:

  1 share premium

  2 revaluation reserve

  3 capital redemption reserve

  4 profits prior to incorporation

- Profits not free for distribution in the form of a cash dividend may be distributed in the form of bonus shares to shareholders.

- Amount of cash available also affects the amount of dividends that a company can pay.

Profits prior to incorporation

- Use a format for the Profit & Loss Account with the following three columns:

  1 period before incorporation

  2 period after incorporation

  3 total for the accounting period

- Apportion gross profit (loss) between the two periods on a turnover basis; do not apportion each individual item in the trading account.

- Do not apportion each item individually; classify the items into:

  1 items apportioned on a turnover basis

  2 items apportioned on a time basis

  3 items apportioned on a different basis

  Charge all items in 1 in one total in the two periods in the Profit & Loss Account; charge all items in 2 in one total in the two periods in the Profit & Loss Account; charge other items individually in the Profit & Loss Account.

- Remember that directors' fees and expenses are incurred by the company and must be charged to the period after incorporation.

Amalgamations

- Three basic ways of amalgamating companies are:

  1 exchanging shares

  2 formation of a holding company and subsidiary companies

  3 one company purchases sundry net assets of other companies which are then liquidated

- Candidates must be able to prepare accounting entries based on the amalgamation scheme agreed by the members of the companies. This may involve calculation of shares allocated, valuation of goodwill, valuation of shares.

Reconstructions and capital reductions

- Debit the capital reconstruction and reduction account with losses on and expenses of capital reconstruction and credit it with any profits

- Losses and expenses may include:

  1 writing off fictitious assets and accumulated losses in Profit & Loss Account

  2 reduction in value of tangible assets

  3 writing off bad debts and increasing provision for doubtful debts

  4 legal and accountancy expenses

  5 making provision for liabilities not in the books (eg arrears of preference dividend payable, damages payable under court action)

- Profits may include:

  1 reduction in nominal value of shares or debentures

2   discounts allowed by creditors

3   agreement by directors to reduce accrued fees and loan accounts owing to them

4   revaluation of assets (usually land and buildings)

4

Accounting for groups of companies

After carefully studying this chapter you should be able to:

1 *prepare consolidated balance sheets;*

2 *make essential calculations in connection with consolidation.*

Accounts for groups of companies tell the shareholders of the holding company the financial position and performance of their company.

The Third Level Accounting syllabus is restricted to holding companies with one or more subsidiary companies. Sub-subsidiary companies, inter-company share-holdings, associated companies and merger accounting are excluded from Third Level Accounting. FRS 3 does not affect the Third Level Accounting syllabus.

The topics to be discussed in this chapter are:

1 *definitions of the headings and the terms used in group balance sheets;*

2 *calculation of:*

    (a) *the goodwill on consolidation (cost of control/capital reserve on consolidation)*

    (b) *the minority interest*

    (c) *the retained earnings of group*

    (d) *the effect of transactions within the group at prices above cost;*

3 *the preparation of group balance sheets incorporating all or any of the above calculations.*

Definitions of the headings and terms used in group balance sheets

The following definitions are used:

1 *Capital reserve on consolidation* This arises where the cost of the purchase of

shares by the holding company in the subsidiary company is *less* than the proportion of sundry net assets attributable to that holding.

- *Cost of shares less attributable value of sundry net assets*

2 *Consolidation* This means the merging of different items (here items in 2 or more balance sheets) to give total figures for each item.

3 *Cost of control or goodwill on consolidation* This arises where the cost of the purchase of shares by the holding company in the subsidiary company is *more* than the proportion of sundry net assets attributable to that purchase of shares.

- *Attributable value of sundry net assets less cost of shares*

4 *Date of acquisition* When the holding company purchases its majority interest in its subsidiary.

5 *Group* Refers to all the companies whose accounts are being consolidated, that is, the holding company and all its subsidiary companies.

6 *Holding company* This is the company that owns 50% or more of the shares in another company.

7 *Inter-company* This signifies transactions between the various companies in the group; it refers to purchases, sales, receipts, payments including payment of dividends.

8 *Majority interest* The book value of the shares held by the holding company in each subsidiary company in the group.

9 *Minority interest* The book value of the shares not held by the holding company.

10 *Profits pre or post acquisition* Indicates profits arising before or after the date at which the holding company purchased the shares in the subsidiary company. It is also referred to as prior, before and after etc.

11 *Retained earnings* This refers to the balance carried forward in respect of profits in the holding company, plus the proportion of the balance carried forward in respect of profits after the date of acquisition of the subsidiary company, attributable to the holding company.

12 *Subsidiary* This is the company 50% or more of whose shares are owned by the holding company.

13 *Sundry net assets* The net book value of a company.

- *Total assets of a company less its total liabilities*

Four basic calculations

There are four basic calculations involved in the preparation of a consolidated balance sheet:

1   goodwill on consolidation

2   minority interest

3   retained earnings of group

4   inter-company profits

Objective

The objective is to show the financial position of a company from the point of view of shareholders of the holding company.

Scenario

Information for these calculations may be derived from many sources. These include:

- the final accounts of the holding and subsidiary companies
- trial balances of those companies
- various schedules of information

All or some of these can be used to construct the final accounts of the individual companies or the consolidated final accounts.

Methods

Goodwill on consolidation

The goodwill on consolidation (cost of control/capital reserve on consolidation) results from a comparison of the cost of the holding company's holdings in the subsidiary company with the holding company's proportion of the sundry net assets of the subsidiary company at the date of acquisition. The calculation of the sundry net assets of the subsidiary company is the total of the share capital plus the balance on reserves at the date of acquisition. Frequently it is necessary to apportion the profits/losses of the subsidiary company between before and after the date of acquisition.

EXAMPLE

On 1 September Year 22 Elsie plc purchased 800,000 ordinary shares in Cia Ltd for £1,100,000. The following information is extracted from the balance sheets of Cia Ltd for Year 22:

	1 January	31 December
	£'000	£'000
Share capital being 1,000,000 shares of £1.00 each	1,000	1,000
Profit & Loss Account being the only reserve	140	200

Note

The average monthly profits accrued during the months of January, February, March and April Year 22, were at twice the average monthly rate for the rest of the year. There were no dividends declared in Year 22.

Required

Calculate the cost of control of Cia Ltd by Elsie plc.

Solution

The cost of control would be calculated as follows:

	£'000	£'000	£'000
Cost of shares bought			1,100
Less sundry net assets at 1 September:			
Share capital		1,000	
Reserves at 1 September			
Profits for year (200,000 – 140,000)	60		
Profits to 31 August (60,000 × (4 × 2) + 4) ÷ (12 + 4)	45		
Reserves 1 January	140	185	
Total sundry net assets		1,185	

Elsie plc's proportion of sundry net assets would be:
total sundry net assets multiplied by Elsie plc's
proportion of total shares:

ie £1,185,000 × (800 ÷ 1,000)	948
Cost of control	152

The minority interest

The minority interest is calculated by attributing to the minority shareholders their proportion of the total assets of the subsidiary company at the balance sheet date. Their interest is not affected by considerations of profits before and after the date the holding company purchased its shares. (As a result, it is a much simpler calculation.)

EXAMPLE

Using the example of Elsie plc and Cia Ltd (*see* above) the minority interest would be calculated as follows:

	£'000
Total sundry net assets of Cia Ltd at 31 December Year 22	
Share capital	1,000
Reserves	200
	1,200
Minority proportion ((200 ÷ 100) × £1,200,000)	240

Retained earnings of group

The retained earnings of the group is the total of the closing profits of the holding company plus the holding company's proportion of the profits of the subsidiary company after the date of acquisition by the holding company.

EXAMPLE

Using the same example as above, the retained earnings of Cia Ltd attributable to the group after the date of acquisition would be calculated as follows:

	£'000
Profits for year (200 – 140)	60
Profits after 1 September ((60,000 × 4) ÷ (12 + 4))	15
Holding company proportion ((800 ÷ 1,000) × £15,000)	12

Intercompany transactions invoiced at prices above cost

There are 3 situations in which intercompany transactions are invoiced at prices above cost.

1   Where the profit accrues on an asset disposed of outside the group before the balance sheet date, the profit element will be ignored as it has been 'realised'.

2   Where the profit accrues on a current asset still held within the group the whole profit will be deducted to reduce the asset to cost.

3   Where the profit accrues on a fixed asset still held within the group the profit will be adjusted by comparing the written-down value of the asset at selling price with the written-down value of the asset at cost price.

In **2** and **3**, if the profit accrues to the holding company deduct the whole profit from the holding company profits; if the profit accrues to the subsidiary, apportion the profit to be deducted from subsidiary company profits between group and minority interest on the basis of their respective holdings in the subsidiary.

The following is an example of this calculation:

EXAMPLE

In the same example as is used above, on 1 July Year 23 Elsie plc bought machinery from Cia Ltd. This machinery was manufactured by Cia Ltd for £80,000 and sold to Elsie plc at a gross profit of 20% on the selling price. Elsie plc, which still owned the machinery at 31 December Year 23, wrote off depreciation at 12% per annum calculated in months from the date of purchase.

Required
Prepare a memorandum journal entry to record the profit to be deducted from the group profits and from the machinery.

Solution

	Cost price 80% £	Profit 20% £	Invoiced price 100% £
Machinery 1 July Year 23	80,000	20,000	100,000
Depreciation to 31 December			
Year 23 at 12% per annum	4,800	1,200	6,000

The memorandum journal entry is:

	£	£
Group Profit & Loss Account	1,200	
Group machinery account		1,200

Problems

Problems arise in making and bringing together the various calculations and different interests involved.

Preparation of group balance sheets

This section deals with the preparation of the consolidated balance sheet and incorporates all or any of the calculations discussed in the previous section. Candidates must ensure that the consolidated balance sheet is laid out correctly, in compliance with current good accounting practice. A question on this topic may ask for a vertical layout consolidated balance sheet.

Objective

The objective of preparing group balance sheets is to merge all the information and previous calculations into one combined balance sheet in order to present the reader with the financial position of the group from the point of view of the group's shareholders.

Scenario

As explained in the previous section, the information may be derived from many sources including:

- the final accounts of the holding and subsidiary companies
- trial balances of those companies
- various schedules of information

Each requires a different method, but the methods have many features in common.

Method

When the basic information has been assembled the balance sheets of all the companies involved are merged or added together, subject to the necessary adjustments for:

1   goodwill on consolidation (cost of control/capital reserve on consolidation)

2   minority interest

3   retained earnings of group

4   intercompany transactions invoiced at prices above cost

Problems

1   Consolidated balance sheets include many detailed calculations. It is therefore essential to prepare adequate workings for each, cross-referenced to the final result.

2   As good layout is required the workings must not appear as part of the final consolidated balance sheet; this means for example that it is incorrect to prepare a '3-column balance sheet' showing side by side the balance sheets of holding and subsidiary companies with the third column being an addition of the previous two columns.

3   The effects of any adjustments must be carefully followed through; for example:

(a)   The final share capital of the group will be that of the holding company as the share capital of the subsidiary is in effect divided between minority interest and calculation of goodwill on consolidation.

(b)   The final balance on the profit and loss account will comprise that of the holding company plus the group's proportion of the subsidiary company's profit earned after the date of consolidation.

(c)   The minority interest will consist of the minority shareholders' proportion of the sundry net assets of the subsidiary company.

(d)   Any assets appearing in the consolidated balance sheet will be adjusted for intercompany profits in them, subject to depreciation.

(e)   Intercompany balances will be offset against each other, any differences being items in transit. For example, stock in transit is added to the stock of the holding and subsidiary company. Similarly, cash in transit is added to the cash of the holding and subsidiary company.

(f)   As a result of the above, the final assets of the group will exclude all intercompany debts and the investment of the holding company in the subsidiary company. The final liabilities of the group will exclude all intercompany liabilities.

EXAMPLE I

Ipa plc bought a majority holding in Codu Ltd on 1 April Year 15. At 31 December Year 15, the following summarised balance sheets were prepared:

	Ipa plc £	Codu Ltd £	Consolidated £
Cost of shares in Codu Ltd	111,000		
Goodwill on consolidation			35,625
Fixed assets	349,000	25,000	374,000
Stock	95,000	30,000	125,000
Debtors	110,000	20,000	130,000
Bank	30,000	10,000	40,000
Current liabilities	−145,000	−5,000	−150,000
	550,000	80,000	554,625
Ordinary shares of £1 each fully paid	500,000	100,000	500,000
Profit & Loss Account	50,000	−20,000	46,625
Minority interest			8,000
	550,000	80,000	554,625

At 1 January Year 15 the profit and loss account of Ipa plc was nil and of Codu Ltd was £15,000 (debit): Codu Ltd has neither paid nor proposed any dividend for Year 15.

Required

(a) Redraft the summarised consolidated balance sheet given above in a vertical layout suitable for publication. Marks will be awarded for suitable subheadings and subtotals.

(b) (i) Show how the percentage minority interest can be calculated at 31 December Year 15.

(ii) Show how the value of the minority interest would have been calculated at 1 April Year 15.

(c) (i) Show how goodwill on consolidation was calculated at 1 April Year 15.

(ii) Briefly comment on how this item should appear in future consolidated balance sheets.

Solution

(a)   **Ipa plc Consolidated Balance Sheet at 31 December Year 15**

	£	£
Fixed assets		
Intangible Goodwill on consolidation		
[offset to Profit & Loss Account]		35,625
Tangible		374,000
		409,625
Current assets		
Stock at lower of cost or net realisable value	125,000	
Debtors	130,000	
Bank	40,000	
	295,000	
Liabilities due within one year	150,000	
Excess of current assets over current liabilities		145,000
		554,625
Represented by		
Share capital and reserves		
Called up share capital		500,000
Profit & loss account		46,625
Minority interest		8,000
		554,625

Note how the question asks the candidate to incorporate the headings used in group accounts in the preparation of the above consolidated balance sheet (in addition to those required in a single company balance sheet).

(b) (i)	Percentage minority interest	£
	Minority interest at 31 December Year 15	8,000
	Sundry net assets of Codu Ltd 31 December Year 15	80,000
	Hence minority shareholders held 10% of the shares	
(ii)	Minority interest at 1 April Year 15 is:	£
	10% × (80,000 + 9 ÷ 12 × (20,000 − 5,000))	8,375
(c) (i)	Goodwill at 1 April Year 15	35,625
	Cost of investment	111,000
	Holding company proportion of sundry net assets	
	(100% − 10%) × (80,000 + (9 ÷ 12 × (20,000 − 15,000)))	75,375

(ii)   It should be written off immediately or amortised on a regular basis.

EXAMPLE 2

Umbrella plc bought 75% of Sati plc's ordinary shares at £1. 10 per share on 1 April Year 9. The companies prepared the following trial balances at 31 December Year 9:

	Umbrella plc		Sati plc	
	£'000	£'000	£'000	£'000
Stock	90		38	
Profit & Loss Account		100		40
Tangible fixed assets	428		180	
Debtors/creditors	42	50	32	28
10% debentures redeemable in two equal instalments				
on 31 December Year 10 and 31 December Year 11		120		
Bank	10			22
Ordinary shares of £1.00 each fully paid		300		160
	570	570	250	250

Notes

1   Umbrella plc had not recorded the purchase of the ordinary shares of Sati plc on 1 April Year 9. This was financed from a special bank loan, upon which 18% per annum interest was payable annually in arrears. Umbrella plc had not accrued this interest. The loan was repayable in 3 years' time.

2   Umbrella plc valued Sati plc's freehold land at £90,000; this is included in the tangible fixed assets of Sati plc at £60,000 on 31 December Year 9.

3   On 1 January Year 9, Sati plc had a credit balance of £44,000 on its Profit & Loss Account; Profits/losses accrued evenly over Year 9.

4   On 31 December Year 9 Umbrella plc declared a dividend of £0.10 per share. Sati plc did not declare any dividend.

Required

Prepare *in good style* a consolidated balance sheet for Umbrella plc and its subsidiary company at 31 December Year 9.

Solution

Umbrella plc and subsidiary
Consolidated Balance Sheet at 31 December Year 9

	£	£	£
Tangible fixed assets			
(428,000 + 180,000 + 30,000)			638,000
Current assets			
Stock (90 + 38)	128,000		
Debtors (42 + 32)	74,000		
Bank	10,000	212,000	
Liabilities payable within 1 year			
Creditors (50 + 28)	78,000		
10% debentures (120 × ½)	60,000		
Bank	22,000		
Proposed dividend (300 × 10%)	30,000		
Interest on special bank loan			
(160,000 × 75% × 1.1 = 132,000 loan)			
(132,000 × 18% × 9/12)	17,820	207,820	4,180
			642,180

	£	£	£
Liabilities payable more than 1 year			
10% debentures (120 × ½)	60,000		
Special bank loan	132,000		192,000
			450,180
Financed by Capital and reserves			
Ordinary shares of £1.00 each			300,000
Capital reserve on consolidation			
(Cost of shares	£132,000		
less S.N.A. 75% (160 + 30 + 40 + (9 ÷ 12 × 4)) £174,750)			42,750
Profit & Loss (100 – 30 – 17,820 – 75% (4 – 1))			49,930
			392,680
Minority (25% (40 + 160 + 30))			57,500
			450,180

PRACTICE QUESTION

4.1   Hello plc has two subsidiary companies:

1   Goodbye Ltd, in which it bought 50% of the shares on 1 January Year 67 at £1.50 each; it still owns these shares and has a controlling interest.

2   Adios Ltd, in which it bought 60% of the shares on 1 January Year 68 at £1.10 each; it still owns these shares.

The following information relates to the subsidiary companies:

	Goodbye Ltd		Adios Ltd	
As at 31 December Year 69	£'000	£'000	£'000	£'000
Debtors/Creditors	80	30	100	90
Bank	10		20	
Stock	160		80	
10% debentures repayable in 5 equal annual instalments from 30 June Year 70		120		
11% debentures repayable in Year 84				60
Fixed assets	100		150	
Ordinary shares of £1.00 each fully paid		150		120
Profit & Loss Account		50		80
	350	350	350	350
For year ended 31 December Year 69				
Sales		1,000		1,500
Cost of goods sold	800		1,000	
Net profit		20		30

Required

(a) Calculate to one decimal place the following ratios for *each* of the subsidiary companies from the information given above:

  (i)   Working capital

  (ii) Acid test

    (iii) Gross profit

    (iv) Return on shareholders' capital employed

    (v) Turnover to fixed assets

As Hello plc is short of cash its directors decide to sell for cash all its shares in *one* of the subsidiary companies.

Revoir plc has offered to buy *either:*

1   All the shares held in Goodbye Ltd for the payment of an amount equal to 50% of the book value of the sundry net assets of Goodbye Ltd after revaluing its fixed assets at 120% of their present value and after creating a provision for doubtful debts of 10% of its debtors; *or*

2   All the shares held in Adios Ltd for the payment of such an amount that 60% of the net profit of Adios Ltd for Year 69 would give a return on Revoir plc's investment of 18% per annum.

Required

  (b) Calculate how much cash Hello plc would receive in respect of each of offers **1** and **2**.

    The trial balance of Hello plc at 31 December Year 69 *before* the sale was:

	£'000	£'000
Fixed assets, including shares in subsidiary companies	800	
Stock	650	
Debtors/Creditors	750	300
Bank overdraft		500
Ordinary shares of £1 each fully paid		1,000
Profit & Loss Account		400
	2,200	2,200

    The directors of Hello plc accepted the offer from Revoir plc for the shares in Adios Ltd.

Required

  (c) Prepare the balance sheet of Hello plc immediately after the sale of the shares in Adios Ltd. Assume no other transactions have taken place since 31 December Year 69.

Hello plc bought its shares in Goodbye Ltd when Goodbye Ltd's balance on Profit & Loss Account, its only reserve, was £55,000.

Required

  (d) Prepare the consolidated balance sheet of Hello plc and its subsidiary Goodbye Ltd immediately after the sale of the shares in Adios Ltd. Assume no other transactions have taken place since 31 December Year 69.

After reviewing the consolidated balance sheet, the directors of Hello plc offered for sale 400,000 Ordinary shares in Hello plc on the following terms:

- 1 March Year 70: application £0.25 per share
- 1 April Year 70: allotment £0.35 per share including premium
- 1 October Year 70: first call £0.25 per share
- 1 March Year 71: second call £0.25 per share

Applications were received for 440,000 shares: on 15 March Year 70 the directors refunded monies received in respect of excess applications. All allotment money was received in full. The first call was fully paid apart from the amount owing by Mr Exe who had been allotted 400 shares; his shares were forfeited on 1 November Year 70. The second call on the remaining shares was fully paid.

Required

(e) Prepare, without narrations, journal entries including those relating to cash to record the issue of shares.

POINTS TO REMEMBER

- *Goodwill on consolidation* (also called cost of control) is: Cost of holding company's shares in subsidiary company *less* proportion of subsidiary company's sundry net assets attributable to holding company at acquisition.

- *Minority interest* is: proportion of subsidiary company sundry net assets at date of consolidated balance sheet.

- *Retained earnings of group* are: final balance on holding company's Profit & Loss Account *plus* holding company's proportion of subsidiary company's net profit earned after date of acquisition.

- *Profits made on intercompany transactions* on assets still held within the group are: deduction of profit on transaction from book value of asset at date of consolidated balance sheet.

- Show all calculations as workings to your answer, but *not* as part of the consolidated balance sheet.

- Eliminate all intercompany current accounts; the differences will be caused by and shown as stock or cash in transit at date of the consolidated balance sheet.

- The consolidated balance sheet will not include:

  (a) The cost of investment by holding company in subsidiary company. This will disappear in calculating goodwill on consolidation.

  (b) Ordinary share capital of subsidiary company. This will be eliminated in calculating the cost of control and the minority interest.

  (c) Intercompany balances.

  (d) Goodwill on consolidation. This must be written off against available profits as soon as possible.

5

Accounting for special circumstances

After carefully studying this chapter you should be able to:

Concerning branches

1 *account for home branches where the double entries are made at head office only;*

2 *account for home branches where full double entries are made at head office and at branch;*

3 *account for home branches where transactions between head office and branch are made at cost price;*

4 *account for home branches where transactions between head office and branch are made at a loaded price or selling price.*

Concerning investments

1 *prepare investment accounts;*

2 *distinguish between fixed interest investments and investments bearing variable income;*

3 *make all calculations for investment accounts.*

Concerning joint ventures

1 *prepare joint venture accounts in the separate books of each joint venturer;*

2 *prepare memorandum joint venture accounts.*

Concerning interest on capital

1 *calculate interest on a debt of varying balance;*

2 *prepare accounts for the capital element of debts and for the revenue element of debts.*

The specific accounting circumstances that come under the heading special circumstances are:

1   *branches (excluding foreign branches);*

2   *investments;*

3   *joint ventures;*

4   *interest on capital.*

As each of the above topics relates to a different aspect of Third Level Accounting, they will be considered individually in the following pages in the order listed.

Branches (excluding foreign branches)

When a business is conducted in more than one business premises, one is considered as the head office and the others are considered as branches. (Foreign branches are not included in the Third Level Accounting syllabus.)

Objectives

The objectives are:

1   to record and control the transactions and sundry net assets of the branch

2   to ascertain the profit/loss of the branch

3   to record the branch transactions with other branches and/or the head office

Scenario

The owners/management of a business identify and decide to exploit an opportunity to expand their business in additional premises, usually in a different area. A branch will usually trade with its head office and with the public.

Methods

There are two main methods of accounting for branches:

1   All the double entry book-keeping is done in the head office books. The branch will probably compile memorandum records but these will not form part of the double entry. This is sometimes called the 'stock and debtors method'.

2   Both head office and branch keep full double entry book-keeping records.

Under both methods, transactions between head office and branch(es) may be at cost price or at cost plus a loading or at selling price.

We will now examine each method in detail:

All the double entry book-keeping is done in the head office

Transactions may be recorded either:

● at cost price or
● at loaded or selling price

If the transactions between head office and branch are at *cost price*, it will be necessary to open two accounts:

1   *Goods sent to branch account* This account will be credited with the cost price of goods sent to the branch; at the end of each financial period it will be closed by transferring its balance to the credit of purchases account or trading account.

2   *Branch stock account* This account will be debited with the cost of the opening balance of stock at the branch and with the cost of goods sent to the branch; it will be credited with the selling price of goods sold and the cost or valuation of the closing stock at the branch. The credit balance carried down at this point on the account is the gross profit of the branch. The expenses of the branch will be charged to give the branch net profit. Note that this is in effect a trading and profit and loss account.

The book-keeping entries in this method in connection with sending goods to the branch are:

Journal

Branch stock account	Debit	£'000
Goods sent to branch account	Credit	£'000

Thereafter all book-keeping entries are the same as in the preparation of a trading and profit and loss account for a sole trader except that the net profit is transferred to the general profit and loss account; the balance on the goods sent to the branch account is credited to purchases account as it represents the amount of purchases by head office which have been 'used' by the branch and not sold by the head office itself.

If the transactions between head office and branch are at *loaded* or *selling price*, it will be necessary to open three accounts:

1   *Goods sent to branch account* This is exactly the same account as 1 above.

2   *Branch stock account* This account is debited with the selling price of opening stocks held at the branch and with the selling price of goods sent to the branch. It is credited with the selling price of goods sold by the branch and with the selling price of closing stock at the branch. As this account is entirely at selling price it should balance exactly, subject to any change in prices, or loss of stock.

3   *Branch stock adjustment account* This account is debited with the gross profit or loading on goods sold at the branch and on closing stock at the branch. It is credited with the gross profit or loading on opening stock of goods at the branch and of goods sent to the branch. As it is entirely at gross profit, it should balance exactly, subject to any change in prices or loss of stock.

The book-keeping entries in this method in connection with sending goods to the branch account are:

Transaction	Journal		
Sending goods to branch	Branch stock account at SP	Debit	
	Goods sent to branch account at CP		Credit
	Branch stock adjustment account at GP		Credit
Selling goods at branch	Debtors and/or cash	Debit	
	Branch stock account		Credit
Goods returned by branch to head office	Goods sent to branch account at CP	Debit	
	Branch stock adjustment account at GP	Debit	
	Branch stock account at SP		Credit
Goods returned by customers to branch	Branch stock account at SP	Debit	
	Debtors and/or cash at SP		Credit
Goods lost at branch	Branch stock adjustment account	Debit	
	Branch Profit & Loss Account	Debit	
	Branch stock account		Credit
Transfer of GP to Profit & Loss	Branch stock adjustment account at GP	Debit	
	Branch Profit & Loss Account		Credit
Provide for GP on unsold stock at branch	Branch stock adjustment account at GP	Debit	
	Branch stock adjustment account		Credit

Note

SP is selling price
CP is cost price
GP is gross profit

The last entry is to bring down the balance on the branch stock account. All other accounts would be balanced in the usual way. Thereafter, all book-keeping entries are as in the normal preparation of a trading and profit and loss account for a sole trader except that the net profit is transferred to the head office or general profit and loss account; the balance on the goods sent to the branch account is credited to the purchases account to represent the amount of goods purchased that are used by the branch and not sold by the head office itself.

Both head office and branch keep full double entry book-keeping records

The essential accounts in this situation are the branch account in the head office books and the head office account in the branch accounts:

- the branch account in the head office books records all transactions between head office and branch from the point of view of the head office
- the head office account in the branch books records all transactions between branch and head office from the point of view of the branch

The format of these accounts is:

In head office books

Branch Account

Opening balance	£'000	Cash received from branch	£'000
Goods sent to branch	£'000	Goods returned from branch	£'000
Fixed assets sent to branch	£'000	Goods sent by branch	
Profit/loss of branch	£'000	to head office	£'000
		Closing balance	£'000
	£'000		£'000

In branch books

Head Office Account

Cash sent to head office	£'000	Opening balance	£'000
Goods returned to head office	£'000	Goods received from head office	£'000
Goods sent to head office	£'000	Fixed assets received	£'000
Closing balance	£'000	Profit/loss of branch	£'000
	£'000		£'000

The book-keeping entries in this method are:

In head office books

Transaction	Journal in head office books		
Branch profit	Branch account	Debit	
	Profit & Loss Account		Credit
Goods sent to branch	Branch account	Debit	
	Goods sent to branch account (or purchases account)		Credit
Cash received from branch	Cash account	Debit	
	Branch account		Credit

In branch books

Transaction	Journal in branch books		
Branch profit	Profit & Loss Account	Debit	
	Head office account		Credit
Goods received from head office	Goods received from head office account (or purchases account)	Debit	
	Head office		Credit
Cash paid to head office	Head office account	Debit	
	Cash account		Credit

At the end of the accounting period

In the trial balance of the head office, the branch account will usually appear as a debit; in the trial balance of the branch the head office account will usually appear as a credit of the same amount.

When the final accounts are prepared, the trial balances of head office and branch will be added together and the accounts in respect of the head office and the branch will be eliminated against each other. If they are of equal amount and on opposite sides of the trial balances, the combined trial balance will still balance when they are eliminated.

Items in one set of books, but not in the other set, will cause a difference when eliminating balances for the final accounts; these are usually cash in transit or goods in transit.

In the head office books, cash in transit from branch to head office will be credited to the branch account and debited to the cash in transit account. It will be shown as a current asset in the combined balance sheet.

In the branch books, goods in transit from head office to branch will be credited to the head office account and debited to the goods in transit account. They will be shown as a current asset in the combined balance sheet.

Problems

The problems arising in connection with branch accounts include:

1   Reading the question to ensure that the method of accounting to be used for the branch is fully understood. The method may be stated in the form of a preamble to the question or in the body of the question. For example if a question gives an opening balance on a branch stock adjustment account, this indicates that the head office invoices the branch at selling price; if it gives opening balances on a head office account and on a branch account these indicate that the branch keeps its own double entry set of accounts.

2   Understanding and applying the price structure if the head office invoices the branch at more than cost. For example a question may state that the head office invoices the branch at a gross profit of 25% on *sales* and that during the year the *cost* of goods sent by the head office to the branch was £1,200,000. If all the double entry book-keeping is maintained at the head office only, the entries to record the goods invoiced by head office to branch would be at selling price, but the question gives only the cost price. If the gross profit is 25% on the sales price it is possible to calculate the selling price thus:

● selling price is cost price plus 25% of selling price
● hence 75% of selling price is cost price and
● the mark-up on cost price therefore is 25% divided by 75%, that is 33.33%

The resultant journal entry could be:

Branch stock account (SP)	£1,600,000	
Goods sent to branch account (CP)		£1,200,000
Branch stock adjustment account (GP)		£400,000

3 Where the head office invoices the branch at loaded or selling price it is necessary to reduce the value of the branch stock to cost price in compiling the final accounts for the business as a whole. For example, assume:
Information given:

(a) the head office invoices the branch at cost price plus 25%;

(b) at the end of the year the stock at the branch was valued at £9,000, being at selling price.

What would the stock be valued at in the company's balance sheet at the year end?
This could be answered as follows:

Reduce the stock to cost price as follows:

	£	£
Stock at branch	9,000	
Less provision for unearned profit at the branch		
((25 ÷ 125) × 9,000)	1,800	7,200

Note
The provision is 20% of the selling price which is the same as 25% of the cost price.

4 Where the branch maintains full double entry book-keeping records and there is a branch account in the head office books and a head office account in the branch books, it will usually be necessary to reconcile these two accounts: they should be of equal amounts but the debit balance on the branch account in the head office books should be reflected by a credit balance on the head office account in the branch accounts.

EXAMPLE

In the double entry records of a company there is in the head office books at the year end a debit balance in respect of the company's branch of £54,321; in the branch books there is a credit balance in respect of the head office of £54,000. The further information states that at the year end there was:

1 Stock sent by the head office to the branch but not yet received by the branch at cost: £149. (This is also called 'stock in transit'.)

2 Cash sent from the branch to the head office at the year end but not yet received by the head office: £172. (This is also called 'cash in transit'.)

Required

(a) Prepare the branch account in the head office books and the head office account in the branch books and then reconcile the two accounts in both books.

(b) Show the entry in the company balance sheet for these items at the year end.

Solution

(a)   **Branch account in head office books**

	£		£
Balance in trial balance	54,321	Cash in transit	172
		Closing balance	54,149
	54,321		54,321

Head office account in the branch books

	£		£
		Balance in trial balance	54,000
Closing balance	54,149	Stock in transit	149
	54,149		54,149

(b) In the company's balance sheet at the year end:

(i) The branch account in the head office books and the head office account in the branch books will not appear. They are equal and opposite and will therefore be eliminated against each other.

(ii) The cash in transit will be added to form part of the total cash of the company or shown as a separate item if significant.

(iii) The stock in transit will be added to form part of the total stock of the company or shown as a separate item if significant.

EXAMPLE I

This example illustrates the situation where all the double entry books of account are maintained at the head office and the branches keep memorandum records only. The branches are invoiced at fixed selling prices. As a result the candidate is required to write up

- goods sent to branches account
- branch stock accounts
- branch stock adjustment accounts

Wabic Ltd has a central warehouse which does not trade with the public. It has three retail branches which do trade with the public. All goods for resale are bought by the central warehouse and invoiced to the retail branches at local selling prices which are determined by adding the following mark-ups on cost:

- 20% at Branch X
- 25% at Branch Y
- 30% at Branch Z

As a result of a computer fault, the central warehouse produced the following printout for Year 42, with blanks indicated by **(1)**, **(2)**, **(3)**, **(4)** and **(5)**.

	Central warehouse £'000	Branch X £'000	Branch Y £'000	Branch Z £'000
Opening stock at cost	100.0			
Opening stocks at selling price		105.0	50.0	39.0
Purchases	1,587.0			
Goods sent to branches at cost	**(1)**			
Goods invoiced by warehouse at selling price		**(4)**	**(2)**	**(3)**
Sales	NIL	**(5)**	640.0	503.1
Closing stock at cost	87.0			
Closing stocks at selling price		168.0	35.0	55.9

In Year 42, Wabic Ltd had no stock differences and did not write any stock off.

Required

(a) Calculate the five missing figures indicated by **(1)** to **(5)** above.

Note

Make all calculations to the nearest £100.

(b) Prepare the following accounts in the central warehouse books:

(i) Stock

(ii) Goods sent to branches

(iii) Branch stock for *each* branch in columnar form

(iv) Branch stock adjustment for *each* branch in columnar form

Solution

(a) Calculation of missing items in printout: £'000

1 $(100 + 1587 - 87)$ — 1,600

2 $(-50 + 640 + 35)$ — 625

3 $(-39 + 503.1 + 55.9)$ — 520

4 $(1600 - (625 \div 125\%) - (520 \div 130\%) = 700 \times 120\%)$ — 840

5 $(105 + 840 - 168)$ — 777

(b)

Account in central warehouse books

(i) Stock account

	£'000		£'000
Balance b/d	100	Goods sent to branches	1,600
Purchases	1,587	Balance c/d	87
	1,687		1,687

(ii) Goods sent to branches

	£'000		£'000
Stock a/c	1,600	Branch X	700
		Y	500
		Z	400
	1,600		1,600

(iii) Branch stock accounts

	X	Y	Z		X	Y	Z
	£'000	£'000	£'000		£'000	£'000	£'000
Bal b/d	105.0	50.0	39.0	Sales	777.0	640.0	503.1
Central warehouse	840.0	625.0	520.0	Bal c/d	168.0	35.0	55.9
	945.0	675.0	559.0		945.0	675.0	559.0

(iv) Branch stock adjustment account

	X	Y	Z		X	Y	Z
Profit & Loss a/c	129.5	128.0	116.1	Bal b/d	17.5	10.0	9.0
Bal c/d	28.0	7.0	12.9	Goods sent	140.0	125.0	120.0
	157.5	135.0	129.0		157.5	135.0	129.0

EXAMPLE 2

This example illustrates the situation where the branch maintains its own full double entry books of account. The head office invoices the branch at a loaded price. These procedures imply the use of a branch account in the head office books and a head office account in the branch books and a branch stock adjustment account which reduces the branch closing stock to cost price in compiling the balance sheet of the company.

Nosetoc plc sells goods at its head office and at the branch it opened on 1 April Year 37. All purchases are made by the head office and goods are invoiced by head office to the branch at cost price. Both head office and branch calculate their selling prices by adding a mark-up of 25% to the cost of goods for sale. Delivery charges to the branch are 4% of the selling price of the goods. The branch had no stock at 31 December Year 37.

Owing to computer errors, the accountant produced the following incomplete trial balance at 31 December Year 37.

	Head office £'000	£'000	Branch £'000	£'000
Sales		800		175
Goods sent to branch/goods from head office		**(1)**	**(1)**	
Delivery expenses of goods sent to branch	**(3)**			
Shop expenses	21		4	
Administration expenses	18			
Shop buildings	33		15	
Shop fittings cost provision for depreciation	31	9	20	
Profit & Loss at 1 January Year 37		21		
Head office account				**(6)**
Branch account	17			
Ordinary shares of £1.00 each fully paid		80		
Stock 1 January Year 37	70			
Purchases	**(4)**			
Creditors		27		
Bank overdraft at Cot Bank plc		6		
Bank account at Eson Bank Ltd			2	
Debtors	26		8	
	(2)	**(2)**	**(5)**	**(5)**

Required

(a) Calculate the figures to fill in the blanks indicated by **(1)**, **(2)**, **(3)**, **(4)**, **(5)** and **(6)**.

The following information is available:

1 Administration expenses will be apportioned between head office and branch on the basis of sales values.

2 There was no stock in transit at 31 December Year 37.

3 Closing stock at the head office is valued at £150,000.

4 No stock was lost during the year.

5 Depreciation is calculated on shop fittings at 25% per annum using the reducing balance method. No shop fittings were purchased or sold during the year except those purchased on 31 March for use in the branch.

6 The directors proposed a dividend of £0.20 per share on the ordinary shares for Year 37.

(b) Prepare, in good style using columnar form, the trading and profit and loss account and appropriation account showing the gross and net profits of the head office, *and of the branch*, for Year 37.

Note
Make all calculations to the nearest £1,000.

(c) Prepare, in good style, the balance sheet for Nosetoc plc at 31 December Year 37.

Note

There is a similarity between this example and Example 1 in that the candidate must first calculate figures to complete the given information and then use them for subsequent parts of the question.

Solution

(a)   £'000

1	(100 ÷ 125 × 175) =	140
2	Trial balance total	1,083
3	(4% × 175)	7
4	Trial balance residual	860
5	Trial balance total	189
6	Trial balance residual	14

(b) Individual trading and profit and loss accounts (in columnar form) for the head office and for the branch are preapred to ascertain the individual profit/loss for head office and branch. The appropriation account for the company as a whole is prepared, beginning with the combined profits/losses derived from the branches.

Nosetoc plc Trading Profit & Loss Account for Year 37

	Head office	Branch
	£'000	£'000
Sales	800	175
Cost of goods sold (800 × 80%)	640	140
Gross profit	160	35
Delivery expenses to branch (charge to branch as goods sent to branch invoiced at cost price)		7
Shop expenses	21	4
Administration expenses (18 ÷ 975) × 800 and (18 ÷ 975 × 175)	15	3
Depreciation (25% × (31 − 9) and (20 × 25%) × 9/12)	6	4
	42	18
Net profit	118	17

Nosetoc plc Profit & Loss Appropriation Account for Year 37

	£'000
Profit for the year (118 + 17)	135
Proposed dividends (80,000 at 20%)	16
Retained profits for the financial year	119

(c)   **Nosetoc plc Balance Sheet at 31 December Year 37**

	£'000 Cost	£'000 Depn	£'000
Tangible fixed assets			
Shop buildings (33 + 15)	48		48
Shop fittings (31 + 20) and (9 + 6 + 4)	51	19	32
	99	19	80
Current assets			
Stock	150		
Debtors (26 + 8)	34		
Bank (Eson)	2	186	
Liabilities within year			
Creditors	27		
Bank overdraft (Cot) (6 – 3)	3		
Dividend	16	46	140
			220
Financed by capital and reserves:			
£1 ordinary shares			80
Profit and Loss (119 + 21)			140
			220

EXAMPLE 3

Toothy Ltd has a head office and three branches – Branch X, Branch Y and Branch Z. The branches keep their own books. They remit their takings gross to the head office. All expenses are paid by the branches from petty cash and reimbursed by head office. In the head office books, there are separate current accounts for each branch. Head office keeps an account at Hoang Bank Ltd. The following balances are extracted from the head office books at 31 December Year 23:

	£ Debit	£ Credit
X Branch current account	10,000	
Y Branch current account	3,830	
Z Branch current account	15,365	
Hoang Bank Ltd		9,600

The following additional information has become available when reconciling the head office and branch books at 31 December Year 23:

1 Cash in transit from head office: to Branch X, £125; to Branch Z, £140.

2 Cash in transit to head office: from Branch X, £2,750; from Branch Y, £2,180; and from Branch Z, £4,780.

3 Stock in transit from Head Office: to Branch X, £375; to Branch Y, £1,970; and to Branch Z, £3,960.

4 Returns in transit to Head Office: from Branch X, £100; and from Branch Y, £460.

5   Accounting errors made by Head Office:

   (a) £250 cash received from Branch X credited to Branch Y;

   (b) £480 goods sent to Branch Y debited to Branch Z.

Required

(a) Prepare journal entries, without narrations but including cash, to adjust the head office books for all items in transit to the head office and for the accounting errors made by the head office.   (6 marks)

(b) Calculate the closing balance at Hoang Bank Ltd in the head office books.
                    (1 mark)

(c) Write up, in *each* set of branch books, the head office current account, adjusting it for items in transit from the head office. Treat the opening balance in each head office current account as a residual.   (10 marks)
                    Total (17 marks)

Solution

(a)   **Journal entries**

	£	£
Bank	9,710	
Branch X		2,750
Branch Y		2,180
Branch Z		4,780
Stock in transit (returns)	560	
Branch X		100
Branch Y		460
Branch Y	250	
Branch X		250
Branch Y	480	
Branch Z		480

(b)   **Hoang Bank Ltd**

	£
Overdraft	−9,600
Cash in transit	9,710
Balance in favour of Toothy Ltd	110

(c)   **Head Office current accounts**

Branch X books

	£		£
Balance c/d		Balance b/d (residual)	6,400
(10,000 – 2,750 – 100 – 250)	6,900	Stock in transit	375
		Cash in transit	125
	6,900		6,900

Branch Y books

	£		£
Balance b/d (residual)	50	Stock in transit	1,970
Balance c/d			
(3,830 – 2,180 – 460 + 480 + 250)	1,920		
	1,970		1,970

Branch Z books

	£		£
Balance c/d		Balance b/d (residual)	6,005
(15,365 – 4,780 – 480)	10,105	Cash in transit	140
		Stock in transit	3,960
	10,105		10,105

Investments

When a company or sole trader invests money in shares in another company the transaction is called an investment. The situation where one company acquires control of another company, known as a majority shareholding, falls under the heading of groups of companies which is considered in Chapter 4.

Objectives

The objectives are:

1   to record the capital invested in stocks and shares

2   to distinguish as far as possible the capital element from the income elements of amounts invested in or derived from the investments in stocks and shares. When stocks and shares carrying a fixed rate of income are bought or sold the amount paid may include an element of 'compensation' for the income accruing from the date at which it was last paid to the date of purchase. The vendor loses and the purchaser gains that income which is automatically reflected in the purchase price.

Scenario

A company has funds in excess of its immediate requirements. The directors of the company decide to invest the excess in stocks and shares which carry either:

(a) a fixed rate of income such as government stocks or fixed income bearing debentures;

(b) a variable rate of income such as ordinary shares in a limited company.

Method

The account used for investments has a 3-column format with the following column headings:

Nominal   Income   Capital   Nominal   Income   Capital

These headings mean:

- *Nominal* Number of stocks or shares involved – purchased, sold or held. These columns are in quantities, ie the number of shares. (These columns do not form part of the double entry book-keeping.)
- *Income* Amount of interest or dividends received or receivable on investment. (These columns form part of the double entry book-keeping.)
- *Capital* Amount of cash paid in respect of purchases of stocks or shares or received in respect of sales of stocks or shares, the value of the stocks or shares held. (These columns form part of the double entry book-keeping.)

The following terms are used:

- 'c.d.' (cum div) – this means the purchaser of the investment is entitled to the next dividend payable on the shares
- 'x.d.' (ex div) – this means the vendor of the investment is entitled to the next dividend payable on the shares.

Transactions are entered in date order in the account as follows:

Transaction	Journal entry
(a) Purchase of investment	Nominal column: debit with number of shares bought Capital column: debit with the capital element of the investment Income column: debit with any accruing interest attributable to vendor but receivable by purchaser *or* credit with any accruing interest attributable to purchaser but receivable by vendor Cash account: credit cash paid
(b) Sale of investment	Cash account: debit with amount received Income column: debit with any accruing interest attributable to purchaser but receivable by vendor *or* credit with any accruing interest attributable to vendor but receivable by purchaser Nominal column: credit with number of shares sold Capital column: credit with the capital element of the investment Any profit or loss on the sale is transferred to the Profit & Loss Account

Transaction	Journal entry
(c) Receipt of interest	Cash account: debit Income column: credit
(d) Receipt of bonus issue on shares held	Nominal column: debit No credit
(e) Take-up of rights issue declared	Nominal column: debit with number of shares bought Capital column: debit with the cash paid Cash account: credit with amount paid
(f) Sale of rights	Cash account: debit Capital column: credit

(g) Any balances on the nominal and capital columns and any interest accrued will be carried forward in the usual way

Problems

Problems arise here with:

1   Treatment of entries that are 'c.d.' and 'x.d.'.

2   The dates of the transactions.

3   When sales take place, it is usual to calculate the cost of the shares sold at an average price of the shares at the date of the sale and then transfer the profit/loss to the profit and loss account at the date of the sale. This calculation must bring into consideration the adjustments for c.d. and x.d. purchases and sales.

4   On a bonus shares issue the shareholder receives shares without payment and therefore the only entry is in the nominal column.

5   If there is a rights issue the existing shareholder is offered the right to buy further shares in the company, usually at a reduced price. If he decides to take up the offer, the accounts will reflect this transaction by debiting the nominal column with the number of shares received and debiting the capital column with any cash paid with a credit to the cash account. It is important to distinguish between bonus issues and rights issues.

6   Distinction between fixed income stocks (such as government bonds) and variable income stocks (such as ordinary shares in a company). The income is apportioned *only* on fixed income stocks.

EXAMPLES

Three examples of investment accounts are given.

The first example demonstrates the calculations and treatment of income earned on an investment bearing a fixed rate of interest. The candidate is required to calculate the income earned in an investor's financial year on an investment in government stocks; the amount of stock held varies during the financial year, due to purchases and sales of the stock.

The second example illustrates *inter alia* transfers to the profit and loss account of the profits/losses of sales of shares forming part of an investment without a fixed rate of interest.

The third example contrasts the treatment of a government bond, bearing a fixed rate of interest, with ordinary shares, bearing a variable dividend.

EXAMPLE I

On 1 January the directors of Ovast Ltd decided to invest surplus company funds in 6% government stock. The interest on this stock was payable 6 months in arrears on 1 February and 1 August. During the year the following transactions in this stock took place:

		Nominal value	
1 Jan	Bought	£50,000	c.d.
15 July	Bought	£30,000	x.d.
15 Aug	Sold	£20,000	c.d.
30 Nov	Sold	£30,000	c.d.

Required

Prepare the income columns in the investment in 6% government stock account in the books of Ovast Ltd from the given information.

Show the adjustments made on purchases and sales of the stock in respect of interest accruing and the total transfer to the profit and loss account in respect of interest gained in the year.

Show calculations in respect of all entries including the closing balance and the transfer to the profit and loss account.

Solution

Preliminary calculations

Note that the interest is 6% per annum, ie ½% per month.

Reason		Capital £	Rate	Months	£
1 Interest accrued on purchase,	1 Nov–31 Dec	50,000	× ½%	× 5	1,250
2 Half-yearly interest,	1 Nov–31 Jan	50,000	× ½%	× 6	1,500
3 Interest accrued on purchase	15 Jul–1 Aug	30,000	× ½%	× ½	75
4 Half-yearly interest,	1 Feb–31 Jul	50,000	× ½%	× 6	1,500
5 Interest accrued on sale,	1 Aug–15 Aug	20,000	× ½%	× ½	50
6 Interest accrued on sale,	1 Aug–30 Nov	30,000	× ½%	× 4	600
7 Interest accrued at year end,	1 Aug–31 Dec	30,000	× ½%	× 5	750
8 Interest gained in the year:					
(a) Interest from initial purchase to purchase 15 July,	1 Jan–15 Jul	50,000	× ½%	× 6½	1,625
(b) Interest from purchase 15 July to sale 15 Aug,	15 Jul–15 Aug	80,000	× ½%	× 1	400
(c) Interest from sale 15 Aug to sale 30 Nov,	15 Aug–30 Nov	60,000	× ½%	× 3½	1,050
(d) Interest from sale 30 Nov to year end,	30 Nov–31 Dec	30,000	× ½%	× 1	150
					3,225

Investment in 6% Government Stock Account

		Income £			Income £
1 Jan 1 Int on c.d. purchase		1,250	2 1 Feb Cash int to date		1,500
			3 15 Jul Int on x.d. purchase		75
			4 1 Aug Cash int to date		1,500
			5 15 Aug Int on c.d. sale		50
			6 30 Nov Int on c.d. sale 6		600
			7 31 Dec Int accrued 7		750
8 Dec 31 Profit & Loss Account Interest for year		3,225			
		4,475			4,475

EXAMPLE 2

Tsavo Ltd is not an investment company. During the financial year ended 31 March Year 27, the following transactions took place in relation to £1 ordinary shares in Crok plc:

Year 26

April 21 Tsavo Ltd purchased 24,000 shares for £1.25 each

June 30 Tsavo Ltd sold 8,000 shares for £1.75 each

Aug 25 Crok plc:

(a) declared a bonus issue of 1 fully paid share for every 5 shares held on 1 August Year 26

(b) gave shareholders the right to apply for 1 share for every 8 shares held on 1 August Year 26 at a price of £1.50 per share (payable £1 on application on 30 September Year 26, the balance on 31 October Year 26)

(c) stated that the new shares from the bonus and rights issues would not rank for dividends declared out of profits for the year to 31 December Year 26

Sept 25 Tsavo Ltd applied for and paid the application money for 800 shares

Sept 30 Tsavo Ltd sold the rights for further entitlement for £0.40 each for cash

Oct 28 Tsavo Ltd paid the balance due on 800 shares

Year 27

Jan 31 Crok plc declared and paid a dividend of £0.15 per share for the year ended 31 December Year 26

March 15 Tsavo Ltd sold 5,000 shares for £2.10 each

Required

Prepare in the books of Tsavo Ltd the investment account (shares in Crok plc) for the year ended 31 March Year 27. Transfer profits/losses to the profit and loss account at the time of sale. Value shares on a weighted average cost basis.

Solution

Shares in Crok plc

DEBIT SIDE

		Nominal	Income	Capital
		£	£	£
Year 26				
April 21	Bank	24,000		30,000
June 30	Profit & Loss Account[1]			4,000
Aug 25	Bonus issue[2]	3,200		
Sept 25	Bank	800		800
Oct 28	Bank[4]			400
Year 27				
March 15	Profit & Loss[6]			5,320
March 31	Profit & Loss		2,400	
		28,000	2,400	40,520

CREDIT SIDE

		Nominal	Income	Capital
Year 26				
June 30	Bank	8,000		14,000
Sept 30	Bank[3]			480
Year 27				
Jan 31[5]			2,400	
March 15		5,000		10,500
March 31[7]		15,000		15,540
		28,000	2,400	40,520

The calculations are as follows:

		£
1	Proceeds of sale 30 June Year 26, 8,000 × (1.75 − 1.25)	= 4,000
2	Bonus issue 30 Sept Year 26, ⅕ × (24,000 − 8,000)	= 3,200
3	Sale of rights 30 Sept Year 26, 0.4 × ((16,000 ÷ 8) − 800)	= 480
4	Payment of balance of rights issue 31 Oct Year 26, 800 × (1.50 − 1.00)	= 400
5	Dividend received 31 Jan Year 27, 16,000 × 0.15	= 2,400
6	Profit on sales of shares on 15 March Year 27,	
	10,500 − (5,000 × ((16,000 × 1.25) + (800 × 1.5) − 480) ÷ (16,000 + 3,200 + 800))	= 5,320
7	Value of closing balance 31 March Year 27,	
	15,000 × ((16,000 × 1.25) + (800 × 1.5) − 480) ÷ (16,000 + 3,200 + 800)	=15,540

EXAMPLE 3

Teen Ltd was formed on 1 January Year 19 to invest in public limited companies. The directors decided to invest any temporarily surplus funds in government bonds, which pay interest half-yearly on 1 February and 1 August.

During Year 19, Teen Ltd's investment transactions were:

1 Jan	Bought £10,000,000 6% government bonds @ 98 x.d.
31 March	Sold £4,000,000 6% government bonds @ 101 c.d. and with the proceeds bought £0.60 ordinary shares in Indust plc @ £0.80 x.d.
30 June	Sold £1,000,000 6% government bonds @ 103 x.d. and with the proceeds bought £0.60 ordinary shares in Indust plc at £0.80 c.d.
15 Aug	Received a dividend of £0.10 per share on the shares in Indust plc.

Any profit/loss on the realisation of an investment was transferred immediately to the profit and loss account.

Required

In the books of Teen Ltd, prepare the investment accounts for Year 19 for:

(a) the 6% government bonds   (14 marks)

(b) the Indust plc shares   (3 marks)

Total (17 marks)

Solution

(a)   **6% Government Bonds**

		Nominal £'000	Income £'000	Capital £'000		Nominal £'000	Income £'000	Capital £'000
Jan 1	Cash	10,000		9,800				
	Interest			50	Interest[1]		50	
				9,850				
Feb 1					No interest[2]			
March 31					Cash[3]	4,000		4,040
	Interest			40	Interest[4]		40	
	Profit & Loss[5]			60				

	Nominal £'000	Income £'000	Capital £'000		Nominal £'000	Income £'000	Capital £'000
June 30				Cash			
				(1,000,000 × 103)	1,000		1,030
Interest		5		Interest[6]			5
Profit & Loss[7]			50				
Aug 1				Cash Interest[8]		180	
Dec 31 Profit & Loss[9]		390		Interest Acc'd[9]		125	
				Balance (9,850 × 50%)	5,000		4,925
	10,000	395	10,000		10,000	395	10,000

(b)   **Indust plc**

		Nominal £'000	Income £'000	Capital £'000		Nominal £'000	Income £'000	Capital £'000
March 31	Cash	5,050		4,040				
June 30	Cash	1,287.50		1,030				
		6,337.50						
Aug 15					Dividend			
					(6,337.5 × £0.10)		633.75	
Dec 31	Profit & Loss		633.75		Balance	6,337.50		5,070
		6,337.50	633.75	5,070		6,337.50	633.75	5,070

The workings are as follows:

1.   Interest $10,000,000 × 6\% × \frac{1}{12} = £50,000$

2.   No interest as x.d. purchase

3.   Cash $4,000,000 × 101 = £4,040,000$

4.   Interest $4,000,000 × 6\% × \frac{2}{12} = £40,000$

5.   Profit on sale $4,040 - 40 - (40\% × 9,850) = £60,000$

6.   Interest $1,000,000 × 6\% × \frac{1}{12} = £5,000$

7.   Profit on sale $1,030 + 5 - (10\% × 9,850) = £50,000$

8.   Interest $6,000,000 × 3\% = £180,000$

9.   *Either* $(10,000 × 3) + (6,000 × 3) + (5,000 × 6) = 78,000 × \frac{1}{2}\% = £390,000$
   or $5,000 × 6\% × \frac{5}{12} = £125,000$

Joint ventures

Joint ventures arise when two or more organisations decide to trade in a temporary partnership. Such partnerships can arise between companies or sole traders.

Objectives

1 to record the transactions of a joint venture in the books of each party to that joint venture

2 to ascertain profits/losses arising from the joint venture

3 to calculate the amount to settle balances between the parties to the joint venture

Scenario

Two or more organisations co-operate to take advantage of business opportunities together without entering into long-term arrangements such as partnerships or the formation of subsidiary companies etc.

Methods

If X and Y enter into a joint venture X will open an account called 'Joint Venture with Y' in his books to record the amounts he puts into the venture (in the form of cash, goods, services etc) and the amounts he withdraws from the venture. Y will open in his books an account called 'Joint Venture with X'. In addition there will be a Memorandum Joint Venture Profit & Loss Account to ascertain the profit/loss arising and to show how it is divided between the joint venturers.

In some circumstances the parties to the joint venture will also open a separate bank account for the joint venture and then the joint venture will keep its own books of account.

Problems

These may include the following:

1 If the joint venturers decide to settle any balance arising between them before the joint venture has ended, it will be necessary to value the sundry net assets of the venture at the time of that settlement and divide the valuation between the venturers in the profit/loss sharing ratio. If a question about a joint venture does not state the value of any assets, it will be necessary to calculate the value. The assets most likely to be valued in these circumstances are tangible fixed assets such as machinery which is subject to depreciation and stock which is calculated on a FIFO or other basis.

In the example given below it is necessary to calculate the value of stock and also to calculate the total value of the sundry net assets and divide it between the joint venturers. These calculations are shown in the preliminary calculations before the answer to the question.

2 When settlements are made between the joint venturers the amount will be the residual amount on the account each joint venturer keeps in respect of the joint venture. This amount must be reconciled between both sets of books. This reconciliation is shown in the example given below.

EXAMPLE I

On 1 January Jay & Ve began a joint venture sharing profits/losses in the ratio of 3 : 2 respectively. They decided not to open a bank account for the joint venture; instead each partner would pay for or deposit into his own bank account any amounts paid for or received on behalf of the joint venture.

Their transactions during the year were as follows:

1 Jan	Jay bought and paid for 1,000 Javes at £5.00 each
	Ve paid £500 for rent on a storage depot for one year
1 March	Jay bought and paid for 2,000 Javes at £6.00 each
To 30 June	Ve sold 2,700 Javes at £11.00 each for cash; he paid the proceeds into his own bank account. He also paid selling expenses for the half-year amounting to £1,400
	The amount owing between the joint venturers to date was paid
1 Aug	Jay bought and paid for 1,500 Javes at £5.50 each
1 Oct	Jay bought and paid for 2,000 Javes at £5.00 each
To 31 Dec	Ve sold 3,400 Javes at £10.50 each for cash; he paid the proceeds into his own bank account. He also paid selling expenses for the half-year amounting to £450
	The amount owing between the joint venturers to date was paid

There was no loss of stock during the year

The joint venturers also agreed:

- to value any stock of Javes held at 30 June and 31 December on a FIFO basis
- to settle any amount owing by one joint venturer to the other at 30 June and at 31 December
- to close the venture at 31 December; Jay will take over any stock left at the end of the venture valued on FIFO basis

Required

Prepare the following:

(a) The memorandum joint venture account showing the profit/loss for the half-year to 30 June and for the half-year to 31 December and its division between the joint venturers.

(b) The joint venture with Ve account in the books of Jay including the settlement of the amount due by one venturer to the other.

(c) The joint venture with Jay account in the books of Ve including the settlement of the amount due by one venturer to the other.

Note

As this question asks for the profit/loss at 30 June and 31 December and a cash settlement between the joint venturers at those dates but no amounts of stock balances are given, the candidate must begin with a preliminary calculation to calculate the amount of stock and its value at 30 June and 31 December. This could be approached by writing up a stock of Javes account.

Solution

Preliminary calculations
Stock of Javes Account

	Units	£
Purchases 1 Jan at £5.00 each	1,000	5,000
Purchases 1 March at £6.00 each	2,000	12,000
Purchases to 30 June	3,000	17,000
Sales to 30 June	2,700	
Stock at 30 June	300	
This would be valued on a FIFO basis at £6.00 each		1,800
Purchases 1 Aug at £5.50 each	1,500	8,250
Purchases 1 Oct at £5.00 each	2,000	10,000
Purchases to 31 Dec	3,500	18,250
Stock at 30 June	300	
	3,800	
Sales to 31 Dec	3,400	
Stock at 31 Dec	400	
This would be valued on a FIFO basis at £5.00 each		2,000

As the joint venturers are settling the balance due at 30 June it is necessary to calculate the value of the sundry net assets of the venture at 30 June. The calculation is as follows:

Sundry Net Assets at 30 June

	£
Stock (see Stock of Javes Account)	1,800
Prepaid rent £500 × ½	250
	2,050
This is divided in profit/loss ratio: Jay 3/5	1,230
Ve 2/5	820
	2,050

(a) The Memorandum Joint Venture Account to 30 June

		£		£
Purchases	3,000 Javes	17,000	Sales 2,700 at £11.00	29,700
Stock	300 Javes	1,800		
		15,200		
Gross profit		14,500		
		29,700		29,700
Rent for half-year		250	Gross profit	14,500
Selling expenses for half-year		1,400		
Net profit: Jay 3/5 7,710				
Ve 2/5 5,140		12,850		
		14,500		14,500

The Memorandum Joint Venture Account to 31 December

		£		£
Opening stock	300 Javes	1,800	Sales 3,400 at £10.50	35,700
Purchases	3,500 Javes	18,250		
		20,050		
Closing stock 400 Javes taken				
over by Jay		2,000		
		18,050		
Gross profit		17,650		
		35,700		35,700
Rent for half-year		250	Gross profit	17,650
Selling expenses for half-year		450		
Net profit:	Jay 3/5 10,170			
	Ve 2/5 6,780	16,950		
		17,650		17,650

(b)   **The Joint Venture with Ve Account in the Books of Jay**

		£			£
Jan 1	Cash	5,000	30 June	Cash (from) Ve*	23,480
March 1	Cash	12,000		Balance	1,230
June 30	Profit & Loss	7,710			
		24,710			24,710
June 30	Balance	1,230	31 Dec	Purchases	2,000
Aug 1	Cash	8,250		Cash*	27,650
Oct 1	Cash	10,000			
Dec 31	Profit & Loss	10,170			
		29,650			29,650

(c)   **The Joint Venture with Jay Account in the Books of Ve**

		£			£
Jan 1	Cash	500	30 June	Cash	29,700
June 30	Cash	1,400		Balance	820
June 30	Profit & Loss	5,140			
June 30	Cash*	23,480			
		30,520			30,520
June 30	Balance	820	31 Dec	Cash	35,700
Dec 31	Cash	450			
Dec 31	Profit & Loss	6,780			
Dec 31	Cash*	27,650			
		35,700			35,700

EXAMPLE 2

On 1 January Year 20 Miss Twist and Mr Bust formed a joint venture to make and sell widgets. They agreed to share profits/losses 3 : 2 respectively. They each contributed £20,000 to buy a widget manufacturing machine for £40,000, which will make 100 batches of 500 widgets each and then have no residual value. They decided to depreciate the machine on the basis of the number of widgets made.

During Year 20, widgets were sold at £7.00 each. The following transactions took place in Year 20:

	No. of widgets made	No. of widgets sold for cash	Total costs excluding depreciation £
1 Jan to 30 April	1,000	1,000	6,000
1 May to 30 Aug	1,500	1,500	8,250
1 Sept to 31 Dec	2,500	2,300	12,750

Miss Twist paid all the costs from her own bank account, paid all the proceeds of sales into her own bank account and sent one-third of the proceeds of sales to Mr Bust. There were no selling or administration expenses. At 31 December Year 21 they decided to value the unsold stock of widgets at its *variable* cost, including depreciation.

Required

Prepare, for Year 20:

   (a) The memorandum joint venture account of Miss Twist and Mr Bust

(11 marks)

   (b) The joint venture with Mr Bust account in Miss Twist's books   (6 marks)

Total (17 marks)

Solution

(a)   **Memorandum Joint Venture Account**

	£	£	£
Sales (1,000 + 1,500 + 2,300) × 7			33,600
Cost of goods sold:			
Costs (6,000 + 8,250 + 12,750)	27,000		
Depreciation (5,000 ÷ 50,000 × 40,000)	4,000		
		31,000	
Stock at variable cost			
Cost excluding depreciation			
((8,250 – 6,000) ÷ (1,500 – 1,000)) = £4.5 unit			
Depreciation (40,000 ÷ (500 × 100)) = 0.8 unit			
2,500 – 2,300 widgets at 5.3 unit		1,060	
			29,940
Net profit:			3,660
Divided: Miss Twist 3/5			2,196
Mr Bust 2/5			1,464
			3,660

(b)   **Miss Twist's Books: Joint Venture with Mr Bust Account**

	£		£
Cash machine	20,000	Cash sales	33,600
Costs	27,000	Machinery[1]	21,600
Bust (33,600 ÷ 3)	11,200	Stock[2]	636
Profit	2,196	Closing balance	4,560
	60,396		60,396

Notes to the accounts

1   $\frac{3}{5} \times (40,000 - 4,000) = 21,600$.

2   $\frac{3}{5} \times 1,060 = 636$.

Interest on capital

Interest on capital arises in many questions which deal with situations where money is borrowed. It could feature as a small section of a large question concerning a company that borrows money as part of a large number of transactions. Alternatively a whole question could be devoted to this topic, as for example, where the management of a company is considering various methods of financing the company's operations.

Objective

When a business borrows money to finance its operations interest will be charged on the amount borrowed and adjusted for any money repaid. Accounting records are necessary to show the amount owing as the basis of calculations of the interest payable. These will show the amounts and the dates on which the amounts were borrowed and repaid and therefore the amount outstanding for the period.

Scenario

The loan or debt giving rise to interest may be short term, such as a temporary bank overdraft, or may be long term in the form of 20-year debentures. The interest may be calculated at a fixed rate or at a variable rate following the terms of the loan agreement; a variable rate may be determined by an external index or by the amount borrowed.

Methods

The records required will be twofold:

1   an account for the loans giving rise to the interest

2   an account for the interest itself

Both of these accounts will be in the usual accounting format, such as:

1 Loan Account

		£			£
June 30	Cash (repaid)	XXXX	1 Jan	Cash (borrowed)	XXXX
	Closing balance	XXXX			
		XXXX			XXXX

2 Interest on Loan Account

		£			£
June 30	Cash	XXXX	30 June	Profit & Loss Account (interest payable)	XXXX

Alternatively both accounts could be combined, giving:

Loan Account

		£			£
June 30	Cash (repaid)	XXXX	1 Jan	Cash (borrowed)	XXXX
	Closing balance	XXXX	30 June	Profit & Loss Account	XXXX
		XXXX			XXXX

Problems

Problems arise in calculating the interest payable as a result of following the actual terms of the loan and the basis upon which interest is payable.

At one end of the scale there is a simple long-term loan in which the whole loan is repayable at the end of a fixed period with simple interest payable annually. At the other end is the more complex situation of a loan that is repayable in instalments with compound interest being calculated on the reducing balance and payable annually. It is essential to understand the exact terms of any loan and the basis of the interest.

EXAMPLES

Three examples are given here to illustrate the various situations possible under the heading of interest.

EXAMPLE 1

On 1 January Year 1 Options Ltd borrowed $100,000 to finance the purchase of a new machine. In the contract with the lenders Options Ltd agreed:

1   to repay each year $12,500 capital from 31 December Year 1 onwards

2   to pay 15% per annum interest on the balance outstanding immediately before the annual repayment

Required

Prepare the loan account including loan interest in the books of Options Ltd for Years 1, 2 and 3.

Solution

Loan Account

		$			$
Year 1			*Year 1*		
Dec 31	Cash (12,500 + 15,000)	27,500	Jan 1	Cash	100,000
	Balance c/d	87,500	Dec 31	P&L	15,000
Year 2			*Year 2*		
Dec 31	Cash (12,500 + 13,125)	25,625	Jan 1	Balance b/d	87,500
	Balance c/d	75,000	Jan 31	Interest	13,125
Year 3			*Year 3*		
Dec 31	Cash (12,500 + 11,250)	23,750	Jan 1	Balance b/d	75,000
	Balance c/d	62,500	Dec 31	Interest	11,250
			Year 4		
			Jan 1	Balance b/d	62,500

EXAMPLE 2

Cashort plc estimates it will have a bank overdraft of £90,000 on 31 December Year 40. Overdraft interest is payable at 12% per annum, calculated on the balance at the end of each month and charged to the account on the first day of the next month. As an alternative to using the bank overdraft as its only source of borrowed finance, Cashort plc is considering reducing the overdraft by issuing to Fince Ltd £90,000 10% debentures (Year 44) at par for cash receivable on 2 January Year 41. For Year 41 Cashort plc budgets the following:

	Jan £	Feb £	March £	April £
Amounts paid into bank				
Receipt from customers	20,000	30,000	20,000	25,000
Sale of fixed assets			80,000	
Amounts paid out of bank				
Supplies and expenses	24,000	26,000	28,000	30,000
Purchase of fixed assets		108,151		

Required

(a) Assuming that Cashort plc has *not* issued any debentures, prepare in columnar form a monthly budgeted bank account from 1 January Year 41 to 1 May Year 41. Include the charges for overdraft interest from 1 January Year 41 to 1 May Year 41.

(b) Assuming that the £90,000 10% debentures were issued at par for cash and paid for by 2 January Year 41, prepare in columnar form a *revised* monthly budgeted bank account from 1 January Year 41 to 1 May Year 41. Include the charges for overdraft interest from 1 January Year 41 to 1 May Year 41.

Note

Make all calculations to the nearest £.

Solution

(a)

Budgeted Bank Account

Month	Bal b/d	Interest	Payments	Subtotal	Receipts	Bal c/d
Jan	90,000	900	24,000	114,900	20,000	94,900
Feb	94,900	949	134,151	230,000	30,000	200,000
March	200,000	2,000	28,000	230,000	100,000	130,000
April	130,000	1,300	30,000	161,300	25,000	136,300
May	136,300	1,363				

(b)

Revised Budgeted Bank Account

Month	Bal b/d	Interest	Payments	Subtotal	Receipts	Bal c/d
Jan	90,000	900	24,000	114,900	110,000	4,900
Feb	4,900	49	134,151	139,100	30,000	109,100
March	109,100	1,091	28,000	138,191	100,000	38,191
April	38,191	382	30,000	68,573	25,000	43,573
May	43,573	436				

EXAMPLE 3

Onyx plc has £900,000 12% debentures which may be redeemed in either of two alternative methods:

1   In 6 equal annual instalments at par from 1 January Year 14. Onyx plc would borrow the funds necessary each year from P Ltd at 7% per annum. The amount borrowed would all be repayable on 1 January Year 22.

2   In one amount at 102% at any time from 1 January Year 14. Onyx plc would borrow the funds necessary from Q plc at 8% per annum, repayable on 1 July Year 17. If Onyx plc redeemed the debentures using this method, it would do so on 1 January Year 14.

Required

(a) Show the entries in the profit and loss account for Years 14, 15, 16 and 17 and in the balance sheet at 31 December Years 14, 15, 16 and 17 using:

(i) Method 1

(ii) Method 2 (14 marks)

(b) Briefly compare the financial effects of the two methods. (3 marks)

Total (17 marks)

Solution

(a) (i) Method 1

	Entries in Profit & Loss Account		Entries in Balance Sheet		
				Liabilities due	
				more than 1 year	within 1 year
		£		£	£
Year					
14	Deb int 750,000 × 12%	90,000	Debs 900,000 ÷ 6 = 150,000 × 4... × 1	600,000	150,000
	Loan int 150,000 × 7%	10,500	Loan P Ltd	150,000	
15	Deb int 600,000 × 12%	72,000	Debs 150,000 × 3... × 1	450,000	150,000
	Loan int 300,000 × 7%	21,000	Loan P Ltd	300,000	
16	Deb int 450,000 × 12%	54,000	Debs 150,000 × 2... × 1	300,000	150,000
	Loan int 450,000 × 7%	31,500	Loan P Ltd	450,000	
17	Deb int 300,000 × 12%	36,000	Debs 150,000 × 1... × 1	150,000	150,000
	Loan int 600,000 × 7%	42,000	Loan P Ltd	600,000	

(a) (ii) Method 2

	Entries in Profit & Loss Account		Entries in Balance Sheet		
				Liabilities due	
				more than 1 year	within 1 year
		£		£	£
Year					
14	Loan int 918,000 × 8%	73,440	Loan Q Ltd 900,000 × 102%	918,000	
	Premium w/o	18,000			
15	Loan int	73,440	Loan Q Ltd	918,000	
16	Loan int	73,440	Loan Q Ltd		918,000
17	Loan int 918,000 × 4%	36,720			

(b) It would be more expensive under Method 1; Method 2 would be cheaper, but it would give the problem of how to repay the £918,000, 1 July Year 17.

PRACTICE QUESTIONS

5.1 Mr Messy, a sole trader, opened his only branch on 1 January Year 41. Although his head office sent the branch all the goods sold by the branch in Year 41, Mr Messy did not record how much was sent and kept no records at the branch other than branch sales.

Owing to local trading circumstances, goods were sold by the head office to the public at a fixed mark-up on cost of 25% and by the branch to the public at a fixed mark-up on cost of 20%.

The following information concerning Year 41 is available:

	£
Stock at head office 1 January Year 41	20,000
Stock at branch (at branch selling price) at 31 December Year 41	12,000
Head office purchases for Year 41	338,333
Total sales for head office and branch	400,000
Gross profit on head office sales to the public	60,000
Total expenses paid by head office for head office and branch★	52,000

Note

★ 50% of these expenses are to be apportioned on the basis of sales turnover and 50% on the basis of floor space; the head office floor space is 4 times as large as that at the branch.

It is assumed that there were no stock differences either at the head office or at the branch for Year 41.

Required

Prepare for Mr Messy for Year 41:

   (a) Head Office Trading and Profit & Loss Account

   (b) Goods Sent to Branch Account

   (c) Branch Stock Account at selling price

   (d) Branch Stock Adjustment Account

   (e) Branch Profit & Loss Account

Note

No trading account is required for the branch. Work to the nearest whole £.

5.2 Strangeloss plc is an import/export agency, making an average annual profit of £100,000. Because of the nature of its business it has large excess funds for temporary investment at certain times in the year. These funds are used to buy government stock; this is sold when the cash is required.

On 1 January Year 88, Strangeloss plc had no government stock. In Year 88 its transactions relating to 8% government stock on which interest is payable 1 January and 1 July were as follows:

Purchases		Sales	
Mar 1	£50,000 stock at 90 c.d.	May 1	£40,000 stock at 90½ c.d.
Jun 1	£70,000 stock at 92 x.d.	Aug 1	£60,000 stock at 60 c.d.

The market price of this stock was 55 x.d. at 31 December Year 88.

Required

   (a) Prepare the investment in 8% government stock account in the books of Strangeloss plc for the year to 31 December Year 88. This stock is normally valued on a FIFO basis.

(b) State how the loss on the 8% government stock might be shown in the published accounts of Strangeloss plc.

Note

Make all calculations to the nearest £.

5.3 Jules and Vernes formed a joint venture on 1 January Year 35 to last to 30 June Year 35 in order to buy and sell units of Jovos. They agreed:

1 To share profits/losses in the ratio Jules 60%, Vernes 40%

2 To value closing stocks on a FIFO basis.

3 Not to open a joint venture bank account.

The following transactions took place:

1 Jan	Vernes paid £600 rent on joint venture warehouse for the half-year
11 Jan	Jules paid for 3,000 units at £5.00 each
23 Feb	Jules paid for 4,000 units at £4.50 each
31 March	Vernes received proceeds of sale of 1,000 units at £6.50 each
30 June	Vernes received proceeds of sale of 5,000 units at £7.00 each
30 June	Vernes paid £1,900 for selling and delivery expenses to date
30 June	Vernes paid Jules £36,000

Required

(a) Prepare for the half-year to 30 June Year 35:

    (i) the memorandum joint venture account

    (ii) the joint venture with Vernes account in the books of Jules

    (iii) the joint venture with Jules account in the books of Vernes

As they considered that the joint venture was successful, Jules and Vernes decided to enter into a formal partnership from 1 July Year 35. The written partnership agreement included the following points:

1 Profits/losses are to be shared equally.

2 Goodwill acquired from the joint venture was valued at £2,000 and brought into the partnership accounts.

3 The stock of the joint venture was taken over at cost.

4 The amount owing between the joint venturers at 30 June Year 35 would be settled by means of a contra entry between the partners' capital accounts.

Required

(b) Prepare the opening entries in the partners' capital accounts.

5.4 Wolf plc's recent sales were:

		£'000		£'000		£'000		£'000
Year 38	Sept	500	Oct	400	Nov	600	Dec	700
Year 39	Jan	800	Feb	400	March	300		

Wolf plc allows its customers to deduct a 5% cash discount if they pay within the first month following the month of sale. 80% (by value) of the sales are paid for in the first month and qualify for the discount; the remaining 20% are paid for in the second month and do not qualify for discount.

Wolf plc calculates its selling price using a mark-up of 25%. Monthly purchases exactly equal the cost of goods sold in the previous month. Wolf plc always pays its suppliers in the second month after purchase and receives a 3% cash discount.

Required

(a) Prepare statements to show for January, February and March Year 39:

   (i)   the cash received from customers

   (ii) the cash paid to suppliers

At the end of each month Wolf plc calculates the difference between the cash received from customers and the cash paid to suppliers. On the first day of the following month the company pays the excess into a 'Special Bank Account' or withdraws any deficit from the same account. This account earns interest of 12% per annum calculated on the balance at the end of each month but only credited to the account on 1 April, 1 July, 1 October and 1 January. There was a credit balance of £100,000 on this account on 1 January Year 39 after the bank had credited 'excess cash' and interest to 31 December Year 38.

Required

(b) Prepare, as it would appear in Wolf plc's books, the 'Special Bank Account' from 1 January Year 39 to 1 April Year 39.

Note

Make all calculations to the nearest £100.

POINTS TO REMEMBER

Branches

- Make quite certain:

  (a) which method of branch accounting is used:

  (i)   either all double entry books are maintained at head office, or

  (ii) branch keeps full double entry records;

  (b) price at which goods are invoiced to branch:

  (i)   either cost price, or

  (ii) cost price plus loading, or

  (iii) selling price

- If all double entry records are maintained at head office and the branch is invoiced at cost price, the following accounts will be used:

  (a) *Goods sent to branch account* This shows as credit entries the cost of goods sent to the branch. It is closed off to purchases account at the end of the accounting period.

  (b) *Branch stock account* This functions as a trading and profit and loss account. Debit it with the cost of opening stock and goods sent from head office and credit it with sales (at selling price) and closing stock at cost. Bring down the gross profit. Debit all expenses and credit any other branch income to give the net profit or loss of the branch.

- If all double entry records are maintained at head office and the branch is invoiced at a loaded price, the following accounts will be used:

  (a) *Goods sent to branch account* This shows as credit entries the cost of goods sent to the branch. It is closed off to purchases account at the end of the accounting period.

  (b) *Branch stock account* All entries in this account will be at the selling price. Debit opening stock and goods received from head office. Credit sales and closing stock.

  (c) *Branch stock adjustment account* All entries in this account will be at the gross profit. Debit gross profit on sales and closing stock. Credit gross profit on opening stock and goods received from head office.

  Prepare the profit and loss account beginning with gross profit brought down from the branch stock adjustment account.

  Note that a journal entry must be made to adjust for stock lost at the branch and that when preparing the balance sheet stock is reduced to cost.

- If the branch maintains full double entry records there will be:

  (a) A head office current account in the branch books to show the transactions between head office and branch from the branch's point of view.

  (b) A branch current account in the head office books to show the transactions between head office and branch from the head office's point of view.

The current accounts are reconciled and eliminated in preparing the final accounts. They must not appear in the balance sheet.

Stock and cash in transit may cause differences: adjust them in whichever set of books is not up to date by credit to the current account and debit to the stock in transit or cash in transit account.

Investments

- Use 3-column layout on both sides of investment account:

  (a) nominal showing number of shares bought, sold or held

  (b) income showing income received and owing

  (c) capital showing value of shares bought, sold, held and profits/losses on sales

- Learn treatment of:

  (a) income accruing on fixed income shares on purchases, sales and end of accounting periods

  (b) bonus shares – no entries in income or capital columns

  (c) rights issues taken up and/or sold

Joint ventures

- Joint venture accounts show transactions with other venturer in each venturer's books from his own point of view.

- Joint venture memorandum profit and loss account calculates the total profit (loss) on joint venture and shares it between venturers. It is a memorandum account and not part of the double entry.

- Closing balances on joint venture accounts may include:

  (a) amount owing by one venturer to the other (which will be equal and opposite)

  (b) each venturer's share of any assets held by the joint venture

Interest on capital

- Remember methods of calculating simple and compound interest: question will indicate which to apply.

- Take care in deducting any repayments when calculating capital amount upon which the interest is based.

- Debenture interest is calculated on the nominal value of the debentures.

6

Cash flow statements

After carefully studying this chapter you should be able to:

1 *apply the definitions and formats used in cash flow statements;*

2 *prepare cash flow statements and schedules;*

3 *make any necessary calculations.*

A cash flow statement shows the reader the inflows and outflows of cash (and cash equivalents). This is vital, because without enough cash to finance its business a company or other trading organisation will be in serious difficulty.

The basic format uses the following headings:

1 *operating activities;*

2 *returns on investment and servicing of finance;*

3 *investing activities;*

4 *financing.*

The examination syllabus of Third Level Accounting of the London Chamber of Commerce and Industry Examinations Board excludes taxation. It is based on current legislation and style but limits questions on cash flow statements to those of single companies (ie those without subsidiary companies). Hence it excludes holding companies, property investment companies, investment companies, banking and insurance companies.

The subject is discussed in relation to limited companies but applies to all trading organisations that prepare cash flow statements.

Cash flows

The following discussion is based on FRS (Financial Reporting Standard) 1 which superseded SSAP (Statement of Standard Accounting Practice) 10.

Objective

To show the effects on the company's cash classified under the following four headings:

(a) operating activities

(b) returns on investments and servicing of finance

(c) investing activities

(d) financing

Scenario

Information is available about the various activities that affect the company's cash flow. It may be in various formats, such as final accounts, or schedules of assets, liabilities, etc from which the cash flow statement is extracted.

Method

The method used will depend on the form in which the basic information is presented:

1   Analyse the information available under the four headings listed under *Objectives* above.

2   Prepare the cash flow statement in the format outlined at the end of the next section, *Problems*.

Problems

The basic definitions which the candidate must know include:

1   *Cash or cash equivalents* Cash in hand, at bank repayable on demand, and investments convertible into cash within 3 months *less* amounts repayable to bankers within 3 months.

2   *Operating activities* The effect on cash of operating or trading transactions.

3   *Returns on investments and servicing of finance* This relates to receipts and payments resulting from owning investments or paying providers of finance.

4   *Investing activities* The amount of cash flowing in or out as a result of acquiring or disposing of fixed assets or current asset investments apart from those classified as cash or cash equivalents.

5   *Financing* Amounts received or paid that relate to main financing, such as the issue of shares, debentures, longer-term borrowings, or the redemption or repayment of any of these.

The format in which the above will be incorporated into the resultant cash flow statement should be similar to the following, depending on the actual circumstances:

Cash Flow Statement for the year ended. . .

Net cash inflow from operating activities	x
Returns on investments and servicing of finance	x
Investing activities (eg payment for tangible fixed assets)	x
Net cash inflow before financing	x
Financing	x
Increase in cash and cash equivalents	x

Supporting schedules or calculations

1 Net cash inflow, being the total of operating profits, depreciation charged, net profit/loss on sale of fixed assets, increase/decrease in stocks, debtors, or creditors.

2 Analysis of change in cash and equivalents in year, being the difference between opening and closing balances.

3 Summary of items comprising opening and closing totals of cash and equivalents.

4 Analysis of financing changes in the year, summarising individual sources/ applications of finance in the year, such as increase of share capital, redemption of debentures etc.

Note: Read 'outflow' for 'inflow' where appropriate above.

EXAMPLE I

A prisoners' charity has offered the governor of Tor Prison a grant of $40,000 to cover the capital expenditure of any welfare programmes in Year 42. The governor can accept such grants provided that welfare programmes are self-financing (ie do not incur losses). He is considering the following estimates in connection with three welfare programmes:

Programme	Capital expenditure[1]	Fixed costs	Variable costs	Hours tuition	Gross income[2]
Word processing	$25,000	$200 p.w.	30% of gross income	200 p.w.	$400 p.w.
Gardening	$ 3,000	$ 10 p.w.	5% of gross income	100 p.w.	$ 30 p.w.
Joinery	$20,000	$100 p.w.	20% of gross income	180 p.w.	$250 p.w.

Notes to estimates

1 Depreciation on capital expenditure is *not* included in the costs given above. All capital expenditure has a life-time of 10 years and no residual value; depreciation is calculated on the straight line basis from the date of acquisition. The prisoners work 50 weeks in a year.

2 Gross income arises from hiring out prisoners' services.

After consideration of the proposals made to him the governor decided to begin all three welfare programmes. Joinery and gardening were started exactly as planned on 1 January Year 42. At first there were not enough prisoners interested in word processing so this programme was not started until later in the year and its capital expenditure was reduced to the amount remaining from the total annual grant after the gardening and joinery programmes had started.

At the end of Year 42 the prison records showed the following information relating to the welfare programmes:

	$
Receipt from prisoners' charity	40,000
Payments for capital expenditure	40,000
Payment of fixed costs:	
Word processing for the last 36 working weeks of Year 42	4,800
Gardening and joinery as originally planned	
Payment of variable costs as planned for all three welfare programmes	
Receipt of gross income:	
Weekly gross income from gardening and joinery as planned	
Gross income from word processing was only $240 per week	
At the end of the year, customers owed 3 weeks for each of gardening and joinery and 6 weeks for word processing	

Required

(a) Prepare, in columnar form, a profit and loss account for *each* of the welfare programmes. Calculate the depreciation for the word processing programme on the basis of the number of weeks the capital items were used in the year.

(b) Prepare in good style, using columnar form, a cash flow statement for *each* welfare programme.

Solution

(a) Tor Prison Profit & Loss Account for year ended 31 December Year 42

	W P $		G $		J $
Gross income (36 × 240)	8,640	(50 × 30)	1,500	(50 × 250)	12,500
Fixed costs	4,800	(50 × 10)	500	(50 × 100)	5,000
Depreciation (17,000 × 36 ÷ 50)	1,224		300		2,000
Variable costs (30% × 8,640)	2,592	(5% × 1,500)	75	(20% × 12,500)	2,500
	8,616		875		9,500
Net profit	24		625		3,000

(b) Tor Prison Cash Flow Statement for year ended 31 December Year 42

	W P $	G $	J $
Net cash inflow from operating activities	−192	835	4,250
Investing activities			
Payment for tangible fixed assets	−17,000	−3,000	−20,000
Net cash inflow before financing	−17,192	−2,165	−15,750
Financing			
Grant	17,000	3,000	20,000
Increase in cash	−192	835	4,250

Supporting Schedules

1 *Net cash inflow from operating activities*

Operating profit			
Net profit	24	625	3,000
Depreciation	1,224	300	2,000
Increase in debtors	−1,440	−90	−750
	−192	835	4,250

2 *Analysis of changes in cash and equivalents*

Balance at 1 Jan Year 42	Nil	Nil	Nil
Net cash inflow/outflow	−192	835	4,250
Balance at 31 Dec Year 42	−192	835	4,250

3 *Analysis of balances of cash and equivalents*

Cash	−192	835	4,250

4 *Analysis of changes in financing* (grant) 17,000   3,000   2,000

EXAMPLE 2

The following information has been extracted from the trial balances of Grumpy plc after the preparation of the annual accounting statements:

31 December Year 8			31 December Year 9	
£'000	£'000		£'000	£'000
40	50	Bills of exchange receivable/payable	60	80
	0	Dividend proposed		90
1,000	400	Machinery at cost/provision for depreciation	?	?
	460	Retained earnings		495
179		Stock	142	
184	162	Debtors/Creditors	191	120
600	300	Fixtures at cost/provision for depreciation	?	?
	42	Bank	21	
2,000	98	Land and buildings at cost/provision for depreciation	?	?

Notes for Year 9:

1   During the year there were no dividends paid or received; no interest expense incurred; no interest income received. All debtors, creditors and bills of exchange relate to operating activities.

2   On 1 January, machinery originally purchased for £200,000 on 1 January Year 6 was sold for £100,000. There were no other purchases or sales of machinery during the year.

3   On 1 July fixtures were purchased for £140,000; there were no other purchases or sales of fixtures during the year.

4   70% of the cost of the land and buildings was in respect of the land. There were no purchases or sales of land and buildings during the year.

5   Depreciation was calculated as follows:

- machinery: 20% pa on a reducing balance basis
- fixtures: 14% pa on a straight line basis, calculated monthly, assuming no residual value
- buildings: 2% pa on a straight line basis, assuming no residual value

Required

Prepare a statement showing the net cash inflow from operating activities for Year 9.

Solution

Grumpy plc Net Cash Flow from operating activities Year 9

Notes		£	£
1	Operating profit		125,000
	Depreciation		
2	Buildings	12,000	
3	Machinery	99,520	
4	Fixtures	93,800	
			205,320
5	Loss on sale of machinery		2,400
6	Decrease in stock	37,000	
7	Increase in bills of exchange receivable	−20,000	
8	Increase in debtors	−7,000	
9	Increase in bills of exchange payable	30,000	
10	Decrease in creditors	−42,000	
			−2,000
			330,720

Notes				£
1	(495,000 – 460,000 + 90,000)			125,000
2	(2,000,000 × 30% × 2%)			12,000
3	Cost price (1,000,000 – 200,000)	= 800,000		
	Depreciation provision (400,000 – 97,600)*	= 302,400		
		497,600 × 20%		99,520

* Depreciation on sale (200,000 – (200,000 × 80% × 80% × 80%) = 97,600

4	Cost price 31 December Year 8			
	(600,000 × 14%)	= 84,000		
	Purchases 1 July Year 9			
	(140,000 × 14% × 6/12)	= 9,800		93,800
5	(200,000 – 97,600 – 100,000)			2,400

		Year 8	Year 9	
		£'000	£'000	
6	Stock	179	–142	37,000
7	Bills of exchange receivable	40	– 60	–20,000
8	Debtors	184	–191	–7,000
9	Bills of exchange payable	50	– 80	30,000
10	Creditors	162	–120	–42,000

PRACTICE QUESTION

6.1 Faras plc has prepared the following trial balance with comparative figures.

Year 8			31 December Year 9	
$'000	$'000		$'000	$'000
	80	Ordinary shares of $1 each fully paid		100
	75	10% debentures		50
	25	Retained profit		30
55	41	Debtors/Creditors	64	40
81		Stock	79	
14		Account with Laurel Bank plc	12	
	21	Account with Hardy Bank Ltd		23
92		Fixed assets	88	
242	242		243	243

Notes

During Year 9:

1 Faras plc paid dividends of $15,000 and interest of $8,000

2 Faras plc depreciated fixed assets by $12,000

3 Fixed assets with a book value of $21,000 were sold at a loss of $8,000

Required

Prepare a cash flow statement for Year 9 in accordance with up-to-date presentation.

POINTS TO REMEMBER

- Remember that a cash flow statement is as follows:

	1	Net cash inflow from operating activities	£'000
+	2	Returns on investments and servicing of finance	£'000
+	3	Investing activities	£'000
=		Net cash inflow before financing	£'000
+	4	Net cash inflow from financing	£'000
=		Increase in cash and cash equivalents	£'000

- A negative inflow is an outflow.

- The meanings of the above terms are:

  1 Operating profits are net profits adjusted for items that do not result in cash receipt/payment, such as depreciation, profit on sale of fixed assets, increase/decrease in stock, debtors, creditors.

  2 Returns on investments include interest/dividends received and paid.

  3 Investing activities are purchase/sale of fixed assets.

  4 Financing is the receipt or redemption of share captial and loan capital of the company.

- The four supporting schedules to cash flow statement are:

  (a) reconciliation of operating profit to net cash inflow from operating activities

  (b) analysis of changes in cash and equivalents during year

  (c) analysis of cash and equivalents in balance sheet

  (d) analysis in changes of financing during the year

7

Budgets, including simple breakeven analysis

After carefully studying this chapter you should be able to:

1 *prepare periodic cash budgets for differing periods;*

2 *prepare final accounts budgets;*

3 *make simple breakeven analyses.*

A budget is a translation into money values of forecasts made by the management and other officers of a business.

Under this heading we include:

1 *monthly cash budget;*

2 *final accounts budget;*

3 *break-even.*

The information and methods of monthly cash budgets, eg the calculations of the timing of sales, or cash received from sales, may well be incorporated into final accounts budgets. Break-even examines a different aspect of budgets.

Monthly cash budget

The discussion that follows refers to monthly budgets but could equally refer to budgets for other periods, such as 2-monthly, or 3-monthly, or half-yearly etc budgets. Monthly budget is also called monthly cash flow.

This topic may appear by itself or may arise as part of a larger question. Parts of this topic may also appear independently.

Objective

The objective is to forecast the cash balance at predetermined intervals, depending upon the needs of management.

Scenario

Information for monthly budgets will be available concerning cash transactions and their timing.

Method

1   Calculate the cash flowing from debtors and other sources and group them into the periods in which they were received.

2   Calculate the cash flowing to creditors and classify them according to the periods of their payment.

3   Assemble the above into a format similar to the following:

	Jan	Feb	March	April	Etc
Receipts					
Debtors for sales	X	X	X	X	X
Cash sales	X	X	X	X	X
Other receipts	X	X	X	X	X
Total receipts **(a)**	X	X	X	X	X
Payments					
Creditors	X	X	X	X	X
Cash purchases	X	X	X	X	X
Other payments	X	X	X	X	X
Total payments **(b)**	X	X	X	X	X
Monthly excess/deficit **(a)** – **(b)**	X	X	X	X	X
Opening balance	X	X	X	X	X
Closing balance	X	X	X	X	X

Problem

The problem is how to ascertain the amounts paid in the period to debtors or received from creditors. For example the information relating to cash flowing from sales may be:

- 30% of the sales are for cash and bear a cash discount of 10%
- 40% pay within one month after the date of the sale and receive a discount of 5%
- 30% pay after one month after date of the sale and receive no discount

EXAMPLE

Tegdub plc prepared the following trial balance at 31 December Year 22 after completing the profit and loss account for Year 22:

	$'000	$'000
Bank	20	
Debtors/Creditors	32	49
Profit & Loss Appropriation Account		15
Ordinary shares of $1.00 each fully paid		100
10% preference shares of $1.00 each fully paid		50
Stock	45	
Freehold buildings	57	
Motor vehicles/Provision for depreciation	113	53
	267	267

On 31 October Year 22 Tegdub plc had offered for sale $75,000 12% debentures at 98. $50 was payable on application on 1 January Year 23 and $48 on allotment on 1 February Year 23. Applications were received in respect of $90,000 debentures and the company returned excess application money on 26 January Year 23 and all money due on allotment was received before the end of February Year 23. In accordance with the terms of the debenture issue, interest was payable from 1 March Year 23.

The company budgets for Year 23 include the following:

1. All sales will continue to be on credit only and will amount to $420,000; the monthly average for each of February and March will be at twice the monthly average for each of the remaining 10 months of the year. Customers will continue to pay in full by the end of the month following that in which the sale took place.

2. The debtors in the trial balance representing sales in December Year 22 will all pay in full during January Year 23.

3. The company will continue to sell goods at the fixed selling price, showing a mark-up of 25%.

4. The company will continue to pay creditors during the second month after the month in which the goods were purchased.

5. The creditors in the trial balance representing purchases in November/December Year 22 will all be paid before the end of February Year 23.

6. Stocks at 31 December Year 23 will be $45,000; purchases will be made evenly over the year.

7. On 1 April Year 23 the company will buy motor vehicles for $48,000, payable in full on 1 May Year 23.

8. Monthly cash expenses of $4,250 will continue to be paid during the month in which they are incurred.

9. Depreciation on motor vehicles will continue to be calculated at $33\frac{1}{3}\%$ on a reducing balance basis; and depreciation on motor vehicles purchased during the year will be calculated in months from the date of purchase.

10 Debenture interest and preference share dividend will be paid on 31 December Year 23.

11 The debentures are repayable in five equal annual instalments the first of which is due 1 March Year 24.

Required

(c) Prepare *in columnar form* a cash budget for Tegdub plc showing the balance at the end of *each* of March, June, September and December Year 23.

Solution

Cash Budget for Year 23

	JFM $	AMJ $	JAS $	OND $
Debtors	*(30 + 32 + 60) = 122,000	(60 + 30 + 30) = 120,000	(30 × 3) = 90,000	90,000
Debentures	73,500			
	195,500	120,000	90,000	90,000
Creditors	# (49 + 28) = 77,000	(28 × 3) = 84,000	84,000	84,000
Expenses	(4.25 × 3) = 12,750	12,750	12,750	12,750
Motor vehicle		48,000		
Debenture interest				7,500§
Preference dividend				5,000
	89,750	144,750	96,750	109,250
Balance b/fwd	20,000	125,750	101,000	94,250
Receipts	195,500	120,000	90,000	90,000
	215,500	245,750	191,000	184,250
Payments	−89,750	−144,750	−96,750	−109,250
Balance c/fwd	125,750	101,000	94,250	75,000

Notes to the budget

$
* 420 ÷ (12 + 2)   = 30,000
# 420 × 100 ÷ 125 ÷ 12 = 28,000
§ 75 × 10 ÷ 12 × 12%   = 7,500

Final accounts budgets

Objective

Find out in advance:

1 in the case of the balance sheet budget: the financial position of an organisation at a future date

2 in the case of the trading profit and loss account budget: the results of the trading operations for a financial period

Scenario

Information is given about the financial position at the beginning of a financial period and the forecast of the trading operations during that period. There may also be information on the financial position at the end of the period.

Method

The method will depend on the actual circumstances of the case, but may combine various techniques such as the preparation of an annual cash budget with incomplete records. As the information available will vary from case to case, so will the method to use. For example, in order to construct a final accounts budget it may be necessary to write up all or some of the following:

(a) cash account or budget for the period to find out the closing cash balance, or the cash received from debtors etc

(b) debtors control account to find out the sales or the closing debtors or the cash received from debtors

(c) creditors control account to find out the purchases or the cash paid to creditors or the closing creditors

(d) stock control account to find out the purchases, or the estimated closing stock or cost price of sales

(e) ratio analysis and application to ascertain figures for the final accounts required

Problems

Problems may include:

1 deciding which controls are necessary;

2 converting cost price into selling price or vice versa;

3 remembering to complete the double entry when concentrating on one aspect of a transaction; for example if you calculate the debits to creditors control account in respect of discounts, do remember to credit those discounts to the profit and loss account;

4 understanding ratios and extracting information for ratios from the facts given.

EXAMPLE I

Ash and Birch are in partnership and have shared profits (losses) in the same way for many years. The following budgeted statements relate to Year 49.

Trading and Profit & Loss Account

		£'000	£'000	£'000
Sales, all on credit				1,000
Cost of goods sold				750
Gross profit				250
Selling expenses			100	
Administration expenses			75	
				175
Net profit				75
Partnership salaries:	Ash		50	
	Birch		30	80
				–5
Residual loss:	Ash		–3	
	Birch		–2	–5
				0

Balance Sheet at 31 December

	£'000	£'000	£'000
Fixed assets			150
Current assets			
Stock	625		
Debtors for sales	200		
Bank	75	900	
Amounts due within one year			
Creditors for purchases	450	450	
			600
Financed by:			
	Ash	*Birch*	
Fixed capital	290	210	500
Current accounts	80	20	100
	370	230	600

Required

(a) Based on the above budgeted statements for Year 49, calculate the following ratios to one decimal place:

   (i) Mark-up

   (ii) Selling expenses to sales

   (iii) Net profit to sales

   (iv) Stock turnover

   (v) Return on closing capital employed

(vi) Debtors turnover

(vii) Acid test

As Ash & Birch are disappointed with the budgeted trading results, they decide to employ Cork as a business adviser. Cork reports to the partners that the following changes to the budget can be made:

1   An increase to the gross profit of 20% while maintaining the same physical sales volume and selling prices.

2   Reduce administration expenses by £6,000.

3   Make a net profit equal to 50% of the new gross profit. This net profit would be *before* deducting Cork's consultancy fee of £4,000 payable before the end of the year.

4   Increase the stock turnover by 40%.

5   Increase the debtors turnover by 20%.

6   Reduce the amount due to creditors to £260,000.

7   Increase the acid test to 1.4

There will be no changes in either the basis of sharing profits/losses or the budgeted drawings.

Required

(b) Prepare, in the same format as shown above, budgeted accounting statements for Year 49 based on Cork's estimates.

Solution

(a)

(i)	Mark-up	(250 ÷ 750)	33.3%
(ii)	Selling expenses to sales	(100 ÷ 1,000)	10.0%
(iii)	Net profit to sales	(75 ÷ 1,000)	7.5%
(iv)	Stock turnover	(750 ÷ 625)	1.2
(v)	Return on closing capital employed	(75 ÷ 600)	12.5%
(vi)	Debtors turnover	(1,000 ÷ 200)	5.0
(vii)	Acid test	(275 ÷ 450)	0.6

(b)   **Budgeted Trading and Profit & Loss Account Year 49**

		£'000	£'000	£'000
Sales all on credit				1,000
Cost of goods sold				700
Gross profit	(250 ÷ 1,000 × 120% × 1,000)			300
Selling expenses	(Residual)		81	
Administration expenses	(75 – 6)		69	
				150
Net profit	(300 × 50%)			150
Cork's fee				4
				146
Partners' salaries	(A: 50; B: 30)			80
				66
Residual profits: A	(3 ÷ 5 × 66)		39.6	
B	(2 ÷ 5 × 66)		26.4	66

Budgeted Balance Sheet end of Year 49

Fixed assets				150
Current assets				
Stock	(700 ÷ (1.2 × 140%))	416.7		
Debtors for sales	(1,000 ÷ (5 × 120%))	166.7		
Bank [(260 × 1.4) – 166.7] *or* (Residual)		197.6	781	
Amounts due within one year Creditors for			260	521
purchases				671

Financed by

	Ash	Birch	
Fixed capital	290	210	500
Current accounts: original budget	80	20	
Add back original loss	+3	+2	
Add revised profit	+39.6	+26.4	
	122.6	48.4	171
	412.6	258.4	671

Break-even

This topic arises in many questions in Third Level Accounting. It frequently forms a small question but also arises as part of a larger question.

Objective

The objective is to ascertain the level of turnover necessary to achieve neither profit nor loss, or to achieve a target profit.

Scenario

Details of the expenses involved will be given. These will include both fixed and variable expenses and the selling price. In some cases, it is necessary to arrive at these figures by analysis of expenses and given revenue accounts; it all depends on the form in which the information is available.

Methods

1 Calculate the amount of each individual expense (such as rent, selling expense, sales director's salary, etc).

2 Group those expenses into fixed and variable expenses.

3 Calculate the variable expenses incurred per unit.

4 Calculate the selling price per unit of the items sold or produced.

5 Deduct the cost per unit of variable expenses from the selling price per unit. This is called the contribution profit per unit.

6 Divide the total of fixed expenses by the contribution per unit to arrive at the number of units required.

Problems

The problems are:

1 analysis of expenses into variable and fixed

2 calculation of selling price from given accounts

EXAMPLE I

On 1 January Year 37, Marino opened a new shop to sell Toms. He agreed with Fenner:

1 to buy Toms at £200 each from Fenner and to sell them at a fixed selling price to show a gross profit of 20% on sales value

2 to pay Fenner 2% of the value of his sales of Toms each year as a contribution to national advertising for Toms, paid for by Fenner.

Marino estimated that his annual expenses regardless of the number of Toms sold would be:

- distribution: £4,700
- administrative: £3,400

Required

(a) Calculate how many Toms would have to be sold in a year for Marino to make neither profit nor loss.

Solution

	£
Selling price (200 × 100 ÷ (100 − 20))	250
Variable cost (200 + (250 × 2%))	205
Variable profit per unit	45
Fixed expenses (4,700 + 3,400)	8,100

Number of units to be sold to make neither profit nor loss

		£
Fixed expenses		8,100
Divided by variable profit per unit (contribution per unit)	÷	45
		180 units

One possible variation to this question could be where the candidate is required to calculate the number of units to make a profit of £900. In this case, the target profit would be added to the fixed expenses. The rest of the calculation would continue as previously:

		£
Fixed expenses as above		8,100
Add target profit		900
		9,000
Divided by variable profit per unit	÷	45
		200 units**

Note

** The number has increased by 20 units, being the target profit of £900 divided by the variable profit per unit of £45.

EXAMPLE 2

David, who was unemployed, decided to work as a self-employed gardener. A shop offered to sell him:

(a) a mower for £500; this had a 10-year life span with a residual value of £40; however its secondhand value after 1 year would be £300

(b) tools for £1,000; these had a 50-year life span with zero residual value; however, their secondhand value after 1 year would be nil

He found out that he could earn £7 per day and could work 5 days per week but would have to pay laundry bills of £5 per week.

Required

(a) Calculate how many weeks David would have to work in each year in order to make neither profit nor loss. (4 marks)

On 1 January Year 10, David withdrew his £1,600 savings and bought the mower and tools at the prices offered. During Year 10 he charged customers £35 per week and received £1,400 cash from customers and he was owed for 2 weeks' work at 31 December Year 10. His actual laundry charges were 20% more than expected for each week he worked and he owed for 3 weeks' laundry at the year end. He also paid insurance £15 for the year and had to pay £31 for mower repairs. During Year 10, he withdrew from the business 80% of the cash received from customers. At the end of Year 10 David sold the mower for £300 cash and gave the tools to a friend free of charge.

Required

(b) Prepare for David for Year 10 a cash account and a profit and loss account.

(10 marks)

(c) Give one reason why the business might have been more profitable in Year 10 if David had continued trading for 2 years. (3 marks)

Total (17 marks)

Solution

The depreciation of the mower can be based on either of the following assumptions:

		Assumption (1) £	Assumption (2) £
Mower:	Residual value after 1 year	300	
	Residual value after 10 years		40
Tools:	Residual value after 1 year	Nil	
	Residual value after 50 years		Nil

		Assumption (1) £		Assumption (2)	£
(a)	Depreciation of: mower (500 – 300)	200	((500 – 40) ÷ 10)		46
	Depreciation of tools (1,000 ÷ 1)	1,000	(1,000 ÷ 50)		20
	Annual fixed cost	1,200			66
	÷ Weekly profit ((5 × £7) – 5)	÷ 30		÷	30
		Weeks		*Weeks*	
	Number of weeks to break even	40		2.2	

(b) Preliminary calculation: David worked $((1{,}400 \div 35) + 2)$ weeks = 42 weeks.

Cash Account for Year 10

		£	£
Savings		1,600	
Takings		1,400	
Sale of mower		300	3,300
Mower		500	
Tools		1,000	
Laundry expenses	$((42 - 3) \times 5 \times 120\%)$	234	
Insurance		15	
Mower repairs		31	
		1,780	
Drawings	$(80\% \times 1{,}400)$	1,120	2,900
Balance			400

Profit & Loss Account for Year 10

		Assumption (1)	Assumption (2)
		£	£
Work done	$(1{,}400 + 70)$	1,470	1,470
Depreciation		1,200	66
Loss on sale of:	mower $(500 - 46 - 300)$		154
	tools $(1{,}000 - 20 - 0)$		980
Laundry	(42×6)	252	252
Insurance		15	15
Mower repairs		31	31
		1,498	1,498
Net loss		28	28

(c) Depreciation of mower and tools would have been spread over Years 10 and 11 instead of being charged entirely to Year 10. This would decrease the annual depreciation charge. However the net loss is £28 in both assumptions as shown in **(b)** above, because the total capital cost must be recovered during the actual life of the business.

PRACTICE QUESTION

7.1 An orchestra is planning to set up a music club on 1 January Year 24. It proposes charging members an annual subscription of $50.00 in return for:

(a) a music club membership card to be renewed annually

(b) a free ticket for the orchestra's concerts for the year

(c) a free ticket for the music club's annual dinner

The music club estimates that it will:

(a) buy blank membership cards at $2 each

(b) pay the orchestra $23 for each music club member

(c) pay $15 for each member for the annual dinner

(d) pay salaries of $4,200 per annum and general expenses of $1,800 per annum

(e) purchase for $7,400 office equipment with an expected 10-year working life and a residual value of $1,400

Required

(a) Calculate how many members the music club will need so that it has neither a surplus nor a deficit on its annual income and expenditure account.

The decision is taken to set up the music club and the following forecasts are made for the first 5 years:

1   Members' annual subscription, cost of blank membership cards, orchestra fees, and annual dinner costs will all remain at the same amount per member.

2   The number of members will be 600 for Year 24 and will increase each year as compared with the previous year as follows:

- Year 25 by 200
- Year 26 by 150
- Year 27 by 100
- Year 28 by 120

3   Salaries will increase each year by 5% on the previous year.

4   General expenses will increase each year by 3% on the previous year.

Required

(b) Prepare budgeted statements in columnar form, showing the excess of income over expenditure (or excess of expenditure over income) of the music club for *each* of its first 5 years.

Make all calculations to the nearest $.

On 31 December Year 24, the summarised records of the club for Year 24 show the following additional information:

1   There were 600 members of the music club on 1 January.

2   The music club received an interest-free loan of $6,000, repayable in Year 29.

3   The music club received subscriptions from members during Year 24:

Period	Number of subscriptions
3 months to March 31	231 members for Year 24
3 months to June 30	145 members for Year 24
3 months to September 30	112 members for Year 24
3 months to December 31	106 members for Year 24
3 months to December 31	7 members for Year 25

4   In January the music club paid:

- $2 each for 3,000 membership cards
- $7,400 for office equipment
- $23 for each member to the orchestra for free tickets for Year 24

5   In November the music club paid $15 for each member for the first year's annual dinner.

6   During the year the music club paid salaries of $350 per month, one month in arrears and general expenses of $150 each month, two months in arrears.

7   On 1 January Year 25, the bank will charge the music club interest of 5% on any overdraft at the end of each of March, June, September and December Year 24.

8   The music club is certain that all outstanding subscriptions for Year 24 will be paid in Year 25.

Required

(c) Prepared a summarised bank account in columnar form showing the balance at the bank at the end of March, June, September and December Year 24 and calculate any interest owing to the bank.

(d) Prepare the music club's income and expenditure account for Year 24 and its balance sheet at 31 December Year 24.

POINTS TO REMEMBER

Monthly cash budget

- Order of basic calculations is:

    1 Sales flow

    2 Stock flow

    3 Purchases flow

    Then cash received from sales after discounts allowed and bad debts and cash paid for purchases after discounts received.

    Then other items including issue of shares or debentures, acquisition or disposal of fixed assets, expenses.

- Remember depreciation is not a cash item and must not be included in a cash budget. If depreciation is included in an expense it must be deducted from the expense before it is inserted in the cash budget.

- Use the columnar format shown, with subtotals for total receipts and total payments.

- Balance off at the beginning and end of each month.

- If a budget is required for a different period, such as weeks or 3 months, make calculations for those periods instead.

Final accounts budget

- Assess the approach required by studying what information is given.

- Be prepared to write up necessary control accounts to ascertain sales or debtors or cash received from customers, etc.

- The final accounts budget will use the same format as year end accounts.

Break-even

- Before beginning, make sure you know what units the question asks for. It could be units of sale, or sales turnover, or machines used.

- Analyse costs into fixed and variable.

- Deduct variable costs from income to give contribution per unit.

- Divide total fixed cost by contribution per unit to give break-even.

- If there is a target profit, add it to the fixed cost, giving a larger break-even.

8

Accounting ratios and working capital statements

After carefully studying this chapter you should be able to:

Concerning ratios

1 *Calculate ratios for liquidity and working capital, profitability, and financial performance;*

2 *interpret the above ratios;*

3 *prepare final accounts and budgets using ratios.*

Concerning working capital statements

1 *prepare working capital statements;*

2 *interpret working capital statements.*

The accounting techniques discussed in this chapter are:

1 *accounting ratios;*

2 *working capital statements.*

These are grouped in the same chapter, as both are used in running businesses and other organisations.

Accounting ratios

Objectives

Accounting ratios are used to:

1 form the basis of management decisions

2 assess previous results

3 compare businesses with each other

4 control liquid assets and working capital flows

5 prepare estimated accounts

Scenario

Accounts have been prepared and on the basis of those accounts the management of a business wants to analyse and interpret the results shown, to decide on future activities or to evaluate the present financial position or past results.

Ratios may also be used to estimate results in the absence of alternative information.

Method

An examination candidate must decide what ratios are necessary if they are not specified in the question and collect the necessary figures before making the calculations with great care.

Problems

The candidate must:

(a) learn the basic ratios. These appear in the table below

(b) be prepared to work out the basis of unusual ratios such as how much income is produced per hour of work or the average amount of time a machine works in a given period

(c) state the formula he has applied to calculate a ratio and show the figures actually used by way of an essential working

(d) read any question very carefully to find what ratios are required and how they are to be calculated. For example, does the question refer to closing capital or average capital?

The candidate must learn the following ten basic ratios:

Current ratio

The current ratio is:

$$\frac{\text{Total current assets}}{\text{Total liabilities due within one year of the balance sheet date}}$$

Total liabilities due within one year of the balance sheet date includes any bank overdraft.

Acid test ratio

The acid test ratio is:

$$\frac{\text{Total liquid assets}}{\text{Total liabilities due within one year of the balance sheet date}}$$

Liquid assets are current assets *less* stock; hence they comprise debtors, bank and cash.

Use of fixed assets ratio

The use of fixed assets ratio is:

$$\frac{\text{Sales}}{\text{Fixed assets}}$$

Fixed assets are net of accumulated depreciation.

Stock turnover ratio

The stock turnover ratio is:

$$\frac{\text{Cost of goods sold}}{\text{Average stock}}$$

An alternative to average stock is closing stock.

Debtors collection ratio in months

The debtors collection ratio in months is:

$$\frac{\text{Debtors} \times 12}{\text{Sales}}$$

This ratio could alternatively be presented in days.

Fixed assets: net worth

The ratio of fixed assets to net worth is:

$$\frac{\text{Fixed assets}}{\text{Total share capital and reserves}}$$

Gross profit (or gross margin) to sales

The ratio of gross profit (or gross margin) to sales is:

$$\frac{\text{Gross profit}}{\text{Sales}}$$

Net profit to sales

The ratio of net profit to sales is:

$$\frac{\text{Net profit}}{\text{Sales}}$$

Return on capital employed

The ratio of return on capital employed is:

$$\frac{\text{Net profit}}{\text{Total share capital and reserves}}$$

Net profit to total assets employed

The ratio of net profit to total assets employed is:

$$\frac{\text{Net profit}}{\text{Tangible and intangible fixed assets plus working capital}}$$

These ratios are usually expressed as percentages.

EXAMPLE 1

The following is the trial balance of Opaque plc at 31 December Year 11:

	£'000	£'000
Plant cost/depreciation	105	62
Bank	20	
Preference shares of £1.00 each fully paid		20
Stock	102	
Profit & Loss Account		40
Land and buildings cost/Provision for depreciation	75	25
Trade creditors (payable 28 February Year 12)		68
Motor vehicles cost/Depreciation	63	38
Ordinary shares of £0.50 each fully paid		50
Debtors	58	
12% debentures repayable in five equal annual instalments at 102 starting from 30 April Year 12		120
	423	423

Required

Calculate the following two ratios to 2 decimal places:

(a) acid test

(b) working capital ratio

Solution

Acid test	$(58 + 20) \div (68 + (120 \times 20\%))$	$= 0.85 : 1$
Working capital ratio	$(20 + 102 + 58) \div 92$	$= 1.95 : 1$

EXAMPLE 2

Cinco began business on 1 January Year 31. He read in a trade journal that his type of business should achieve the following ratios:

1   Gross profit 50%

2   Stock turnover 10 times per annum

3   Debtors credit period of 1.5 months

4   Creditors credit period of 2.0 months

5   Return on average capital employed 15%

6   Acid test 1 : 1

Cinco's summarised bank account for Year 31 is:

	$'000	$'000
Capital introduced 1 January Year 31		100
Customers for sales		220
		320
Suppliers for goods purchased for resale	100	
General expenses	12	
Rent of shop for the 18 months to 30 June Year 32	60	
Distribution expenses	39	
Drawings	25	
Fixtures bought 1 January Year 31, which are expected to last for 10 years with a residual value of $8,000	88	324
Overdraft 31 December Year 31		4

His records show at 31 December Year 31:

1   He owed $24,000 for goods purchased and $1,000 for general expenses.

2   His customers owed him $20,000 for goods sold to them.

3   His stock of goods for resale cost $14,000 and had a net realisable value of $25,000.

Required

(a) Prepare in good style Cinco's trading and profit and loss account for Year 31 and balance sheet at 31 December Year 31.

(b) Calculate to 1 decimal place, from your answer to (a) the 6 ratios that are listed in the trade journal.

(c) Compare 1 of the ratios calculated in (b) with the corresponding ratio in the trade journal and comment on Cinco's performance as compared with the ratio in the trade journal.

Observation

Three different accounting techniques must be used in answering this question:

(a) incomplete records

(b) calculation of accounting ratios

(c) discussion of one ratio achieved

Solution

(a)   **Cinco Trading Profit & Loss Account for Year 31**

	$'000	$'000
Sales (220 + 20)		240
Cost of goods sold		
Purchases (100 + 24)	124	
Stock 31 December	14	110
Gross profit		130
General expenses (12 + 1)	13	
Rent (60 × 12 ÷ 18)	40	
Distribution expenses	39	
Depreciation ((88 − 8) ÷ 10)	8	100
Net profit		30

Cinco Balance Sheet at 31 December Year 31

	$'000	$'000	$'000
Fixed assets: Fixtures		88	
Less depreciation		8	80
Current assets			
Stock	14		
Prepaid rent	20		
Debtors	20	54	
Liabilities due within one year			
Creditors	24		
General expenses	1		
Bank	4	29	
			25
			105
Financed by			
Capital introduced			100
Add net profit			30
			130
Less drawings			25
			105

(b)

	Formula	Calculation	Actual	Target[1]
1	Gross profit			
	Gross profit : sales	130 ÷ 240	54.2%	50.0%
2	Stock turnover			
	Cost of goods sold : closing stock	110 ÷ 14	7.9	10.0
3	Debtors credit period			
	Debtors × 12 : sales	(20 × 12) ÷ 240	1.0	1.5
4	Creditors credit period[2]			
	Creditors × 12 : purchases	(24 × 12) ÷ 124	2.3	2.0
5	Return of average capital[3]			
	Net profit : average capital	30 ÷ [(100 + 105) ÷ 2]	29.3%	15%
6	Acid test			
	Liquid assets: Liabilities due within one year of balance sheet date	20 ÷ 29	0.7 : 1	1 : 1
	(Alternatively[4]	40 ÷ 29	1.4 : 1	1 : 1)

Notes to the ratios

1 The target column is an exact copy of the information given in the question; it is tabulated here to facilitate comparison of actual results achieved with the target.

2 The period here is calculated in months. If the question asked for weeks it would be necessary to substitute 52 for 12 in the calculation.

3 The average capital is calculated by adding opening and closing capital together and dividing by 2. If the question asked for the ratio to be based on closing capital instead of on average balances it would be necessary to use the closing capital, ie $105,000.

4 Two alternative calculations of the current assets are given. The first one is debtors only; the second one includes prepaid rent. If there were a favourable bank balance, this would be included in both cases.

Note: The candidate must work out what to include in those ratios that are not given in the '10 basic ratios'. He must be prepared to work out ratios 'unknown' to him previously.

(c) Consider the stock turnover ratio

Cinco has turned his stock over 7.9 times; the target is 10 times. This means Cinco turned his stock over less times in the year than he aimed to do. Therefore he had more capital tied up in stock to finance. This is to his disadvantage as the more quickly the stock is turned over the better it will usually be for the business.

EXAMPLE 3

At the board meeting of Hen plc, to discuss proposals for the annual general meeting relating to Year 14, the chairman stated:

"The company has a satisfactory financial position.

1 *Reserves* It has reserves of £80,000 brought forward from Year 13 available for distribution and in Year 14 it made a profit of £10,000, although the accounts will show a loss because of the charge of £60,000 for depreciation.

2 *Liquidity* The cash brought forward from Year 13 was £110,000. It declined in Year 14 because £30,000 was invested, to increase the stock from the opening stock of £70,000 and £60,000 was invested in new machinery. Both debtors and creditors decreased by £15,000 from their levels of £45,000 and £35,000 respectively at 1 January Year 14. As in previous years, our working capital consists entirely of stock, debtors, cash and creditors.

3 *Capital structure* This remained unchanged in Year 14 at £175,000, being the ordinary shares of £0.50 each and the £75,000 12% preference shares."

Required

Calculate for Hen plc to 1 decimal place the following:

(a) profit/loss shown in the Profit & Loss Account for Year 14

(b) cash at 31 December Year 14

(c) maximum ordinary dividend in pence per share in Year 14 payable from the available cash (assuming no cash is borrowed)

(d) maximum ordinary dividend in pence per share in Year 14 payable from the available profits

(e) Maximum dividend yield per ordinary share for Year 14 based on a market value of £0.70 per share, using your own answer in **(d)** above

(f) acid test ratio at beginning and end of Year 14

(g) working capital ratio at beginning and end of Year 14

(h) gearing ratio at the end of Year 14, before any dividend is declared

(17 marks)

Solution

(a) Profit & Loss Account
'Profit' – depreciation
10,000 – 60,000   –£50,000

(b) Cash
Opening balance + profit   – more stock – more debtors
  [110,000] + 10,000 –   30,000   –   60,000   £30,000

(c) Ordinary dividend from available cash
Cash (b) – pref dividend ÷ no of ordinary shares
(30,000   – 9,000)   ÷   (100,000 ÷ 0.5)   10.5p

(d) Ordinary dividends from available profits
Opening reserves –   loss   – pref dividend ÷ no of ordinary shares
  (80,000   – 50,000 –   9,000   ÷   (100,000 ÷ 0.5)   10.5p

(e) Dividend yield on market value
Dividend ÷ market value
  10.5   ÷ 70%   15%

(f) Acid test
                    Cash + debtors ÷ creditors
Beginning of Year 14   (110 +   45) ÷   35   4.4 : 1
End of Year 14   (30 +   30) ÷   20   3.0 : 1

(g) Working capital
                    Cash + debtors + stock ÷ creditors
Beginning of Year 14 (110 + 45   + 70) ÷ 35   6.4 : 1
End of Year 14   (30 + 30   + 100 ÷ 20   8.0 : 1

(h) Gearing
Preference shares + ordinary shares + profit and loss
        75   ÷   (100   +   30)   0.6 : 1

Working capital statements

Objective

In order to facilitate trading activities, it is necessary for a business to have sufficient working capital. The objective here is to assess the adequacy of the working capital of a business.

Scenario

The management of a business must ensure the business has sufficient working capital both at present and as far as possible in the future. This may not be immediately apparent. For example there may not be final accounts prepared, or accounts have simply been taken to a trial balance stage or the balance sheet is prepared in a horizontal layout. Hence it is necessary to extract the figures required for the working capital statement from the information available.

Method

The method used will depend on the information available and on how it is presented. The method will be to ascertain the total current assets and deduct from it the total liabilities due within one year of the balance sheet date. If final accounts are available, the working capital may be shown; if no accounts have been prepared, the figures must be extracted from the books or trial balance or other available source.

Problems

The candidate must know what to include in the working capital statement and be able to find this information. In a given list of balances there may be items that are not relevant to a working capital statement and therefore need to be excluded from the statement. In addition information may be given that leads to the balances required such as rent paid for an 18-month period that extends beyond the financial year end and needs to be apportioned between before and after the year end. It is essential to know which assets and liabilities to include.

Assets

The assets to include are those which a business already holds in the form of cash or expects to turn into cash or use within one year in the normal course of trading. These assets are:

- stock
- work in progress
- debtors (and prepaid expenses)
- bills receivable
- cash at bank
- cash in transit
- cash in hand

Liabilities

The liabilities to include are those that *fall due for payment within one year of the balance sheet date*. These liabilities are:

- trade creditors
- bills payable
- unpaid expenses
- debentures and loans (or instalments of debentures and loans)
- bank overdrafts due within one year of the balance sheet date

EXAMPLE 4

Verney extracted the following balances from his accounting records at 31 December Year 94:

	£
Goodwill at cost	1,500
Cash in hand	160
Bank overdraft	2,315
Plant and machinery at cost	3,654
Debtors for sales	4,523
Delivery van at cost *less* depreciation to 31 December Year 94	1,249
Expenses owing	561
Loan repayable in 10 equal annual instalments, the first of which falls due 30 November Year 95	20,000
Trade creditors	2,486
Cash drawn from the business by Verney for private expenses during Year 94	9,483

Additional information was also available:

		£
1	In November Year 94, Verney paid rent for the 6-month period ending 30 April Year 95	450
2	Cash in transit from Verney's branch to his head office at 31 December Year 94	96
3	Stock at cost at head office and at branch at 31 December Year 94	3,809
4	Verney decided to increase provisions to the following amounts:	
	● provision for depreciation on plant and machinery	1,793
	● provision for doubtful debts	532

Note that some of the information given above is not relevant to working capital and must not be included in the answer.

Required

Prepare a statement to show Verney's working capital at 31 December Year 94.

Solution

(a) list current assets

(b) list liabilities falling due within one year of the balance sheet date

(c) prepare the statement of working capital in the format shown below

Verney Statement of Working Capital at 31 December Year 94

	£	£	£
Current assets			
Stock at head office and branch cost		3,809	
Debtors	4,523		
Provision for bad debts	532	3,991	
Rent paid in advance (450 × 4 ÷ 6)		300	
Cash in transit from branch to head office		96	
Cash in hand		160	
			8,356
Liabilities falling due within one year			
Loan instalments payable in Year 95 (20,000 ÷ 10)		2,000	
Expenses		561	
Trade creditors		2,486	
Bank overdraft		2,315	
			7,362
Working capital			994

PRACTICE QUESTIONS

8.1 Mr Oitar's business has a head office and two shops at Xmouth and Yarville. He invoices goods to the shops so that there is a mark-up of 25% at Xmouth shop and 33.33% at Yarville shop. All expenses are paid at the head office and charged to the shops on the following bases:

1   general administration expenses Xmouth shop 60% and Yarville shop 40%

2   selling expenses on basis of sales values at each shop

3   distribution expenses are allocated between:

(a)   deliveries to the shops, 30% of the total

(b)   deliveries from the shops to the customers, 70% of the total.

They are then charged to the shops:

● deliveries to the shops on the basis of the cost of goods sold at each shop

● deliveries from the shops on the basis of the sales value of goods sold at each shop.

Mr Oitar's trial balance at 31 December Year 99 includes:

	$	$
Total sales, the sales value from shop Xmouth was twice the sales value of that from shop Yarville		360,000
Stocks at cost price at 1 January Year 99: Shop Xmouth	15,000	
Shop Yarville	14,000	
General administration expenses	6,500	
Selling expenses		39,600
Distribution expenses		40,000
Bad debts: Shop Xmouth		1,363
Shop Yarville		1,027

The stocks at cost price at 31 December Year 99 were:

- Shop Xmouth: $16,000
- Shop Yarville: $17,000

Required

(a) Prepare *in columnar form* the trading profit and loss accounts of the shop at Xmouth and the shop at Yarville. Make all calculations to the nearest $.

(b) Calculate to 1 decimal place the number of times the average stock of each shop was turned over.

8.2 F plc is a retailer selling for *cash only*.

In the Finance Director's report the following appears:

On 31 December Year 9 the company's stock of goods for resale was £99,000 and suppliers for goods for resale were the only liability due within one year.

The acid test ratio of 2 : 1 and the working capital ratio of 3½ : 1 were both considered satisfactory.

Required

(a) Prepare an extract from the balance sheet of F plc at 31 December Year 9 showing the company's working capital.

The report continues:

As a result of a sales project in Year 10 it is necessary to increase the stocks of goods for resale by 80%. Suppliers will allow this to be done by extending the present credit limit by half the amount of the stock increase. The cash balance would remain the same apart from the payment of £100,000 for capital expenditure in connection with the sales project.

Required

(b) Prepare an extract from F plc's budgeted balance sheet at 31 December Year 10 taking into consideration the sales project, showing the budgeted working capital.

The report concludes:

> In order to finance the capital expenditure on the sales project I propose F plc should issue 1000, 12% debentures of £100 each at a premium of 5% payable £30 on application, £45 (including the premium) on allotment and the balance on a first and final call.

F plc issued the offered debentures for sale and received £42,500 cash with applications. It refunded excess application money and proceeded with the allotment and call. All amounts due on allotment and call were received in full.

Required

(c) Prepare without narratives, *in date order*, journal entries to record the debenture issue.

POINTS TO REMEMBER

Accounting Ratios

- When presenting a ratio in an examination answer, show the figures that have been used in its calculation.

- Present the answer in the format usually used for the ratio. For example, gross profit is usually presented in the form of a percentage, whereas stock turnover is presented as a number of times in a year.

- Present the answer to the number of decimal places specified in the question.

- Learn the ratios given in this chapter, but be prepared to work out what is necessary to calculate any other ratio required.

- Remember to compare like with like. For example, in calculating a stock turnover ratio, compare the cost of goods sold with the cost of stock.

- In calculating working capital and acid test ratios, remember that a bank overdraft is a liability and not a negative asset.

Working Capital Statements

- Learn carefully what is included in working capital.

- Note that debentures and other loans usually of a long-term basis will become part of the working capital, when they become repayable within one year of the balance sheet date. Split instalments on such loans between those due within the next financial year and those due after the end.

9

Disclosure of accounting policies

After carefully studying this chapter you should be able to:

Make appropriate disclosures in accordance with Appendix 3.

This chapter discusses the accounting policies for published accounts. It refers mainly to the accounts of limited companies, but many of the principles are being applied increasingly to other business entities, such as partnerships or sole traders.

Candidates must be aware that the Third Level Accounting syllabus states that final accounts must be prepared 'in accordance with basic accounting conventions and current accounting practice as specified in the Companies Acts and in the Statements of Standard Accounting Practice'.

Third Level Accounting examination papers use the terms 'good accounting style' and 'minimum information required for publication' to instruct candidates to prepare final accounts based on acceptable relevant accounting policies such as those outlined in the latest Companies Acts and the Statements of Standard Accounting Practice (SSAP) and the Financial Reporting Standards (FRS).

Objective

The objective is to ensure that published accounts are meaningful and consistent and make full disclosure of the factors contributing to the financial position and trading results of a limited company.

Scenario

There are many methods of preparing accounts. If different accounting policies are used it will become impossible to compare the results and financial positions of the same business in different years or between different businesses in the same year. For example in a period of rising prices, a business might overstate its profits by using a LIFO basis of stock valuation in one year and change to a FIFO basis in the subsequent year.

Methods

The Third Level Accounting syllabus refers to the following methods:

1   disclosure of accounting policies

2   stocks and long-term contracts

3   accounting for depreciation

4   cash flow statements

5   group accounts

This chapter considers *disclosure of accounting policies*

Methods for the other items are discussed elsewhere in the text as follows:

- stocks and long-term contracts in Chapter 10
- accounting for depreciation in Chapter 11
- cash flow statements in Chapter 6
- group accounts in Chapter 4

Disclosure of accounting policies

The following definitions are summarised from SSAP 2. They should be used in considering the disclosure of accounting policies:

1   *Fundamental accounting concepts* These are the basic broad assumptions underlying the periodic accounts of business enterprises. These are:

    (a)   Going concern: assume the business will continue trading in the foreseeable future.

    (b)   Accruals: match revenue on an earned basis and costs on an incurred basis (instead of on the basis of cash received or paid). If, however, the application of this concept contradicts the prudence concept, the prudence concept is applied.

    (c)   Consistency: the same items are treated in the same way in different accounting periods.

    (d)   Prudence: do not anticipate revenue, unless it is reasonable to assume it will ultimately be settled in cash. Provide for all known liabilities even if the amount is not certain by estimating on the basis of available information.

2   *Accounting bases* These are the methods of applying the fundamental accounting concepts to determine in which accounting period to include revenue and costs in both profit and loss account and balance sheet.

3   *Accounting policies* These are the specific accounting bases the management of a business considers most appropriate to use in its final accounts.

Problems

The problems that arise in examinations are:

(a) giving the definitions and explanations of accounting policies, fundamental accounting concepts and accounting bases

(b) preparation of accounts applying accounting policies

(c) ascertaining accounting bases used

EXAMPLE 1

Horus Ltd has decided to change its computer program from the 'Alexis' used until now, to the 'Biancus' in order to produce its consolidated balance sheet on 31 December Year 99.

The accountant has prepared the consolidated balance sheet on both bases and notices the following different book values at 31 December Year 99 arising from each program:

		Alexis £	*Biancus* £
1	Machinery bought for £120,000 by Horus Ltd on 1 January Year 98. This type of machinery has a 7-year life span and a residual value of £15,980	67,500	90,280
2	Debts at £42,000 upon which the directors consider there should be made a provision for doubtful debts of 5% and a provision for discounts allowable of 3%	38,640	38,703

Required

State, with supporting calculations, the different accounting methods used by each program in respect of *both* of the *two* items listed above.

Solution

1   **Machinery**

			Alexis £	*Biancus* £
Cost price			120,000	120,000
Less depreciation:				
(a)	Straight line basis			
	Cost	120,000		
	Less residual value	15,980		
		104,020 ÷ 7 = 14,860 pa		
Two years' depreciation		× 2		29,720
Balance at 31 December Year 99 using Biancus				90,280

(b)   Reducing balance

As 7-year life and residual value of £15,000
  try 25% pa *or* apply formula

Depreciation Year 98 120,000 × 25%	30,000
	90,000
Depreciation Year 99 90,000 × 25%	22,500
Balance at 31 December Year 99 using Alexis	67,500

Methods used by Alexis: reducing balance
Method used by Biancus: straight line

2   Debts

	Gross debtors	42,000	42,000
(a)	Provision of 5% for doubtful debts		2,100
			39,900
	Provision for discounts allowable: 39,900 × 3%		1,197
	Balance at 31 December Year 99 using Biancus		38,703
(b)	Combined provision for doubtful debts and discounts		
	allowable: 42,000 × (5% + 3%)	3,360	
	Balance at 31 December Year 99 using Alexis	38,640	

Method used by Alexis: deduct combined provision
Method used by Biancus: deduct provision for doubtful debts then
  calculate provision for discounts

EXAMPLE 2

Mad plc appointed three assistant accountants (Mr Major, Mrs Augmen, Ms Dimin) at the beginning of the year to strengthen its accounting department. Soon after 31 December Year 41, they produced independently final accounts for publication based on the company's accounting records for the year ended on that date. The following table shows the differences in the accounts they produced:

	Mr Major £	Mrs Augmen £	Ms Dimin £
Balance sheet			
Fixed assets			
Plant Y[1]	843,750	800,000	500,000
Current assets			
Bank[2]	152,000	151,000	148,000
Stock X[3]	120,000	100,000	150,000
Debtors[4]	1,153,200	1,154,440	1,138,000

Notes

1   Plant Y was bought on 1 January Year 39 for £2,000,000; it has a residual value of £23,750. No additions or sales have taken place in connection with Plant Y. It appeared in the balance sheets of Mad plc at 31 December

Year 39 valued at £1,500,000 and at 31 December Year 40 valued at £1,125,000.

		£
2	Balance at 31 December Year 41 in bank statement, in favour of Mad plc	152,000
	Cheques drawn before 31 December Year 41, presented for payment to bank on 5 January Year 42	13,000
	Cash paid into bank before 31 December Year 41, credited by bank on 2 January Year 42	9,000
	Bank charges in bank statements before 31 December Year 41 but not yet entered in the cash book	3,000
	The cashier intended drawing cheques payable to creditors before 31 December Year 41 but forgot to do so	5,432
	Balance, in favour of Mad plc, in company's cash book at 31 December Year 41	151,000

3   Stock X is priced by Mad plc per unit as follows:

	£
Variable cost	200
Fixed manufacturing cost allocation	40
Manufacturing profit	60
Credit sale price	300
Cash discount allowed	6
Cash sale price	294

There were 500 units of Stock X held at 31 December Year 41

4   The debtors at 31 December Year 41 amounted to £1,240,000; provisions were made for doubtful debts of 5% and for discounts allowable of 2%. The provision for doubtful debts at 31 December Year 40 amounted to £100,000; bad debts written off in Year 41 were £71,000.

Required

State what should be recorded in Mad plc's balance sheet at 31 December Year 41 in respect of each of the 4 items listed above. Given full reasons for your choice and show all calculations.

Solution

(1)   Plant Y

Select reducing balance basis	£843,750

In Years 39 and 40 a reducing balance method of depreciation has been applied.
Adopt a consistent basis for Year 41

Workings	Year 39 2,000,000 × 75% =	£1,500,000
	Year 40 1,500,000 × 75% =	1,125,000
	Year 41 1,125,000 × 75% =	843,750

(2) Balance at bank

Select amount in favour of Mad plc, taking into consideration amounts
    not entered in bank statements at 31 December Year 41   £148,000
(Workings: 152,000 – 13,000 + 9,000 = £148,000)

(3) Stock X

Select variable cost including allocation of fixed cost, but excluding
    discounts profit or allowable (SSAP 9)   £120,000
(Workings: 500 units at £(200 + 40))

(4) Debtors

Select most prudent policy which is to anticipate doubtful debts
    and discounts allowable   £1,154,440
(Workings: 1,240,000 × 95% × 98% = 1,154,440)

EXAMPLE 3

Minor has decided to change his accounting policies when preparing his final
accounts at the end of his second year of business. His accounting policies are:

	Year 1	**Year 2**
Land and buildings	Show at cost	Show at cost less depreciation on buildings at 2% pa on cost
Debtors	Show at amount owing, *less* provision for specific bad debts	Show at amount owing, *less* provision for specific bad debts and *less* a general provision at a fixed proportion for any other possible bad debts
Vehicles	Show at cost, *less* depreciation on a straight line basis	Show at cost *less* depreciation on a reducing balance basis
Stock	Show at the lower of cost or net realisable value	Show at the lowest of cost, net realisable value or replacement cost
Creditors	Show at amount owing, *less* provision of 3% for discounts receivable	Show at amount owing

Minor's balance sheets included the following at 31 December:

	Year 1 (old policies)		Year 2 (new policies after making prior year adjustments)	
	£	£	£	£
Land and buildings[1]		1,200,000		1,192,000
Debtors	40,000		50,000	
Provisions				
Specific	−800		−1,400	
General	0	39,200	−2,430	46,170
Vehicles at cost	300,000		300,000	
Depreciation	−57,000	243,000	−209,250	90,750
Stock[2]		67,000		72,000
Creditors		33,950		48,000

Notes

1   There were no sales or purchases of land or buildings in the second year.

2   Replacement cost of stock at end of first year was £70,000.

Required

Calculate, for Minor:

(a) the revised figures for the balance sheet at the end of the first year on the basis of the accounting policies used for the second year (11 marks)

(b) the value of tangible fixed assets at the end of the first year on the same basis as in **(a)** above (2 marks)

(c) the effect of applying the new accounting policies on the profits for the first year (4 marks)

Total (17 marks)

Solution

(a) Revised figures for the balance sheet at the end of the first year on the basis of the accounting policies used for the second year

		£	£
(i)	Land and buildings		
	Cost	1,200,000	
	Less 1 year's depreciation, being half of the total depreciation written off by the end of the second year: ½ × (1,200,000 − 1,192,000)	4,000	1,196,000

		£	£
(ii)	Debtors	40,000	
	Less		
	Provision		
	Specific	−800	
	General, being same rate as in new policy		
	2430 ÷ (50,000 − 1,400)%, ie 5%		
	5% of (40,000 − 800)	−1,960	37,240

(iii) Vehicles at cost *less* depreciation at rate used in new policy for one year only. Work out rate used in new policy. Assume reducing balance method of depreciation:
net book value at end of second year is square root of
90,750 ÷ 3,000,000 = 55% (3,000,000 × 55% × 55% = 90,750).
Net book value of 55% of cost at end of first year:
300,000 × 55%   165,000

(iv) Stock
Unchanged as replacement cost is greater than book value   67,000

(v) Creditors
Calculate gross amount before provision for discount receivable:
33,950 ÷ 97%   35,000

(b) Tangible fixed assets at end of first year: 1,196,000 + 165,000   1,361,000

(c) Effect of applying the new accounting policies on the profits for the first year would be:

	Old policy	*+ New policy*	*Net effect*
	£	£	£
Land and buildings	−1,200,000	+ 1,196,000	−4,000
Debtors	−39,200	+ 37,240	−1,960
Vehicles	−243,000	+ 165,000	−78,000
Creditors	(−33,950	+ 35,000)	−1,050
Net effect			−85,010

PRACTICE QUESTION

9.1 SSAP 2 defines four 'fundamental accounting concepts'. The following concepts/conventions might be regarded as equally important when preparing accounting statements:

1   accounting period (or time interval)

2   entity

3   money measurement

4   materiality

Required

(a) Identify the four concepts referred to in SSAP 2.

(b) Briefly explain the four concepts referred to in **1** to **4** above and state why each is important.

POINTS TO REMEMBER

- Essential accounting policies to remember are:

    1 disclosure of accounting policies

    2 stocks and long-term contracts

    3 accounting for depreciation

    4 cash flow statements

    5 group accounts

- *Understand* and *apply* the policies in the examination.

- It is *not* necessary to be able to repeat from memory the exact wording of the SSAP or FRS.

10

Stocks and long-term contracts

After carefully studying this chapter you should be able to:

1 *value stocks at lower of cost or net realisable value;*

2 *distinguish acceptable cost bases;*

3 *define long-term contracts and understand the principles of allocation of profits and overheads between different periods and between different contracts;*

4 *understand the effect of prudence and consistency on the above;*

5 *prepare stock accounts;*

6 *value stocks using perpetual and periodic stock methods;*

7 *ascertain stock in absence of physical stock-taking.*

The topics that will be considered in this chapter are:

1 *stocks valuation in preparation of final accounts;*

2 *long-term contracts in preparation of final accounts;*

3 *stock accounts: actual book-keeping methods used for stocks or long-term contracts during the financial year;*

4 *calculation of stock in absence of physical stock-taking.*

Stocks

Objectives

The objective of the valuation of stock and long-term contracts is to provide the amount for inclusion in the year end accounts for publication. The stock accounts and long-term contract accounts are running controls of the stocks and work in progress.

Scenario

In order to determine profits within an accounting period, it is necessary to match costs with related revenues. Therefore if stocks remain at the end of the accounting period they represent accumulated costs which are being carried forward to be matched against the relevant revenue. The stocks include:

- goods for resale
- consumable stores
- raw materials
- components to be used in products for resale
- products in various stages of completion
- long-term contract balances and finished goods

Methods

In order to ascertain the quantities of stock of a business, the stocks are counted at the year end. If this is not possible, the stock is counted as near as possible to the year end and then additions or subtractions are made to arrive at the year end figure. This figure also may be calculated by reference to perpetual stock accounts in which the transactions in stocks are recorded on a running daily basis with test counts on some of the stocks taking place during the year.

The quantity of each item of stock is then multiplied by the value per unit to give its valuation; then the valuations of the individual items are added together to arrive at the grand total valuation of stock.

Problems

For balance sheet purposes stocks are valued on the basis of the lower of cost and net realisable value. These are defined below.

Cost

There are many different bases of cost. Some are acceptable under SSAP 9: others are unacceptable.

1   *Bases of cost acceptable under SSAP 9*

   (a)   Average cost: the average cost per unit of stock is calculated by dividing the total cost of the stock by the total number of units.

   (b)   FIFO (First in, first out): the cost per unit is based on the cost of the latest purchases.

   (c)   Replacement cost: the cost is what identical items would cost to be purchased or manufactured.

   (d)   Standard cost: the cost of stocks is based on predetermined costs calculated from management's estimates of expected levels of costs and operations.

2   *Bases of cost not acceptable under SSAP 9*

   (a)   Base stock: in this method the original unit cost for each item of stock is applied to a predetermined quantity of stock. Any excess over the predetermined quantity is valued on a different basis. If the quantity of closing stock is less than the predetermined quantity, apply the original cost for each unit.

(b)   LIFO: the cost per unit is based on the cost of the earliest purchases.

Net realisable value

The net realisable value is what the business expects to realise on selling the stock in the course of its business, less any expenses connected with selling the stock.

EXAMPLES

Three examples are given in connection with the valuation of stock.

EXAMPLE 1

Steven Victor is preparing his accounts for the year ended 31 December Year 25. His stock account for material Venro shows:

		Units	Cost per unit £
Jan 1	Stock from previous year	100	5.00
Feb 1	Purchases	500	4.00
March 1	Issue to production	300	
April 1	Purchases	600	5.50
May 1	Issue to production	200	
June 1	Purchases	400	5.25
July 1	Issue to production	250	
Oct 1	Issue to production	350	
Dec 1	Issue to production	450	
Dec 31	Balance	50	

Note to the accounts

There was no delivery charge in Year 24 but, on 31 December Year 25, the supplier made a delivery charge of £750 for the 1,500 units of Venro delivered.

Steven Victor is uncertain how he should value the closing stock of 50 units. His three book-keepers suggested:

(i)   £250.00

(ii)   £262.50

(iii) £287.50

Required

(a) Determine, showing calculations, the basis of each of these three alternative valuations.

(b) Write up the stock account for material Venro using each of these three bases in turn, showing the cost of each transfer to production.

Solution

Basis

(a) Basis **(i)** £250.00 ÷ 50 units =   £5.00 per unit

This is based on the opening stock; hence: LIFO

     Basis **(ii)** £262.50 ÷ 50 units =   £5.25 per unit

This is based on the last invoice received in

     Year 25; hence: FIFO

Basis **(iii)** This is £25 more than the previous

     basis £25 ÷ 50 units =   £0.50 per unit

This is based on the delivery cost *divided by*

     the total number of units purchased during

     the year: £750 ÷ (500 + 600 + 400) =   £0.50 per unit

Hence: FIFO +

     delivery charge

(b)

		Units	LIFO	FIFO	FIFO + delivery charge
			£	£	£
Jan 1	Stock from previous year	100	500	500	500
Feb 1	Purchases	500	2,000	2,000	2,000
March 1	Issue to production	–300	–1,200	–1,300	–1,400*
April 1	Purchases	600	3,300	3,300	3,300
May 1	Issue to production	–200	–1,100	–800	–900
June 1	Purchases	400	2,100	2,100	2,100
July 1	Issue to production	–250	–1,313	–1,225	–1,350
Oct 1	Issue to production	–350	–1,887	–1,925	–2,100
Dec 1	Issue to production	–450	–2,150	–2,388	–2,612
Dec 31	Delivery charge				750
Dec 31	Balance	50	250	262	288

Note

★ Including £100 delivery charge *only* as the first 100 units are from opening stock and the remaining 200 units are from the purchases on 1 February.

EXAMPLE 2

Lead, Moly and Nitro obtained the sole distribution rights in their area for a brand of canned beer. On 1 January Year 9 they put their savings into a bank account under the name of LMN Partnership for the purposes of distributing cans of beer. They decided to operate from their house and not to charge any overheads.

Although they understood from their supplier that the price they would pay for the cans of beer was likely to vary, they decided to offer their customers a stable price of £0.45 per can during their first 6 months of operation. The following transactions took place to 30 June Year 9:

Month	Cans bought	Cans sold
Jan	10,000 @ £0.300 each	5,000
Feb	5,000 @ £0.360 each	5,000
March	10,000 @ £0.300 each	
April		10,000
May	5,000 @ £0.330 each	5,000
June	5,000 @ £0.375 each	5,000

During July, each partner independently calculated the partnership profits to the nearest £. Lead calculated £4,050; Moly calculated £3,675 and Nitro calculated £3,793.

Required

(a) Demonstrate (showing supporting calculations) which method each of the partners probably used to value the closing stock and to arrive at their total profit figure. You may assume the partners' calculations were arithmetically correct. Note: make calculations to the nearest £.

(b) After further discussion, the partners decided to adopt the FIFO method of stock valuation because 'unless we use the earliest purchases first, the labels tend to fade'. Comment briefly on this way of choosing the basis of valuation.

Solution

(a) Prepare a statement for each partner using a columnar layout and the following formulae:

$$\text{Sales } \textit{less} \text{ gross profit} = \text{Cost of goods sold}$$
$$\text{Purchases } \textit{less} \text{ cost of goods sold} = \text{Closing stock}$$

Calculate the value of stock using the better-known bases of stock valuation and compare these with the valuations arrived at by the partners to determine the basis each partner used. Note: as there are no expenses, assume gross profit is the net profit given in the question.

Preliminary calculations

	Units
Calculation of closing stock in quantities	
Purchases: (10,000 + 5,000 + 10,000 + 5,000 + 5,000) =	35,000
Sales: (5,000 + 5,000 + 10,000 + 5,000 + 5,000) =	30,000
Closing stock	5,000

	£
Sales: (30,000 @ £0.45) =	13,500.0
Purchases: (10,000 × 0.3) + (5,000 × 0.36) + (10,000 × 0.3) + (5,000 × 0.33) + (5,000 × 0.375) =	11,325.0

Closing stock using the better-known bases:

		£
(i)	FIFO: (5000 x 0.375) =	1,875.0
(ii)	LIFO: (5,000 x 0.300) =	1,500.0
(iii)	Periodic average cost: (5,000 × 11,325 ÷ 35,000) =	1,617.9

	Lead	Moly	Nitro
	£	£	£
Sales	13,500	13,500	13,500
Gross/net profit	4,050	3,675	3,793
Cost of goods sold	9,450	9,825	9,707
Purchases	11,325	11,325	11,325
Closing stock	1,875	1,500	1,618
Bases used	FIFO	LIFO	Periodic average cost

(b) There is no necessary connection between actual physical flow and stock valuation method. The method should be chosen on the basis of its effect on profit, effect on the balance sheet, consistency, ease of recording, etc.

EXAMPLE 3

On 1 January Year 17, Mr Steen started in business as a dealer in widgets. In addition to introducing his own capital, he borrowed £300,000 from the Homid Bank at 15% interest pa. On 5 January Year 17 he bought all the following (identical) widgets for resale:

Supplier	Quantity of widgets	Cost of widgets	
	Units	£	
A Ltd	25,000	3.21	per unit less £0.02 trade discount per unit plus carriage of £0.70 per unit
B plc	38,000	4.01	per unit including carriage
C Suppliers	15,000	4.02	per unit less 5% discount for paying cash on delivery
D Warehouse	50,000	3.81	per unit. Mr Steen collected these himself, driving 125 kilometres each way to D Warehouse at £2.00 per kilometre
E Orders	32,000	4.03	per unit for the first 20,000 units
		3.95	per unit for any more units
F Company	40,000	3.80	per unit plus £1,600 total carriage charge

During January Year 17, Mr Steen made no further purchases of widgets. During January Year 17, he sold 172,000 units at £4.40 each, paying an average of £0.10 postage on each unit sold; his general expenses and advertisement costs amounted to £8,280 and £13,015 respectively.

At 31 January Year 17, the resale value of widgets had fallen to £3.95 each.

Required

(a) Calculate the cost of purchases that would appear in Mr Steen's trading account for January Year 17   (7 marks)

(b) Calculate the value of the stock that would appear in Mr Steen's balance sheet at 31 January Year 17, using the periodic weighted average cost basis   (3 marks)

(c) Using your answers to **(a)** and **(b)** above, prepare a trading and profit and loss account for January Year 17   (7 marks)

                                                Total (17 marks)

Solution

(a) Cost of Purchases in Mr Steen's Trading Account for January Year 17

	Units		£	£
A Ltd	25,000 × (3.21 + 0.70 − 0.02)			97,250
B plc	38,000 × 4.01			152,380
C Suppliers	15,000 × 4.02			60,300
D Warehouse	50,000 × 3.81 + (125 × 2 × 2)			191,000
E Orders	20,000	× 4.03	80,600	
	12,000	× 3.95	47,400	
	32,000			128,000
F Company	40,000 × 3.80 + 1,600			153,600
	200,000			782,530

(b) Value of stock that would appear in Mr Steen's balance sheet at 31 January Year 17, using the periodic weighted average cost basis. As these are simultaneous purchases, compare average cost with net resale value:

Average cost: (782,530 ÷ 200,000)	3.91
Net resale value	3.85
Therefore adopt net resale value	
Hence (200,000 − 172,000) × (3.95 − 0.10)	107,800

(c)   **Trading and Profit & Loss Account for January Year 17**

	£	£
Sales (172,000 × £4.40)		756,800
Cost of goods sold		
Purchases		782,530
Stock		107,800
		674,730
Gross profit		82,070
Discounts received from C Suppliers (60,300 × 5%)		3,015
		85,085
Postage (172,000 × 0.10)	17,200	
Advertisements	13,015	
General expenses	8,280	
Interest (300,000 × 1/12 × 15%)	3,750	
		42,245
Net profit		42,840

Long-term contracts

Objectives

The objectives here are basically the same as those outlined for stocks: that it is valuation of an asset in order to obtain the information for final accounts.

Scenario

A business undertakes contracts that fall within two or more accounting periods: usually, the contracts are for more than one year.

Profits and/or losses may accrue throughout the life of the contracts. If the profits/losses were taken to profit and loss account only when each individual contract was completed and paid for, the profit/loss shown for any accounting period would be distorted and would give a false impression of the profitability of the business. In the case of a company distributing profits by way of annual cash dividend, the directors may propose and the members may declare dividends from declared profits that do not exist; to do this would be illegal. In this scenario a loss arising on a long-term contract might be ignored.

Method

If the eventual outcome of a contract can be determined with reasonable certainty, profits may be transferred annually to the profit and loss account. The amount to transfer is based upon how far the contract has progressed at the end of the accounting period. It is essential to adopt a prudent policy in determining whether or not to take profits in any accounting period. Losses must be anticipated.

Problems

The problems in determining the profit/loss that may arise on a long-term contract include:

(a) the basis of allocation of overheads arising between different accounting periods

(b) the basis of allocation of overheads between different contracts within an accounting period

(c) the use of a prudent formula to determine what proportion of profits accruing to take to the annual profit and loss account

The same bases and formulae would be used in subsequent years unless there were exceptional circumstances.

From the point of view of a candidate for the Third Level Accounting examination, the problem must be resolved within the examination question itself as the question itself must give either the bases of allocation and formulae or the method of ascertaining them. Candidates must read and carefully apply such bases and formulae. In the example given below, the question itself gives the bases and formulae.

EXAMPLE 4

Egg plc is a building contractor engaged in the construction of public buildings which usually take between two and four years to complete. It is at present working on the following contracts:

| | Contract | | |
| | L | A | Y |
	£'000	£'000	£'000
Contract price	20,400	8,000	24,000
Total costs (other than depreciation) up to			
31 December Year 5	4,800	Nil	Nil
Estimated costs to completion (including depreciation)			
at 31 December Year 5	10,400	Nil	Nil
Plant and equipment			
Written-down value at 31 December Year 5	1,600	Nil	Nil
Purchases during year to 31 December Year 5	2,000	Nil	Nil
Total costs (other than depreciation) up to			
31 December Year 6	10,650	2,400	16,100
Estimated costs to completion (including depreciation)			
at 31 December Year 6	4,000	3,250	9,000
Plant and equipment			
Written down value at 31 December Year 6	1,450	1,200	350
Purchases during year to 31 December Year 6	800	2,050	2,250

Work in progress should be valued at the end of each year as the total of costs to date plus 'attributable profits' on any contract over half completed (as measured on a cost basis).

Attributable profit is calculated as follows:

$$\text{Total anticipated profit} \times \frac{\text{Total costs incurred to date}}{\text{Total costs } \star}$$

$\star$ Incurred to date plus anticipated costs to completion.

The draft Profit & Loss Account of Egg plc for the year ending 31 December Year 6 showed the following entry:

	£'000	£'000	£'000
Profit on Contract L	750		
Profit on Contract A	1,700	2,450	
Less loss on Contract Y		2,000	
			450

Required

Show for *each* of the contracts L, A and Y how the entry in the Profit & Loss Account must have been calculated. In each case, state whether or not the company's figures are correct and, where necessary, calculate revised figures.

Solution

(a) Calculate how the actual transfer for each contract was calculated.

(b) Calculate how the transfer for each contract should have been calculated.

(c) State whether or not the company's figures for each contract are correct and any revised figures that are necessary.

(a)   **Contract A, Year 6**

	£'000	£'000
Price		8,000
Costs to date	2,400	
Depreciation (2,050 – 1,200)	850	
	3,250	
Estimated costs to complete	3,250	6,500
Total anticipated profit		1,500
Profit attributable (1,500 × 3,250 ÷ 6,500)		750

(b) As the contract is less than half complete no profit should be taken.

(c) Therefore for Contract A the company's figure is incorrect. It should be NIL.

(a)   **Contract L, Year 6**

	£'000	£'000
Price		20,400
Costs to date	10,650	
Depreciation ((2,000 – 1,600) + (1,600 + 800 – 1,450))	1,350	
	12,000	
Estimated costs to complete	4,000	16,000
Total anticipated profit		4,400
Profit attributable (4,400 × 12,000 ÷ 16,000)		3,300

As this exceeds the profit in the Profit & Loss Account for Year 6 some profit must have been taken to the Profit & Loss Account for Year 5.

Therefore calculate what profit was transferred to the Profit & Loss Account for Contract L for Year 5 as follows:

Contract L, Year 5

	£'000	£'000
Price		20,400
Costs to date	4,800	
Depreciation (2,000 – 1,600)	400	
	5,200	
Estimated costs to complete	10,400	15,600
Total anticipated profit		4,800
Profit attributable (4,800 × 5,200 ÷ 15,600)		1,600

Therefore in Year 6 profit transferred to the Profit & Loss Account was calculated as £3,300,000 less £1,700,000, being £1,600,000.

(b) *No* profit should have been transferred to the Profit & Loss Account in Year 5 because the contract was then less than half completed.

(c) Therefore for Contract L the company's figure is incorrect. The company should transfer the whole profit of £3,300,000 in Year 6.

(a)   **Contract Y, Year 6**

	£'000	£'000
Price		24,000
Costs to date	16,100	
Depreciation (2,250 – 350)	1,900	
	18,000	
Estimated costs to complete	9,000	27,000
Total anticipated loss		–3,000
Therefore loss attributable		
(–3,000,000 × 18,000,000 ÷ 27,000,000)		–2,000

(b) Calculation of the transfer would be the same calculation but as there is a loss anticipated on this contract it should all be provided for, not simply the loss attributable to Year 6.

(c) Therefore for Contract Y the company's figure is incorrect.

Stock accounts

Objectives

The objectives of keeping stock accounts include:

1   management control over the stock held, received and issued

2   basis for preparation of both interim and final accounts

3   instructions to store-keepers of when to re-order stocks by use of maximum and minimum re-order levels

Scenario

Businesses require a stock of goods for:

- resale
- consumption in production of goods for resale
- own use in running the business activities

It is not usually possible or desirable to replenish these goods on a daily basis so the business will hold stocks. The amounts of stocks held will vary on a daily basis due to supply and demand. It is necessary to determine the value of stocks held at the end of financial periods in order to prepare periodic accounts.

Methods

The actual book-keeping methods include:

- simple manually prepared accounts showing volume of stock only
- accounts with many analysis columns
- computer-produced information with a large amount of statistical information

From a candidate's point of view, the system required will be indicated by the examiner or implied in the question (eg by reference to the information made available or the number of marks allocated to the question).

Problems

A candidate is usually required in this type of question to use a given basis for pricing out issues of stock and valuing closing stocks. The various bases must be fully known and then readily applied.

EXAMPLE 5

Copper, a wholesaler, started trading on 1 September Year 8. During her first year of business, the following transactions occurred in respect of Article B, the only article she dealt in:

Month		No of units	Cost price per unit £	Selling price per unit £
Year 8				
Sept	Purchased	2,000	30.0	–
Oct	Purchased	2,000	34.0	–
Dec	Sold	1,600	–	38.0
Year 9				
April	Purchased	4,000	40.0	–
May	Sold	6,000	–	45.0
July	Purchased	2,000	34.6	–

Copper uses a *perpetual* stock recording system (making transfers from stock to cost of goods sold at the time of each sale). All necessary calculations are on a weighted average cost basis.

On 31 August Year 9, a physical stock check showed that 2,300 units of Article B were held. By then the unit purchase price of Article B had fallen to £28 and its net realisable value to £32 per unit. Selling and administrative expenses for the year totalled £36,000.

Required

(a) Prepare Copper's stock account (in a form suited to your calculations) for Article B for the year ended 31 August Year 9.

(b) Calculate Copper's gross and net profits for the year on the above basis.

(c) Calculate to what extent the gross and net profits of Copper would have been different if she had used a *periodic* stock recording system.

(d) Briefly outline the additional advantages (ie other than those revealed by (b) and (c) above) usually claimed for a *perpetual* stock recording system.

Solution

(a)   **Copper's Stock Account for Article B for the Year**

Month		Units	Unit cost £	Value £
Sept	Creditors	2,000	30.00	60,000
Oct	Creditors	2,000	34.00	68,000
		4,000	32.00	128,000
Dec	Cost of goods sold	–1,600	32.00	–51,200
		2,400	32.00	76,800
April	Creditors	4,000	40.00	160,000
		6,400	37.00	236,800
May	Cost of goods sold	–6,000	37.00	–222,000
		400	37.00	14,800
July	Creditors	2,000	34.60	69,200
		2,400	35.00	84,000
Aug	Profit & Loss Account for stock lost*	–100	35.00	–3,500
	Profit & Loss Account for stock write down**		3.00	–6,900
	Closing balance	–2,300	32.00	73,600

Notes to the accounts

★ This is charged to the Profit & Loss Account and is calculated on the same basis as the cost of goods sold would have been at this stage.

★★ This is charged to the Profit & Loss Account and is to reduce the price of the remaining stock to the net realisable value at 31 August, that is £32 per unit.

(b) Copper's gross and net profits for the year using the above stock figures would be calculated by preparing a brief Trading and Profit & Loss Account for Copper as follows:

	£	£
Sales (1,600 × £38) + (6,000 × £45)		330,800
Cost of goods sold (51,200 + 222,000)		273,200
Gross profit		57,600
Less Stock loss	3,500	
Stock write down	6,900	
Selling and administrative expenses	36,000	46,400
Net profit		11,200

Note the stock loss and stock write down are both charged to the Profit & Loss Account

(c) Cost of goods sold using the periodic stock system

Weighted average cost per unit is:

$$\frac{60,000 + 68,000 + 160,000 + 69,200}{2,000 + 2,000 + 4,000 + 2,000} = \frac{£357,200}{10,000}$$

This gives £35.72 per unit. As £35.72 per unit is greater than the net realisable value at 31 August Year 8 we must value the closing stock at the net realisable value of £32.00 per unit. Value of closing stock is 2,300 × £32.00 = £73,600. (Stock is valued at the lower of cost and net realisable value.)

Trading and Profit and Loss Account

	£
Sales as in (b) above	330,800
Cost of goods sold (357,200 – 73,600)	283,600
Gross profit	47,200
Less selling and administrative expenses	36,000
Net profit	11,200

Hence the profit would be the same using the periodic stock system as it is using the perpetual stock system.

Notes

1   It may be observed that as the stock is valued at the same price per unit using the perpetual stock recording system and the periodic stock recording system, the net profit must be the same.

2   Alternatively a quick way of arriving at this conclusion would be:

	£
Cost of goods sold using weighted average cost basis	273,200
Add: Stock loss	3,500
Stock write down	6,900
Cost of goods sold using periodic stock basis	283,600

(d) Additional advantages for a *perpetual* stock recording system include:

(i) It enables the business to control the quantities of the stock by maintaining an up-to-date record showing how much stock it should hold in the stores at any given date.

(ii) Interim accounts can be prepared more easily as it will not be necessary to await the outcome of stocktaking.

(iii) The perpetual stock system will provide information for budgeting.

Calculation of stock in absence of physical stocktaking at financial year end

Objective

In many businesses it is impracticable to halt normal trading activities (production or services to customers, etc) in order to take stock at the financial year end or in connection with the preparation of interim accounts. If the business maintains perpetual stock records, these may be used to supply the figure of stock at the end of the financial period. In the absence of such records the business may take stock at the nearest possible date to that required and adjust the figure thus obtained for movement of stock between the date of stocktaking and the financial year end.

Scenario

The information available will be:

1   stock quantities at time of stock taking

2   stock received and issued between stocktaking date and financial year end

3   information to enable the candidate to value stock

4   bases of converting stocks given at prices other than cost to cost

Method

The method is to prepare a schedule which will:

(a) begin with the stocktaking figures

(b) add stock to be included

(c) deduct stock to be excluded

As far as possible work in relation to the total stock; but, if this is not possible, information will be available to calculate individual items of stock.

Problems

Problems include making adjustments for the profit element included in stock quoted at selling prices, stock held on sale or return or out on sale or return, and accounting errors.

EXAMPLE 6

The annual stocktaking of Shannon plc was delayed one week (from 31 March Year 10 to 7 April Year 10) because of staff illness. However, the resultant figure of £48,000 was still used in the preparation of the company's draft trading account and draft balance sheet. The draft accounts showed a gross profit of £320,000, a net profit of £65,000 and working capital of £50,000.

Analysis of the relevant ledger accounts showed that, during the week's delay, the following transactions affecting stock took place:

1   sales: at selling price £11,000, of which £1,000 had still to be delivered when stocktaking took place

2   purchases: all received, £8,000

3   returns outwards: £400

4   returns inwards: £200

Shannon plc achieves a constant rate of gross profit of 20% on all sales revenue.

In addition it was discovered that:

1   A stock sheet, prepared on 7 April Year 10, had been overadded by £300.

2   The stock valuation on 7 April Year 10 included goods costing £1,500. These were sold on 15 April Year 10 for £1,200 and it had cost £100 to deliver them to the customer.

3   Included in the stock value of £48,000 was the company's office stationery stock, costing £3,800. During the week's delay, it was estimated that £800 of stationery had been used but none had been purchased.

4   The valuation on 7 April Year 10 had omitted goods costing Shannon plc £1,600, sent on a sale or return basis to Dart Ltd in March Year 10. Half of these goods, in value, were purchased by Dart Ltd on 30 March Year 10

and the remainder were returned to Shannon plc on 12 April Year 10. The sale had not been recorded in Shannon plc's draft accounts.

Required

(a) Calculate the corrected stock valuation for Shannon plc's balance sheet at 31 March Year 10.

(b) Incorporating your answer to (a) above, calculate the corrected figures of Shannon plc's gross profit and net profit for the year ended 31 March Year 10 and the corrected figure of Shannon plc's working capital at 31 March Year 10.

Solution

(a)

		£	£
Stocks as in draft accounts			48,000
Add Net sales at cost omitted (11,000 − 1,000 − 200) × 80%		7,840	
Stock on sale or return (1,600 × ½)		800	
			8,640
			56,640
Less Purchases included (8,000 − 400)		7,600	
Addition error		300	
Write-down of stock (1,500 − 1,200 + 100)		400	
Stationery stock included		3,800	
			12,100
			44,540

(b)

	Gross profit £	Net profit £	Working capital £
Balances per draft accounts	320,000	65,000	50,000
Stock adjustment			
(12,100 − 8,640)	−3,460	−3,460	−3,460
Stationery (3,800 + 800)		+4,600	+4,600
Sales/debtors (1,600 × 1.25 × ½)	+1,000	+1,000	+1,000
	317,540	67,140	52,140

PRACTICE QUESTIONS

10.1 Lemon plc trades from its head office in Mond and its branch in Lee. Its accountant is experiencing difficulty in deciding on the value of its stock, for balance sheet purposes. The stock comprises the following four items:

1 *Stock M 300 units* These were bought by Mond from the Lee branch for £100 per unit but at the balance sheet date have a net realisable value of £97 per unit, due to a temporary depression of the market. Lee branch had calculated the price per unit on the following basis:

	£
Labour	30
Materials	40
Factory Overhead Allocation	20
Profit	_10_
	_100_

2   *Stock O* This comprises the following five categories bought from outside suppliers:

Category	Cost £	NRV £
1	5,000	6,000
2	7,500	7,200
3	4,000	5,100
4	9,100	10,000
5	_14,300_	_13,400_
	_39,900_	_41,700_

3   *Stock N* This was bought by the Lee branch from Mond at an invoice price of £10,000 which included Mond gross profit of 25% on cost price. The Lee branch will use it in a manufacturing process instead of purchasing an alternative material costing £12,500 on the open market.

4   *Stock D* Mond has held 15,400 units of this stock in its warehouse for many years; it originally cost £7.00 per unit, but now has a replacement cost of £11.00 per unit. Mond has found a buyer for this stock who is prepared to pay £12.00 per unit after Mond has carried out processing on $\frac{1}{11}$ of this stock at a cost of £1.00 per unit. This process has now been completed.

Required

Calculate, to 1 decimal place, the total value to be included in the balance sheet in respect of each of the four items of stock. Give your reasons and show your workings.

10.2   Bergman Ltd started business on 1 January Year 42 as a dealer in electronic games. During Year 42, the company made the following purchases of Game X:

- February: 2,000   units   at £5.00 each
- May: 2,500   units   at £6.00 each
- August: 2,000   units   at £6.50 each
- November: 1,500   units   at £7.50 each

The company was undecided whether to adopt the First In First Out (FIFO) basis of stock valuation or the Last In First Out (LIFO) basis of stock valuation. On 31 December Year 42, the units of Game X in stock had cost Bergman Ltd £17,750 using the FIFO basis or £13,000 using the LIFO basis. Bergman Ltd has used the periodic system of recording stock.

Required

(a)   Calculate how many units of Game X from each of the above purchases were assumed, for calculation purposes, to be in stock at the end of Year 42, using alternatively:

    (i)   a stock valuation based on the FIFO basis

    (ii)   a stock valuation based on the LIFO basis

During Year 43, the company purchased 1,000 units of Game X at £8.00 each and a further 500 units of Game X at £8.50 each. On 31 December Year 43, there were 2,000 units of Game X in stock.

Throughout Years 42 and 43, the selling price of Game X was £15 per unit and no units were lost or destroyed.

Required

  (b) Calculate the gross profit on sales of Game X during Year 43, using alternatively:

    (i)   a stock valuation based on the FIFO basis

    (ii)   a stock valuation based on the LIFO basis

  (c) Recalculate the two profit figures from **(b)** above, assuming that all data remain the same except that, on 31 December Year 43, Bergman Ltd had purchased an additional 1,000 units of Game X at £10.00 each and there were 3,000 units of Game X in stock on that date.

10.3 Derwent Manufacturing Ltd uses two raw materials, A and B, which it purchases from Usk Ltd. The materials accounts for December Year 10 were as follows:

		A kg	A $	B kg	B $			A kg	A $	B kg	B $
Dec 1	Balances	100	250	200	1,000	Dec 6	Work in progress	120	(1)		
Dec 4	Usk Ltd	100	300			Dec 12	Work in progress			100	(2)
Dec 13	Work in progress			10	(3)	Dec 26	Work in progress	30	(4)		
Dec 24	Usk Ltd			200	1,200	Dec 28	Work in progress			140	(5)
						31 Dec	Profit & loss	–	–	(6)	(7)
							Balances	50	(8)	150	(9)
		200	550	410	(10)			200	550	(11)	(12)

Stocks at 31 December were checked by a physical stocktaking. In the case of B, some wastage occurs when making issues, so 10% is added to the cost of all issues.

Required

Copy out the above accounts twice and fill in the spaces marked

(1), (2), (3), (4), (5), (6), (7), (8), (9), (10), (11) and **(12)**

assuming alternatively that issues are recorded on:

  (a) a FIFO basis

  (b) a LIFO basis

POINTS TO REMEMBER

Stocks valuation for final accounts

- Stock is valued at the lower of cost or net realisable value.

- *Cost* bases of stock valuation acceptable under SSAP 9 are:

    1   Average cost

    2   FIFO

    3   Standard cost

- *Net realisable value* is the expected amount from selling stock in the course of business.

Long-term contracts valuation

- Take care in allocation of overheads between periods and contracts.

- Apply formula given in question to determine proportion of profits taken to Profit & Loss Account.

Book-keeping methods for stock and long-term contracts

- Read carefully the method of pricing stock issues given in the question.

- Use columns for:

    - Units

    - Unit cost

    - Value.

- Show your calculations of:

    - cost of goods taken to production or sales

    - stock lost

    - closing stock.

Absence of physical stocktaking

- Adjust actual stocktaking figures for movement of stock between date of stocktaking and date of balance sheet.

- Take care to make all adjustments at cost price, even if the information is given at selling price.

11

Accounting for depreciation

After carefully studying this chapter you should be able to:

1 *define depreciation and state the objectives of accounting for depreciation;*

2 *apply the important accounting bases of depreciation;*

3 *prepare accounts for depreciation;*

4 *make the necessary disclosures for depreciation;*

5 *identify the basis of depreciation used.*

Depreciation is the measure of the wearing out, consumption, or other reduction in the useful economic life of a fixed asset whether arising from use, effluxion of time or obsolescence through technological or other market changes (SSAP 12).

Objectives

The objectives of providing for depreciation include:

1   To present a true and fair view of tangible fixed assets in a balance sheet. If no provision is made for depreciation the tangible fixed assets will be overvalued in the balance sheet.

2   To present a true and fair view of expenses in a trading and profit and loss account. If no provision is made for depreciation, the net profit will be overstated.

3   To calculate the cost of production when preparing quotations for potential customers. If no provision is made for depreciation the quotations will not reflect the actual costs.

Scenario

In order to carry out its trading activities, a business will acquire various tangible assets. There are two categories of tangible assets:

1   *Current assets* The assets that the business trades in are classified as current assets; these assets will be held for as short a time as possible and will be converted into cash as soon as they can. They include stock, work in progress, debtors, bills receivable, cash at bank and cash in hand.

2   *Fixed assets* The assets that the business intends to hold for a long time because it uses them are classified as fixed assets. They include land and buildings, plant and machinery and motor vehicles.

This chapter is concerned only with tangible fixed assets. As they have a limited economic life but one that extends beyond the usual accounting period, it is necessary to apportion the cost of these assets over the accounting periods in which they are used. The amount apportioned to each year is called the depreciation for that year.

Method

In connection with the topic of depreciation the term 'method' can be applied to:

1   the different bases of calculating depreciation

2   the different accounting procedures for depreciation, and

3   the disclosures required in respect of depreciation

These will be considered individually:

The different bases of calculating depreciation

There are many bases available for allocating depreciation to the relevant accounting periods; the management of a business must choose the basis most suitable to the type of asset and to the type of business. Usually a business will use many different bases of calculating depreciation, as the management will take into consideration the nature and use of each asset concerned. For example, depreciation may relate to:

● the use of an asset in producing goods for resale
● the delivery of those goods to customers
● the simple passage of time
● the availability of more efficient or cheaper assets than those owned by the business

The following bases of depreciation are examinable in Third Level Accounting:

1   *Straight line* In this basis, depreciation is calculated by dividing the cost of the asset less residual value by the number of years of economic life the asset is expected to have. For example, *see* Example 1.

2   *Reducing balance* In this basis, depreciation is calculated by multiplying the net cost of the asset, or the closing balance on the asset at the beginning of the accounting period, by a predetermined rate of depreciation (based on the expected economic life of the asset). For example, *see* Example 1.

3   *Unit cost* In this basis, depreciation is calculated by dividing the cost of the asset less residual value by the number of units the asset is expected to produce to give a cost per unit of production. In each accounting period the actual number of units produced is multiplied by the cost per unit to give the depreciation for that period. This basis is applied to machinery, etc. For example, *see* Example 1.

4   *Depletion unit* This basis applies the unit cost basis to mines, quarries, oil wells and similar assets which contain material such as coal or sand or oil. In this basis, depreciation is calculated by dividing the cost of the asset less residual value by the quantity of coal, sand or oil, etc it is expected to produce, to give a cost per tonne or barrel of production. In each accounting period the actual tonnes or barrels produced is multiplied by the cost per tonne or barrel to give the depreciation for that period.

5   *Machine hour* This basis applies the unit cost basis to machines and similar assets which can be used for a determined number of hours. In this basis, depreciation is calculated by dividing the cost of the asset less residual value by the number of hours it is expected to work, to give a cost per hour worked. In each accounting period the actual number of hours worked is multiplied by the cost per hour to give the depreciation for that period.

6   *Sum of the year's digits* In this basis, depreciation is calculated by giving the last year of life of the asset 'digit' 1; the year before 'digit' 2; the year before that 'digit' 3, etc. The digits are added to give the total of digits. Then the cost of the asset less residual value is divided by the total of digits to give a cost per digit. In each accounting period the depreciation is calculated by multiplying the digit of that year by the cost per digit. For example, *see* Example 1.

7   *Annual revaluation of asset* In this basis depreciation is calculated by valuing the asset at the end of the accounting period and deducting that valuation from the valuation at the beginning of the accounting period.

The different accounting procedures for depreciation

The different accounting procedures concern the book-keeping aspects of accounting for depreciation. This topic was considered in the previous 2 volumes of this series of book-keeping and accounting texts. The two methods available are:

1   Credit the depreciation annually to the asset account with a debit to depreciation account or to manufacturing or profit & loss account.

2   Credit depreciation to the provision for depreciation account where it is accumulated for the period in which the asset is retained. The accumulated depreciation is then offset against the asset to ascertain its net book value on disposal of the asset.

The disclosures required in respect of depreciation

SSAP 12 requires published accounts of limited companies to disclose the following in respect of depreciation:

● the basis used to calculate depreciation

- the useful economic life of each asset or group of assets
- the depreciation rates used in the calculation
- the total depreciation for the accounting period
- the gross amount of depreciable assets and accumulated depreciation

Problems

Problems arising include:

(a) definitions used in connection with depreciation

(b) change in the basis of calculation of depreciation of an asset

Definitions

The following definitions are used in discussing depreciation:

1   *Obsolescence* An asset becomes uneconomic to use due to its age or the development of alternative means of production.

2   *Effective cost of an asset* This is the cost upon which depreciation calculations are based. It includes the cost of purchasing the asset plus transportation and installation. If the owner of the asset undertakes installation etc, the cost may include wages, materials, overheads etc incurred, ascertained by analysis of the total expenditure of the business. The estimated realisable value will be deducted in using all bases of calculating depreciation other than the reducing balance basis.

3   *Useful economic life* This is the period over which the present owner will derive economic benefits from the use of an asset. It is difficult to forecast how long an asset will last and be useful, especially in view of the incidence of obsolescence. An asset's useful economic life may be:

(a)   predetermined as in the case of a lease

(b)   directly governed by extraction or consumption as in the case of a mine

(c)   dependent upon its physical deterioration through use or effluxion of time

(d)   reduced by economic or technological obsolescence

4   *Residual value* In order to allocate the effective cost of an asset over its economic life it is necessary to estimate its value at the end. This is difficult to anticipate.

5   *Recoverable amount* This is the greater of the net realisable value of an asset and (where appropriate) the amount recoverable from its further use.

6   *Carrying amount* This is the value brought forward at the beginning of an accounting period upon which the current year's depreciation is based; in the case of the first year of use of an asset, it is the cost.

Change in the basis of depreciation

Changes may arise in the basis of depreciation of an asset. For example, depreciation may have been based originally on an estimated 10-year useful economic life of an asset, but at the end of the 5th year it may become necessary to revise the total economic life of the asset to just 7 years. If this happens, depreciation for Year 6 and Year 7 will be based on the net book value at the end of Year 5. Alternatively, the management of a business may decide that, due to the changed circumstances of that business, it has become more appropriate to calculate depreciation on a straight line basis instead of the previous basis. Here too the new basis will be applied to the net book value at the date of the change of basis.

EXAMPLE I

Aurum purchased machine X for £3,000 and spent £200 installing it. The machine has an economic life of 5 years and an estimated scrap value of £100. The number of units the machine is expected to produce each year is as follows:

Year 1	4,000
Year 2	5,000
Year 3	9,000
Year 4	7,000
Year 5	6,000

Aurum has read a textbook and discovered that the annual credit to accumulated depreciation account in respect of the machine could:

1   remain the same

2   fluctuate

3   decline sharply every year

4   decline gradually every year

Required

(a) Identify a depreciation policy that will produce *each* of the four patterns shown in Aurum's textbook.

(b) Using the above information, prepare calculations to show that each of the four policies you have identified for **1** to **4** produces the intended pattern of annual credits to accumulated depreciation account.

Solution

(a)   **Identification of depreciation policies used**

Annual credit to accumulated depreciation	*Policy used*
1 remain the same	Straight line
2 fluctuate	Unit cost (usage)
3 decline sharply every year	Reducing balance
4 decline gradually every year	Sum of the years' digits

(b)

1		**Straight line**	**Credit**
Cost	– residual value ÷ years of economic life		per annum
(£3,000 + 200) – 100	÷ 5		£ 620
Total depreciation			£3,100

2		**Unit cost**	
Cost *less*	residual value divided by number of units		per unit
(£3,000 + 200) – 100	÷ (4,000 + 5,000 + 9,000 +		
	7,000 + 6,000)		£0.10

Credits to accumulated depreciation account would be:

			£
Year 1	4,000 units	× £0.10 =	400
Year 2	5,000 units	× £0.10 =	500
Year 3	9,000 units	× £0.10 =	900
Year 4	7,000 units	× £0.10 =	700
Year 5	6,000 units	× £0.10 =	600
Total depreciation			3,100

3		**Reducing balance**	
	Carrying amount	× rate of depreciation	annual depreciation
	£		£
Year 1	3,200	× 50%	1,600
Year 2	3,200 – 1,600	× 50%	800
Year 3	1,600 – 800	× 50%	400
Year 4	800 – 400	× 50%	200
Year 5	400 – 200	× 50%	100
Total depreciation			3,100

4			**Sum of the years' digits**			
	Net cost	times	'digit' for year	divided by	total digits	£
Year 1	£3,100	×	5	÷	15	1,033
Year 2	£3,100	×	4	÷	15	827
Year 3	£3,100	×	3	÷	15	620
Year 4	£3,100	×	2	÷	15	413
Year 5	£3,100	×	1	÷	15	207
Total digits			15	Total depreciation		3,100

Note to the example

The 'digits' for the each year are weighted in favour of the earlier years. As the economic life of machine X is 5 years: Year 1 is given 5; Year 2 is given 4; Year 3 is given 3; Year 4 is given 2; Year 5 is given 1.

EXAMPLE 2

Whole plc owns 70% of the ordinary share capital of Sub Ltd and 90% of the ordinary share capital of Idiary Ltd.

The plant and machinery of the group in the consolidated balance sheet at 31 December Year 38 comprised:

	Cost £'000	Invoice price £'000	Cumulative depreciation £'000
Whole plc	10,000		4,000
Sub Ltd		6,000	3,000
Idiary Ltd		5,200	1,560

All plant and machinery at 'invoice price' was bought by Sub Ltd from Whole plc at cost price plus a 25% mark-up and all plant and machinery at 'invoice price' was bought by Idiary Ltd from Whole plc at cost price plus a 30% mark-up.

Required

Calculate the total value to be included in the consolidated balance sheet of Whole plc and subsidiaries at 31 December Year 38 for plant and machinery cost, cumulative depreciation and net book value.

Solution

Plant and machinery

	Cost £	Depn £	£
Whole plc	10,000,000	4,000,000	6,000,000
Sub Ltd	6,000,000	3,000,000	3,000,000
Inter-co profits 25/125	1,200,000	600,000	600,000
	4,800,000	2,400,000	2,400,000
Idiary Ltd	5,200,000	1,560,000	3,640,000
Inter-co profits 30/130	1,200,000	360,000	840,000
	4,000,000	1,200,000	2,800,000
	18,800,000	7,600,000	11,200,000

The unrealised profits included must be eliminated.

EXAMPLE 3

Aung and Bui own a small car hire business. At 31 December Year 8, before the preparation of the annual final accounts, there is a balance of $35,220 on the partnership's Cars account. This consists of the cost price of Car no 8, which was bought for cash on 1 January Year 8, together with the *written-down values* at that date of their other cars, details of which are as follows:

Car no	Cost price $	Year purchased
4	6,400	5
5	8,800	5
6	9,700	6
7	10,400	7

Car no 5 was sold for $4,100 in November Year 8, but no entry in respect of its sale has yet been recorded in the Cars account. Depreciation on cars has always been calculated on the basis of an estimated useful life of 5 years. Aung and Bui now decide to change the basis to an estimated life of 8 years, as from the depreciation to be calculated for Year 8. As previously, they intend using the straight line basis, ignoring residual values, and charging a full year's depreciation in the year of purchase, but no depreciation in the year of sale.

Required

(a) Prepare the firm's Cars account for Year 8 on the new basis, showing as its closing balance the total written-down value of cars then held after the year's depreciation has been charged.

(b) State, with a brief explanation, whether the change in the firm's assessment of the useful life of cars requires an adjustment to be made to profits of prior years.

(c) State the total amount of depreciation to be charged in Year 9, assuming no purchases or sales of cars during that year.

Solution

(a) Preliminary calculations

Cost of car no 8

					$
Balance on Cars account at 31 December Year 8					35,220
Less opening balances for other cars					

Car no	Cost	Remaining years	Years of life	Balance	
	$			$	
4	6,400	× 2	÷ 5	2,560	
5	8,800	× 2	÷ 5	3,520	
6	9,700	× 3	÷ 5	5,820	
7	10,400	× 4	÷ 5	8,320	20,220
8	Residual				15,000

Depreciation for Year 8

Car no	Opening balance/cost	Remaining years	
	$		$
4	2,560	÷ 5	512
6	5,820	÷ 6	970
7	8,320	÷ 7	1,189
8	15,000	÷ 8	1,875
			4,546

Cars Account for Year 8

	$		$
Opening balance	20,220	Sale of car	3,520
		Profit & Loss Account	4,546
Bank (purchase)	15,000	Closing balance	27,154
	35,220		35,220

(b) No adjustment is required to profits of prior years, because future depreciation is based upon the written-down value of the cars at the beginning of Year 8.

(c) As Aung and Bui are using the straight line basis for calculating depreciation the depreciation for Year 9 will be the same as that calculated for Year 8, namely $4,546.

EXAMPLE 4

The following is an extract from the accounting policies of Elve plc:

Freehold land is stated at historical cost.

Freehold buildings are stated at historical cost; depreciation is calculated on a straight line basis, assuming a useful life of 50 years and a zero residual value.

Machinery is stated at historical cost; depreciation is calculated on the basis of units produced.

Vehicles are stated at historical cost; depreciation is calculated on a straight line basis, assuming an estimated useful life of 6 years and a residual value of 10% of cost.

Computers are stated at historical cost; depreciation is calculated on a reducing balance basis, assuming an annual rate of 30%.

The trial balance of Elve plc at 1 January Year 12 included:

	£'000	£'000
Freehold land at cost[1]	1,000	
Freehold buildings at cost/provision for depreciation[1]	500	200
Machinery at cost/Provision for depreciation[2]	450	210
Vehicles at cost/Provision for depreciation[3]	150	105
Computers at cost/Provision for depreciation[1]	90	65

Notes to the balance sheet

1   During Year 12, there were no purchases or sales of freehold land, freehold buildings or computers.

2   During Year 12 Elve plc used 'model X' machinery for the first time. This is included at cost £50,000 in the trial balance at 1 January Year 12. It is estimated that model X will produce 20,000 units in its useful life. In Year 12, the total production of Elve plc was 10,000 units, out of which 'model

X' produced 10%. The provision for depreciation of machinery represents a production of 63,000 units up to 31 December Year 11.

3   During Year 12 Elve plc sold for £9,500 vehicles which had cost £50,000 and on which depreciation of £40,000 had been provided to 31 December Year 11; it also bought vehicles for £30,000. Depreciation is calculated on the basis of all vehicles held at the end of the year.

Required

Show all the entries relating to fixed assets as they would appear in Elve plc's:

(a) Profit and loss account for Year 12   (10 marks)

(b) Balance sheet at 31 December Year 12   (7 marks)

Total (17 marks)

Solution

(a)   **Profit and Loss entries**

		£	£	£
Loss on sale of vehicles (50,000 − 40,000 − 9,500)				500
Depreciation				
Buildings	500,000 ÷ 50		10,000	
Machinery				
Model X	1,000 units @ 50,000 ÷ 20,000	2,500		
Other machinery	9,000 units @ 210,000 ÷ 63,000	30,000	32,500	
	10,000			
Vehicles	(150,000 − 50,000 + 30,000) × 0.9 ÷ 6		19,500	
Computers	(90,000 − 65,000) × 0.3		7,500	69,500
				70,000

(b)   **Balance Sheet entries**

	Cost		Depreciation	
	£		£	£
Tangible fixed assets				
Land	1,000,000			1,000,000
Buildings	500,000	200,000 + 10,000	210,000	290,000
Machinery	450,000	210,000 + 32,500	242,500	207,500
Vehicles (150,000 − 50,000 + 30,000)	130,000	(105,000 + 19,500 − 40,000)	84,500	45,500
Computers	90,000	(65,000 + 7,500)	72,500	17,500
	2,170,000		609,500	1,560,500

PRACTICE QUESTIONS

11.1 The following table relates to the depreciation of some of the fixed assets of Carrot Ltd:

	Motor lorry	Drilling machine	Building	Robot
Date bought	1 Jan Year 30	1 Jan Year 30	1 Jan Year 20	1 Jan Year 33
Cost	£13,000	£20,000	£60,000	£25,000
Residual value	£1,000	**(3)**	nil	£3,000
Method	Straight line	Reducing balance	Straight line	**(7)**
Working life	**(1)**	10 years	50 years	**(8)**
Annual depreciation	**(2)**	30%	**(5)**	£5,500
Balance sheet value at 31 December Year 35	£4,000	**(4)**	**(6)**	**(9)**

Required

(a) Give the entries for each of the nine items **(1)–(9)** required to complete the table. Show workings, which should be to the nearest £.

(b) Briefly define 'depreciation'.

11.2 Leopard Deliveries Ltd owned three vans on 1 April Year 26. Their details were as follows:

- Van P cost £23,400 in May Year 22
- Van Q cost £14,700 in June Year 24
- Van R cost £36,600 in January Year 26

Depreciation is calculated using the straight line method, assuming a 5-year economic life and zero scrap value. A full year's depreciation is charged in the year of purchase but none in the year of disposal.

During the year to 31 March Year 27, the following transactions took place:

1 June Year 26: Van Q written off due to an accident; £7,875 was received from the insurance company in full compensation.

2 July Year 26: Van S purchased for £24,600.

3 August Year 26: Van P sold for £5,250.

4 October Year 26: Van T purchased for £29,250.

5 January Year 27: after testing, Van T was considered unsuitable and exchanged for Van U, valued at £28,200; no depreciation was written off Van T.

Required

(a) Show the following accounts as they would appear in the books of Leopard Deliveries Ltd for the year ended 31 March Year 27:

(i) vans at cost

(ii) accumulated depreciation on vans

(iii) van disposal (one account for each disposal)

(b) Explain briefly why the reducing balance method is often preferred to the straight line method of calculating depreciation for vans.

11.3 On 1 July Year 15, the fixed assets of Flamingo Ltd were valued in the company's books as follows:

	Cost £	Depreciation £	Net £
Freehold land	270,000		270,000
Freehold buildings	180,000	4,500	175,500
Factory machinery	592,800	357,150	235,650
Vehicles	48,250	27,600	20,650
	1,091,050	389,250	701,800

It is company policy to calculate depreciation on a straight line basis, assuming no residual value, and to provide a full year's depreciation in the year of purchase but none in the year of sale. The following information relates to the year ended 30 June Year 16:

1   Buildings are being written off on a straight line basis over 40 years. The freehold land and buildings were professionally revalued at £570,000 on 30 June Year 16. This valuation included £240,000 in respect of the buildings. The directors have decided to show the revalued amounts in the company's balance sheet.

2   Factory machinery is being depreciated at 10% per annum on a straight line basis. An item of machinery, purchased for £126,000 in September Year 11, is now recognised as having an economic life of at least 20 years from its purchase date. Machinery, originally purchased for £108,000 has been fully depreciated and will be scrapped in August Year 16. The remaining machinery is less than 10 years old.

3   Vehicles have been depreciated at 12½% per annum on a straight line basis. A vehicle purchased in January Year 11 for £6,000 was traded in part exchange for a new vehicle costing £9,600. The old vehicle was valued at £2,000 for this purpose. All vehicles are less than 8 years old. It has now been decided to depreciate vehicles on a diminishing balance basis at a 25% rate.

Required

(a) Assuming that no prior year adjustments are considered to be necessary, calculate Flamingo Ltd's depreciation expense for the year ended 30 June Year 16 in respect of:

   (i)   freehold buildings

   (ii)   factory machinery

   (iii)   vehicles

(b) Calculate the other effects of the fixed asset transactions on the non-distributable and distributable reserves of Flamingo Ltd at 30 June Year 16.

POINTS TO REMEMBER

- Learn the following bases of calculating depreciation:

Straight line	Cost less residual value divided by economic life
Reducing balance	Cost/book value multiplied by given rate
Unit cost	Cost less residual value divided by total units
Depletion unit	Cost less residual value divided by total tonnage
Machine hour	Cost less residual value divided by total hours
Sum of the years' digits	Cost less residual value divided by total digits
Annual revaluation	Reduction in valuation at year end

- In connection with depreciation, the published accounts of limited companies must disclose:

  – basis

  – useful economic life

  – rate

  – total depreciation for year

  – total cost and depreciation

- If the basis of depreciation is changed, calculate subsequent depreciation on the book value of the asset, immediately before the change.

- Calculate depreciation for fixed assets in a consolidated balance sheet on the net cost to the group of the asset, after eliminating any inter-company loading.

APPENDIX I
How to approach LCCIEB Question I

This appendix considers how to approach Question 1 of the London Chamber of Commerce and Industry Third Level Accounting examination.

This is an extended question carrying a significant proportion of the total marks of an examination paper and must be attempted, since it is compulsory. The question is allocated 49% of the marks.

This appendix reproduces part 1 of an article written for the LCCIEB *Link* magazine in 1993, to encourage candidates for Third Level Accounting to attempt Question 1 of the paper. The example given at the end of the article has been changed.

How to approach Question I

I Marks available

Candidates must be aware of the importance of attempting this question. Since it is compulsory, it is impossible for any candidate not attempting Question 1 to pass the examination.

2 Format

The question is effectively a collection of small items based on a common set of circumstances. It enables the examiner to cover a number of important syllabus areas within the framework of one extended question. Each section should lead naturally and sequentially into the next, thereby steering the candidate through the information given.

3 Mistakes

Candidates should not worry unduly, as they work through the question, if they feel they may have made one or two early mistakes. Candidates will not be penalised more than once for an error which makes subsequent figures wrong. Examiners mark on the 'own figure' rule, whereby the initial error is penalised, but subsequent errors are marked according to the correctness of the treatment of the figure resulting from the initial error.

To use a basic arithmetic example:

> $4 \times 2 = 7$ is wrong and would lose a mark
> *but* a consequent calculation –
> $7 \times 5 = 35$ is correct and could gain a mark for the correct treatment of the wrong initial figure, ie 7.

It is worth remembering that, in many instances, figures from earlier requirements are not used subsequently anyway.

4 Time allocation

Candidates should allocate 50% of the available time to this question and should be disciplined about allocating the time in accordance with the number of marks available for each section. The marks available for each section are always printed at the end of the section.

5 Reading the question

Another important examination technique relates to reading the question. There is no advantage to be gained from reading the whole question through and then returning to the beginning. Each section can be read in turn, thus saving valuable reading time. The text printed before REQUIRED **(a)**, will contain all the information needed to answer REQUIRED **(a)** and so on.

In this connection, note particularly the words at the beginning of **(c)** in the following example: 'based on your answer to **(b)**'.

6 Workings

In all examinations involving calculations, candidates should show the basis of their calculations. The candidate who shows workings but ends up with the wrong answer may earn some of the marks available, whereas the candidate who produces an incorrect answer without showing any workings is not likely to earn any marks at all.

7 Preparation

There is now a reasonably large stock of past question papers featuring the extended question. Candidates are urged to obtain these papers, in order to test both their accounting skills and their examination technique.

8 Example

The following is an example of Question 1 and the suggested approach to answering it.

Do try the question and then compare your answer with that given.

Sour Ltd bought 40% of the ordinary shares of Crowt Ltd many years ago, when the capital structure of Crowt Ltd consisted of 200,000 ordinary shares of £0.50 each fully paid less a debit balance of £5,000 on profit and loss account, its only reserve.

During October Year 41, Sour Ltd was notified that, due to the death of Crowt Ltd's managing director, who held 30% of the ordinary shares, the remaining directors were considering liquidating Crowt Ltd unless a buyer could be found for the shares previously held by the managing director.

Sour Ltd is considering buying the whole of the 30% shareholding of the managing director at the agreed offer price of £68,500, of which £46,500 would be payable in cash and the balance by means of £20,000 9% debentures Years 60/61. The accountants of the two companies have prepared the following budgeted information at 31 December Year 41:

	Sour Ltd £'000	Crowt Ltd £'000
Stock	70	30
Debtors (including inter-company debt £4,000)	75	25
Account at Cabbage Bank plc	45	
40% shareholding in Crowt Ltd at cost	70	
Land and buildings	60	45
Machinery	90	50
	410	150
Overdraft at Cabbage Bank plc		5
Creditors (including inter-company debt £4,000)	30	10
Ordinary shares of £0.50 each fully paid	200	100
Profit & Loss Account – Sour Ltd (balance at 1 January Year 41 was £10,000 debit)	30	
Profit & Loss Account – Crowt Ltd (balance at 1 January Year 41 was £20,000 credit)		35
10% Debentures redeemable April Year 42	150	
	410	150

Required

(a) Prepare a journal entry in the books of Sour Ltd, without narratives, to record the acquisition by Sour Ltd of the additional 30% shareholding in Crowt Ltd for cash and debentures.

(b) Prepare, in good style, the consolidated balance sheet at 31 December Year 41 of Sour Ltd (and its subsidiary) on the assumption that Sour Ltd acquired the shares in Crowt Ltd on 31 December Year 41 and all forecasts were completely accurate.

(c) Calculate, to 1 decimal place, the following 10 ratios based on your answer to (b) and the other information given above:

  (i) in respect of Sour Ltd and Crowt Ltd and the group as a whole:
      1 working capital
      2 acid test

  (ii) in respect of Sour Ltd and Crowt Ltd only:
      3 % return on opening capital employed
      4 % earnings per share (in pence)

(d) Comment on the proposal, using your ratios from (c) above, where appropriate.

Solution

(a) **Journal entry**

	£	£
Shares in Crowt Ltd	68,500	
Bank		46,500
Debentures		20,000
Premium on debentures		2,000

Notes to part (a)

1   The total consideration is £68,500, but the cash plus nominal value of the debentures allocated amounts to £66,500 (46,500 + 20,000). The difference of £2,000 is assumed to be debenture premium in the absence of any information to the contrary.

2   Although the question specifies 'a journal entry', that is ONE only, a candidate might gain some marks (but not all) by submitting as an alternative presentation two or more journal entries thus:

	£	£
Shares in Crowt Ltd	68,500	
Executors of Crowt Ltd director		68,500
Executors of Crowt Ltd director	68,500	
Bank		46,500
Debentures		20,000
Premium on debentures		2,000

(b) **Consolidated Balance Sheet at 31 December Year 41**

	£	£	£
Fixed assets			
Intangible: Cost of control of subsidiary company			60,000
Tangible: Land and buildings (60 + 45)		105,000	
Machinery (90 + 50)		140,000	
			245,000
			305,000
Current assets			
Stock (70 + 30)		100,000	
Debtors (75 + 25 – 4)		96,000	
			196,000
Creditors due within one year			
10% debentures (April Year 42)		150,000	
Suppliers (30 + 10 – 4)		36,000	
Bank overdraft (5,000 – 45,000 + 46,500)		6,500	
			192,500

	£	£	£
Working capital			3,500
Total assets less creditors due within one year			308,500
Creditors due more than one year			
9% debentures Years 60/61			20,000
			288,500
Financed by capital and reserves			
400,000 ordinary shares of £0.50 each			200,000
Debenture premium			2,000
Profit & Loss Account			46,000
			248,000
Minority interest			40,500
			288,500

Notes to part (b)

1 The candidate must prepare the following essential workings and submit them to the examiner, making it quite clear that they are workings and do *not* form part of the consolidated balance sheet for publication. This enables the examiner to award part-marks where a candidate has applied the correct accounting technique but made an error in arithmetic:

(i)

	Cost of shares	Proportion of sundry net assets	Goodwill
	£		£
Original holding	70,000	40% × (100,000 − 5,000)	32,000
Additional	68,500	30% × (100,000 + 35,000)	28,000
			60,000

(ii)   **Minority interest**

(100% − 40% − 30%) × (100 + 35)	40,500

(iii)   **Profit & Loss Account**

Sour Ltd closing balance	30,000
Crowt Ltd 40% × (35,000 + 5,000)	16,000
	46,000

2 The debentures are classified differently:

- Under 'Creditors due after more than one year', are the debentures payable Years 60/61.

- Under 'Creditors due within one year', are the debentures payable April Year 42.

3 Do give full headings and subheadings with their appropriate subtotals as these are allocated marks.

(c) *Sour Ltd*   *Crowt Ltd*   *Group*

1 Working capital

$$\frac{(70 + 75)}{(30 + 46.5 - 45 + 150)} = 0.8 : 1 \qquad \frac{(30 + 25)}{(5 + 10)} = 3.7 : 1 \qquad \frac{196}{192.5} = 1.0 : 1$$

2 Acid test

$$\frac{75}{(30 + 46.5 - 45 + 150)} = 0.4 : 1 \qquad \frac{25}{(5 + 10)} = 1.7 : 1 \qquad \frac{96}{192.5} = 0.5 : 1$$

3 % Return on Opening Capital Employed

$$\frac{[30 + 10 + (40\% \times \{35 - 20\})]}{(200 - 10) + 40\% (20 + 5)} = 23.0\% \qquad \frac{(35 - 20)}{(100 + 20)} = 12.5\%$$

4 % Earnings per Share (in pence)

$$\frac{[30 + 10 + (40\% \{35 - 20\})]}{(200 \times 2)} = 11.5 \qquad \frac{(35 - 20)}{(100 \times 2)} = 7.5$$

Notes to part (c)

1   A columnar layout has been used; this saves the candidate rewriting the headings many times and also makes it easier for the examiner.

2   The workings are given for each ratio, so that part-marks may be awarded in case of errors of arithmetic. As this statement refers to ratios and not to final accounts for publication, the workings appear with the final figures in the form of fractions.

(d) Two comments on the proposal could be selected from the following:

1   *Social* Ensures continuity of employment for Crowt Ltd employees.

2   *Accounting* Gives Sour Ltd controlling interest, hence a consolidated balance sheet has become necessary.

3   *Financial* Creates bank overdraft in Sour Ltd and the group as a whole.

4   *Investment* Reduces Sour Ltd % return on opening capital employed, as that of Crowt Ltd is lower than that of Sour Ltd.

5   *Investment* Cost of control appears to be high.

APPENDIX 2
Two complete examination papers

Appendix 2 contains two complete papers of LCCIEB Third Level standard to illustrate the breadth and application of the syllabus in the context of an actual examination.

How to use Appendix 2

Candidates are strongly advised to work through the questions in each paper as if in the actual examination, that is:

1   do not at first refer to the answers given

2   work each paper at one sitting

3   do not refer to any study material

4   keep to the 3½ hours time limit which will apply in the examination room.

Then when you have completed each paper

5   compare your answers with the ones given

6   investigate the reasons behind any differences.

Sources of errors

They could be due to:

1   Careless errors, eg errors of arithmetic. If this is the reason, do try to take more care in your work.

2   Points in Third Level Accountancy that you do not understand. If this is the reason do refer back to this text or those relating to First and Second Levels to make sure you understand the principles involved.

3   Third Level Accounting techniques that you have not practised sufficiently. If this is the case you must work through as many questions as you can on the particular technique.

PAPER I

1 Boms Ltd owns one shop divided into three departments called Bin department, Odd department and Mun department. Each department sells only one product. The following is the company's trial balance at 31 December Year 33.

	£'000	£'000
Sales[1]		1,800
Departmental wages[2]	195	
General expenses[3]	126	
Debtors/creditors[4]	150	240
Buildings	166	
Fixtures/Provision for depreciation, 1 January Year 33[5]	100	30
Office wages and expenses[6]	18	
Bank		145
Stocks at 1 January Year 33:		
Unissued at cost price	210	
Issued at selling price[7]	150	
Provision for unrealised profit on stock held by departments at 1 January Year 33[7]		30
Purchases	1,480	
Bank charges[8]	11	
Discounts allowed/received[8]	4	5
Debenture interest[8]	10	
Directors' fees[8]	6	
Ordinary shares of £1.00 each fully paid		200
Profit & Loss Account 1 January Year 33		76
10% debentures (repayable in Year 35)		100
	2,626	2,626

Notes to trial balance

1 Sales were: Bin £500,000; Odd: £600,000 and Mun: £700,000.

2 Departmental wages are charged to departments on the basis of the number of employees in each department; Bin has 6 employees; Odd has 5 employees; and Mun has 4 employees.

3 General expenses are charged to departments on the basis of shelves in each department. Bin has 40 shelves, Odd has 50 shelves and Mun has 50 shelves.

4 Make a provision for doubtful debts of 2% of the debtors at 31 December Year 33. This cost should not be allocated between the three departments.

5 Depreciation is calculated on fixtures at 10% per annum using the reducing balance basis. Depreciation is charged to departments on the same basis as general expenses.

6 Office wages and expenses are charged to departments on the basis of the average number of hours per week of office staff time used in each department. This is 8.5 hours for Bin department; 10.2 hours for Odd department; and 11.9 hours for Mun department.

7 Each department has the same gross profit percentage on sales and this remains constant for all years. There were no stock losses or write offs in Year 33.

8 These items should *not* be allocated between the three departments.

Required

(a) Prepare, in columnar form, the trading profit & loss and appropriation account for Year 33 of Boms plc showing the gross profit and the net profit for *each* department, after charging departmental wages, general expenses, depreciation and office wages and expenses.

(b) Prepare *in good style* the balance sheet of Boms Ltd at 31 December Year 33.

(c) (i) For each department, calculate to 2 decimal places the ratio that the total expenses allocated to that department has to the sales of that department.

(ii) Calculate what annual sales Bin department must make and what annual sales Odd department must make so that neither department has either a profit or a loss. Assume that the level of expenses allocated between the departments will not be affected by the level of sales and will be the same total amount each year.

(iii) Calculate to 2 decimal places Boms Ltd's acid test ratio at 31 December Year 33.

With court approval, the directors of Boms Ltd made the following arrangements with the company's bank, 10% debenture holders, creditors and shareholders:

1. The bank agreed that 80% of the amount owing to it would be converted into a 15% loan, repayable in Year 45, secured on the company's buildings.

2. The 10% debenture holders agreed that their debentures would be replaced by 12.5% debentures with the nominal value reduced from £100 to £80 each.

3. The creditors agreed to allow a special reduction of 15% in return for payment within 3 months.

4. The ordinary shareholders agreed that their shares would be reduced to £0.65 paid up and that the remaining £0.35 would be immediately called up.

5. That the buildings would be written down to £40,000.

Required

(d) Prepare journal entries to record *each* of the 5 items above.

Solution

(a)   Trading Profit & Loss Account, Year ending 31 December Year 33

	Bin	Odd	Mun
	£'000	£'000	£'000
Sales	500	600	700
Cost of goods sold (residual amount)	400	480	560
Gross profit[1]	100	120	140
Departmental wages[2]	78	65	52
General expenses[3]	36	45	45
Depreciation[4]	2.0	2.5	2.5
Office wages and expenses[5]	5	6	7
	121	118.5	106.5
Net profit/loss before 'special items'	−21	1.5	33.5

		£'000	Total £'000
Net profit/loss before 'special items'	Bin	−21.0	
	Odd	1.5	
	Mun	33.5	
			14
Discounts received			5
			19
Provision for bad debts (150 × 2%)		3	
Discounts allowed		4	
Bank charges		11	
Debenture interest		10	
Directors fees		6	
			34
Net loss			−15
Balance 1 January Year 33			76
Balance 31 December Year 33			61

Notes on the allocation of specific items

1   The allocation of gross profit is based on the provision for unrealised profit on stock at 1 January Year 33 of £30,000 ÷ £150,000, ie 20% of sales of £500,000, £600,000, £700,000 are £100,000, £120,000 and £140,000.

2   Departmental wages are apportioned on the basis of:
    Bin: 6 ÷ (6 + 5 + 4) × £195,000 = £78,000
    Odd: 5 ÷ (6 + 5 + 4) × £195,000 = £65,000
    Mun: 4 ÷ (6 + 5 + 4) × £195,000 = £52,000

3   General expenses are apportioned on the basis of:
    Bin: 40 ÷ (40 + 50 + 50) × £126,000 = £36,000
    Odd: 50 ÷ (40 + 50 + 50) × £126,000 = £45,000
    Mun: 50 ÷ (40 + 50 + 50) × £126,000 = £45,000

4   The total depreciation to be allocated is:
    10% × (£100,000 − 30,000) ie £7,000
    This will be allocated on the same basis as general expenses:
    Bin: 40 ÷ (40 + 50 + 50) × £7,000 = £2,000
    Odd: 50 ÷ (40 + 50 + 50) × £7,000 = £2,500
    Mun: 50 ÷ (40 + 50 + 50) × £7,000 = £2,500

5 Office wages and expenses are apportioned on the basis of:
   Bin: $8.5 \div (8.5 + 10.2 + 11.9) \times £18,000 = £5,000$
   Odd: $10.2 \div (8.5 + 10.2 + 11.9) \times £18,000 = £6,000$
   Mun: $11.9 \div (8.5 + 10.2 + 11.9) \times £18,000 = £7,000$

(b)   **Balance Sheet at 31 December Year 33**

		£'000 Cost	£'000 Cum'l Dep'n	£'000
Tangible fixed assets				
Buildings		166		166
Fixtures		100	(30 + 7) 37	63
		266	37	229
Current assets				
Stock★		370		
Debtors	(150 − 3)	147	517	
Liabilities due within one year				
Creditors		240		
Bank		145	385	132
				361
Liabilities due more than one year				
10% debentures				100
				261
Financed by capital and reserves				
200,000 ordinary shares of £1.00 each				200
Profit and loss account				61
				261

Note to the balance sheet

★The value of stock at 31 December Year 33 is calculated as follows:

	£'000
Opening stock	
Unissued	210
Issued reduced to cost price (£150,000 − 30,000)	120
Add purchases in Year 33	1,480
	1,810
Less sales in Year 33 reduced to cost price (£1,800,000 × 80%)	1,440
Closing stock	370

(c) (i) The ratio of expenses for each department to the sales of that department: the total expenses allocated to each department are derived from the answer given above in part **(a)**.

Bin:	(121,000 ÷ 500,000%)	=	24.20%
Odd:	(118,500 ÷ 600,000%)		19.75%
Mun:	(106,500 ÷ 700,000%)		15.21%

(ii) In this case as all expenses are fixed, we will calculate the break-even point on the basis of the total expenses specifically allocated to each department compared with the gross profit margin on sales. The gross profit margin on sales has already been calculated at 20%.

Expenses ÷ Gross profit margin

		$£$
Break-even of Bin:	$£121,000 ÷ 20\%$	605,000
Break-even of Odd:	$£118,500 ÷ 20\%$	592,500

(iii) Acid test $(147 ÷ (240 + 145))$ $= 0.38 : 1$

(d)   **Journal entries**

		$£'000$	$£'000$
1	Bank account (145 × 80%)	116	
	15% loan		116
2	10% debentures	100	
	12.5% debentures		80
	Reconstruction		20
	(Note that as the 10% debentures are replaced by 15.5% debentures we must close off the 10% debenture account.)		
3	Creditors (240 × 15%)	36	
	Reconstruction		36
4	£1.00 paid-up ordinary shares	200	
	Reconstruction		70
	£0.65 (paid-up ordinary shares)		130
	Cash (200 × 0.35)	70	
	Ordinary shares		70
5	Reconstruction (166 − 40)	126	
	Buildings		126

2   Mrs Ownfig began trading 1 January Year 51. Her business plan was:

1 To achieve monthly sales in November and December at twice the monthly average for the rest of the year.

2 To sell goods on credit only.

3 For debtors to pay in full in the month following the month of sale.

4 For selling prices to be calculated giving a mark-up of 50%.

5 To purchase on credit only and spread purchases evenly throughout the year.

6 To turn over stock based on closing stock, 10 times per annum.

7 To pay creditors in the second month following the month of purchase.

8 For selling expenses, caused by sales to be 10% of sales value and to be paid during the year.

9 For general expenses to be £8,000 per annum for any level of sales value, all to be paid during the year.

10 For rent of the shop and fittings to be £7,500 per annum, all to be paid in advance on 1 January each year.

11 To introduce cash of £20,000 as capital on 1 January Year 51.

12 To draw £700 monthly.

The only business records Mrs Ownfig kept were copies of the invoices sent to customers; she destroyed these copy invoices as the customers paid. From the copies of the invoices remaining, Mrs Ownfig calculated her debtors at 31 December Year 51 to be £15,000.

Required

(a) Assuming Mrs Ownfig achieved her business plan, prepare:

  (i)   the trading and profit and loss account for Year 51

  (ii) the summarised cash account for Year 51

  (iii) the balance sheet at 31 December Year 51

(b) Calculate to the nearest £1,000 the sales turnover that would produce neither profit nor loss for Mrs Ownfig's business.

Solution

(a) (i) **Trading and Profit & Loss Account Year 51**

		£
Sales [1]		105,000
Cost of goods sold[2]		70,000
Gross profit (residual figure)		35,000
General expenses	8,000	
Rent of shop and fittings	7,500	
Sales expenses[3]	10,500	26,000
Net profit		9,000

Notes to the accounts

1	Sales	£	
	Sales for December	15,000	(December debtors from unpaid invoices)
	Sales for November	15,000	(same as December)
	Sales for other months	75,000	(15,000 ÷ 2 × 10)
		105,000	

2 Cost of goods sold   105,000 ÷ 150% = £70,000

3 Sales expenses   105,000 × 10% = £10,500

(a) (ii) **Summarised Cash Account**

	£	£
Capital introduced		20,000
Debtors (105,000 − 15,000)		90,000
		110,000
Creditors★	64,167	
Drawings	8,400	
General expenses	8,000	
Rent of shop and fittings	7,500	
Sales expenses	10,500	98,567
Closing balance of cash		11,433

213

(a) (iii)   **Balance Sheet at 31 December Year 51**

	£	£
Current assets		
Stock (70,000 ÷ 10)	7,000	
Debtors	15,000	
Cash	11,433	33,433
Liabilities payable within year		
Creditors★		12,833
		20,600
Financed by		
Capital introduced		20,000
Net profit		9,000
		29,000
Drawings		8,400
		20,600

Note to part (a)(ii) and (a)(iii)

★Amount paid to creditors is:

	£
● cost of goods sold	70,000
● cost of closing stock held	7,000
● total purchases in year	77,000
● 10 months paid 77,000 × 10 ÷ 12	64,167
● closing creditors	12,833

(b) Fixed expenses (8,000 + 7,500)	15,500
Selling price	100.0%
Less Variable expenses	
Cost of goods sold	66.6%
Selling expenses	10.0%
	76.6%
Recovered	23.4%
Turnover needed £15,500 ÷ 23.4% to nearest £1,000	£67,000

3 Pre and Lude were in partnership for many years. On 1 January Year 20, Min became a partner and the following journal entry was passed through the partnership books in respect of goodwill:

	£'000	£'000
Pre	30	
Lude	20	
Min	10	
Pre		36
Lude		24

On 31 August Year 20, Strel their sales manager became a partner. From that date the profit/loss sharing ratio was agreed as Pre : Lude : Min : Strel 2 : 2 : 1 : 1 respectively.

It was also agreed that Strel's salary as a partner would be £9,000 *less* than his salary as Sales Manager. Although Strel's salary as Sales Manager was stopped on 31 August Year 20, he still continued to receive salary payments each month at the reduced rate, in addition to making drawings. Goodwill was revalued at £72,000 on 31 August Year 20. The following is the partnership's trial balance at 31 December Year 20 *before* making any adjustment for goodwill on Strel's admission as a partner:

	£'000	£'000
Sales		103
Current assets	58	
Strel's salary payments for Year 20	9	
Expenses	11	
Liabilities due within one year		5
Tangible fixed assets at book value	144	
Cost of goods sold	44	
Drawings/Capital: Pre	15	70
Lude	10	50
Min	8	40
Drawings/Capital introduced by Strel	2	33
	301	301

Required

(a) Prepare without narrations, journal entries to show the adjustment for goodwill upon the introduction of Strel as a partner. It was decided that goodwill would remain unrecorded.

(b) Calculate Strel's annual salary *before* becoming a partner and his annual salary *after* becoming a partner.

(c) Prepare for the partnership trading, profit and loss and appropriation accounts for the year ended 31 December Year 20 and a balance sheet at 31 December Year 20.

Solution

(a)   **Journal Entry**

		£'000	£'000
Pre	$\frac{2}{6} \times 72,000$	24	
Lude	$\frac{2}{6} \times 72,000$	24	
Min	$\frac{1}{6} \times 72,000$	12	
Strel	$\frac{1}{6} \times 72,000$	12	
Pre	$\frac{3}{6} \times 72$		36
Lude	$\frac{2}{6} \times 72$		24
Min	$\frac{1}{6} \times 72$		12

(b) Salaries of Strel

The salary payments to Strel in the trial balance represents his salary as manager for the 8 months to 31 August Year 20 plus his salary as partner for the 4 months to 31 December. The annual rate of salary is £9,000 less as a partner than as a manager.

Therefore **(i)** $\frac{8}{12}$ of the salary as manager plus $\frac{4}{12}$ of the salary as partner adds up to whole salary of £9,000

and **(ii)** salary as manager less salary as partner is £9,000 per annum.

Simplifying this we have:

(i) $\frac{8}{12}$ M $+$ $\frac{4}{12}$ P $=$ £ 9,000
8 M $+$ 4 P $=$ £108,000
12 M $=$ £144,000

(ii) M $-$ P $=$ £ 9,000
4 M $-$ 4 P $=$ £36,000

Therefore:

- managerial salary is £12,000 per annum and
- partnership salary is £3,000 per annum

(c)   **Trading, Profit & Loss and Appropriation Account**

	£'000
Sales	103
Cost of goods sold	44
Gross profit	59
Expenses (excluding salary)	11
Net profit	48

	Pre, Lude, Min	*Pre, Lude, Min, Strel*
	£'000	£'000
Net profit[1]	32,000	16,000
Strel's salaries[2]	8,000	1,000
	24,000	15,000

Ratio	*Before*	*After*		
Residual	£24,000 and	£15,000		
Pre	$\frac{3}{6}$	$\frac{2}{6}$	12,000	5,000
Lude	$\frac{2}{6}$	$\frac{2}{6}$	8,000	5,000
Min	$\frac{1}{6}$	$\frac{1}{6}$	4,000	2,500
Strel		$\frac{1}{6}$		2,500
			24,000	15,000

Notes to the accounts

1. The profit of £48,000 is apportioned between the period before and after Strel's admission as a partner on a time basis:

   - before admission: $\frac{8}{12} \times$ £48,000 $=$ £32,000
   - after admission: $\frac{4}{12} \times$ £48,000 $=$ £16,000

2. The managerial salary will be charged to the period before admission and the partnership salary will be charged to the period after admission thus:

	£'000
Before: 8 months at £12,000 per annum	8,000
After: 4 months at £3,000 per annum	1,000
	9,000

Balance Sheet

	£'000	£'000
Tangible fixed assets		144
Current assets	58	
Liabilities due within one year	5	
		53
		197

Financed by Capital	Pre £	Lude £	Min £	Strel £	
Opening balance	70,000	50,000	40,000		
Cash introduced				33,000	
Goodwill brought in	36,000	24,000	12,000		
Goodwill taken out	−24,000	−24,000	−12,000	−12,000	
Net profit to 31 Aug	12,000	8,000	4,000		
Net profit from 31 Aug	5,000	5,000	2,500	2,500	
Drawings	−15,000	−10,000	−8,000	−2,000	
	84,000	53,000	38,500	21,500	197

4 The following items have been extracted from the trial balance of Quizi plc on 1 January Year 52.

	£'000	£'000
Profit & Loss Account, the company's *only* reserve		1,500
Machinery cost/Provision for depreciation	3,000	1,200
Buildings cost	1,100	
Vehicles cost/Provision for depreciation	1,400	600
Shares in Game Ltd	290	
11% debentures		750
Working capital	52	

The Directors' Report of Quizi plc prepared after the end of Year 52 stated:

'Your company had a good year. The net profit was £600,000, after charging £225,000 depreciation on machinery and £120,000 depreciation on vehicles and the £20,000 loss when some of the shares in Game Ltd were sold for £130,000. The total funds raised were used to buy additional buildings £200,000; additional machinery £300,000; additional vehicles £50,000; and to redeem part of the 11% debentures at 105 for £262,500 and to pay the full dividend of £80,000 on the company's 10% preference shares and the year's dividend of £200,000 being £0.10 per share on the company's £0.50 ordinary shares. The balance remaining increased your company's working capital.'

There were no issues or redemptions of *shares* in Year 52.

Required

Calculate the balances at 31 December Year 52 for:

1   Profit & Loss Account

2   Machinery and provision for depreciation of machinery

3   Vehicles and provision for depreciation of vehicles

4   Shares in Game Ltd

5   11% debentures

6   Buildings

7   10% preference shares

8   Ordinary share capital

9   Working capital

Solution

1 Profit & Loss Account

	£		£
Preference shares dividend	80,000	Opening balance	1,500,000
Ordinary share dividend	200,000	Net profit in Year 52	600,000
Closing balance	1,820,000		
	2,100,000		2,100,000

2 Machinery

Opening balance	3,000,000		
Cash	300,000	Closing balance	3,300,000
	3,300,000		3,300,000

Provision for depreciation of machinery

		Opening balance	1,200,000
Closing balance	1,425,000	Profit & Loss Account	225,000
	1,425,000		1,425,000

3 Vehicles

Opening balance	1,400,000		
Cash	50,000	Closing balance	1,450,000
	1,450,000		1,450,000

Provision for depreciation of vehicles

		Opening balance	600,000
Closing balance	720,000	Profit & Loss Account	120,000
	720,000		720,000

4 Shares in Game Ltd

Opening balance	290,000	Cash	130,000
		Profit & Loss Account	20,000
		Closing balance	140,000
	290,000		290,000

5 11% debentures

Cash	262,500	Opening balance	750,000
Closing balance	500,000	Premium on redemption	
		(262,500 × 5 ÷ 105)	12,500
	762,500		762,500

6 Buildings

Opening balance	1,100,000		
Cash	200,000	Closing balance	1,300,000
	1,390,000		1,300,000

7 10% preference shares

	Opening balance	
	£80,000 ÷ 10%	800,000

8 Ordinary share capital

	Opening balance	
	£200,000 ÷ 0.1 × 0.5	1,000,000

9 Working capital

Opening balance	52,000	Purchase of machinery	300,000
Net profit	600,000	vehicles	50,000
Depreciation machinery	225,000	buildings	200,000
Depreciation vehicles	120,000	Dividends	
Premium on debentures	12,500	Preference shares	80,000
Sale of shares in Game Ltd.	130,000	Ordinary shares	200,000
Loss on above	20,000	Redemption of debentures	262,500
		Closing balance	67,000
	1,159,500		1,159,500

5 Soma Stores Ltd calculates cost of goods sold by adding opening stock and purchases and deducting closing stock. The stock values are obtained from the annual stocktaking. The draft summarised balance sheet at 31 March Year 24 is as follows:

	£		£
Share capital	100,000	Freehold property	51,000
Retained earnings	39,000	Fixtures and fittings	45,000
Creditors	14,300	Stock for resale	28,500
Proposed dividend	9,000	Debtors	23,100
		Bank	14,700
	162,300		162,300

Since preparing the above balance sheet the following errors and omissions have been discovered:

1 The annual stocktaking had been delayed until 6 April Year 24. Between 1 April and 5 April the following transactions took place:

- purchases, all received, £9,400
- returns inwards, all received, £600★
- sales, all despatched, £32,000★
- returns outwards, all despatched, £360

★ Soma Stores Ltd sets selling prices, by adding 33⅓% to cost.

2 Goods supplied, received by Soma Stores Ltd from Victoria in February Year 24, on a sale or return basis, were returned in May Year 24. However, they had been recorded as purchases of £1,800 and at 31 March Year 24, were included in stock at that value.

3 One of the stock sheets prepared on 6 April Year 24 had been overadded by £900.

4 Two cheques had not been recorded in the books. They had not been presented at 31 March Year 24. The first was for £500 in respect of stationery used up before 31 March Year 24. The second was for £700 in respect of a payment in advance for stock for resale, delivered in June Year 24.

5 Cash discounts allowed to debtors of £650 in March Year 24 had still not been recorded.

6 A bulk purchase of stationery costing £1,500, from an office supplies merchant, remained unused. However, it had been included in fixtures and fittings at 31 March Year 24 and 10% of its value had been written off as depreciation.

7 The freehold property had been professionally revalued on 31 March Year 24 at £65,000. This value should have been incorporated in the accounts.

Required

(a) Calculate the corrected amount for Soma Stores Ltd's stock for resale at 31 March Year 24.

(b) Incorporating the *change* in stock value from (a) above, and other relevant items, calculate the corrected amount for Soma Stores Ltd's retained earnings at 31 March Year 24.

(c) Incorporating the answers to (a) and (b) above, redraft the summarised balance sheet of Soma Stores Ltd at 31 March Year 24.

Solution

				£
(a)	Stock per the draft balance sheet			28,500
	Less purchases *less* returns	(9,400 − 360)		9,040
				19,460
	Add sales *less* returns	(32,000 − 600)	£31,400	
	Less gross profit thereon	(31,400 × 25%)	7,850	23,550
				43,010
	Less goods received on a sale or return basis			1,800
				41,210
	Less addition error			900
	Corrected amount of stock at 31 March Year 24			40,310

				£
(b)	Retained earnings per the draft balance sheet			39,000
	Add increase in stock from **(a)** as above		£40,310	
	Less as in draft balance sheet		28,500	11,810
				50,810
	Add reduction in purchases arising from goods received on a sale or return basis			1,800
				52,610
	Less stationery cost			500
				52,110
	Less cash discounts allowed			650
				51,460
	Add depreciation written off stationery	(10% × 1,500)		150
	Corrected amount of retained earnings at 31 March Year 24			51,610

Redraft of summarised Balance Sheet

	£	£	£
Tangible fixed assets			
Freehold property			65,000
Fixtures and fittings (45,000 − [1,500 × 90%])			43,650
			108,650
Current assets			
Stocks (1,500 + 40,310)	41,810		
Debtors and prepaid expenses (23,100 − 650 + 700)	23,150		
Cash at bank (14,700 − 1,200)	13,500	78,460	
Liabilities due within one year			
Creditors (14,300 − 1,800)	12,500		
Dividends proposed	9,000	21,500	
			56,960
			165,610
Financed by capital and reserves			
Share capital			100,000
Revaluation reserve (65,000 − 51,000)			14,000
Retained earnings			51,610
			165,610

PAPER 2

1   Doreen looks after her sick father, who pays all her living expenses when she is at home. During Year 9, she had a **3-week** working holiday at a hotel in Buckland. She prepared the following profit and loss account for the holiday:

	£	£
Wages from hotel (for 25 hours' work each week)		150
Less Return train fare to Buckland	50	
Taxi fares	5	
Cost of meals not provided by hotel	35	
Cost of nurse to visit father	40	130
Net profit		20

Doreen has found out that in Year 10:

1   Under a new system of paying holiday staff at the hotel, her wages would increase by 60% but, instead of receiving free accommodation she would be charged £20 per week for bed and breakfast.

2   Her return train fare would increase by 12%.

3   Taxi fares would increase by £3 in total.

4   The cost of meals not provided by the hotel would increase by £16.

5   The nurse would charge £18 per week to visit Doreen's father.

Required

(a)   Prepare a budgeted profit and loss account for Doreen's 3-week working holiday in Buckland in Year 10. Show comparative figures for Year 9.

Doreen read the following advertisement:

> 'Pay for a 4-week holiday in Year 10 in Buckland by buying a box of 300 "Watifs" for £2,400 and selling each Watif for £10.'

Doreen is thinking of doing this, instead of her hotel work, and found out that, for Year 10:

1   She would have to hire a car to carry the Watifs to Buckland; this would cost her £87 for hire charge for the 4-week period and a £30 refundable deposit plus £0.50 for petrol and oil per kilometre. Buckland is 110 kilometres away from Doreen's home. Car insurance would cost £3 per week.

2   Her hotel bills including all meals and car parking would be £85 for Week 1 and 80% of that amount for each of Weeks 2, 3 and 4.

3   The nurse would still charge £18 per week to visit Doreen's father.

Required

(b)   Assuming Doreen can sell a whole box of 300 Watifs in 4 weeks, prepare a budgeted trading profit and loss account for the working holiday in Year 10.

(c)   Calculate:

    (i)   how many Watifs Doreen must sell during the 4-week period, so that she makes neither a profit nor a loss;

    (ii) how much Doreen must charge for each of the 300 Watifs to make a total profit of £60.

After considering the various alternatives Doreen bought a box of 300 Watifs and sold 280 of them at £10 each during the 4-week period at Buckland, keeping the rest as stock for next year. It takes on average 1 hour to sell each Watif. All transactions were made in cash and all expenses were as budgeted.

Required

    (d) Assuming the refundable deposit on the car is not returned until Year 11, prepare for Year 10, Doreen's:

        (i) trading profit and loss account

        (ii) cash account

        (iii) cash flow statement (showing the changes in the different elements of Doreen's working capital)

    (e) Calculate to 2 decimal places Doreen's profit or loss per hour in £ for Year 10:

        (i) from the budgeted profit and loss account in **(a)**

        (ii) from the budgeted profit and loss account in **(b)**

        (iii) from the actual profit and loss account in **(d)(i)**

    (f) Give 2 comments on Doreen's decision to sell Watifs in Year 10.

Solution

(a)   **Budgeted Profit & Loss Account Year 10**

Year 9 £			Year 10 £	£
150	Wages	(£150 × 160%)		240
50	*Less* Return train fare	(£50 × 112%)	56	
5	Taxi fares	(£5 + £3)	8	
35	Meals outside hotel	(£35 + £16)	51	
40	Cost of nurse	(£18 × 3)	54	
	Bed and breakfast	(£20 × 3)	60	
130				229
20	Net profit			11

(b)   **Budgeted Profit & Loss Account selling Watifs in Year 10**

			£	£
Sales		(300 × £10)		3,000
Cost of box of Watifs				2,400
Gross profit				600
Less Car expenses:	hire charge		87	
	petrol & oil	(110 × 2 × £0.5)	110	
	insurance	(£3 × 4)	12	
Hotel		(£85 + [£85 × 80% × 3])	289	
Nurse		(£18 × 4)	72	
				570
Net profit				30

Note to part (b)

The refundable deposit on car hire is not an expense; if a balance sheet were prepared it would appear as an asset.

(c) (i) How many Watifs must Doreen sell during the 4-week period so that she makes neither a profit nor a loss? Sales quantity necessary:

Fixed expenses	£570
Divided by profit per Watif (£10–8)	÷ £2
Watifs that Doreen must sell	285

(ii) Amount Doreen must charge for each of the 300 Watifs to make a total profit of £60:

	£
Purchase price for 300 Watifs	2,400
Fixed expenses	570
Target profit	60
Total sales revenue required	£3,030
Divide by number of Watifs to be sold	÷ 300
Selling price that Doreen must charge for each Watif	10.1

(d) (i) **Trading Profit & Loss Account for Year 10**

			£	£
Sales		280 @ £10		2,800
Cost of goods sold	Watifs purchased	300 @ £8	2,400	
	Less closing stock	20 @ £8	160	
				2,240
Gross profit				560
Expenses as in **(b)**				570
Net loss				10

(ii) **Cash Account for Year 10**

	£	£
Sales	2,800	
Cost of purchases		2,400
Expenses		570
Refundable deposit on hired car		30
Cash deficit	200	
	3,000	3,000

(iii) **Cash Flow Statement for Year 10**

	£	£
Net loss		−10
Increase in stock	160	
Increase in debtor (being the refundable deposit on the car which was not refunded until Year 11)	30	
	190	
Decrease in cash	−200	
		−10

Notes to the cash flow statement

1 This statement will show the sources of cash expressed in terms of Doreen's closing assets and liabilities resulting from her trading in Watifs in Year 10.

2 As this is the first trading period and there were no opening balances of stock debtors or cash all closing balances must represent an increase or decrease and the net total must equal the net loss for the period.

(e) Doreen's profit or loss per hour in £ for Year 10:

   (i) in the budgeted profit and loss account in (a)

   (ii) in the budged profit and loss account in (b)

   (iii) in the actual profit and loss account in (d)(i)

Profit/loss ÷ Hours worked = Profits/loss per hour

	£	*Number of hours*	£
(i)	+11	(25 × 3)	0.15
(ii)	+30	(300 × 1)	0.10
(iii)	−10	(280 × 1)	−0.04

(f) The two comments could refer to any of the following:

1 the total loss or the hourly loss arising by selling Watifs as compared with the profit arising from hotel work

2 whether or not Doreen has sufficient cash to finance the cash deficit

3 the disposal of closing stock; does she want to sell Watifs in Year 11?

4 can Doreen store the remaining Watifs? are Watifs perishable?

5 can Doreen afford to lose the income derived from hotel work?

6 Doreen did not sell all 300 Watifs in Year 10; would it be possible to sell 300 or more Watifs in Year 11?

7 is it safe to leave father for a fourth week?

2 Miss Take established a business on 1 January Year 11. She decided to prepare monthly accounts but had little knowledge of book-keeping. She prepared the following for January Year 11:

Cash account

	£		£
Cash sales for January	270	Staff wages (including £100 unpaid wages at end of January)	850
Receipts from credit customers (although total sales were £1,180)	980	Office rent for January	150
Cash balance at end of January	150	Fixtures, bought 1 January	200
	1,400		1,200

She says:

1   I have not included the £400 I borrowed free of interest from cousin Fool.

2   I counted the cash at the end of January and it amounted to £150.

3   I also bought stationery on 1 January for £93. I have not included it as I have not paid for it and still had £72 of it left on 31 January.

4   I think the fixtures will last 8 years and then I can sell them for £8.

5   I have also paid, in January, the same amount of office rent for February and for March but I have left them out because they do not belong to January.

Required

(a) Redraft Miss Take's cash account for the month of January Year 11.

(b) Prepare Miss Take's profit and loss account the month of January Year 11.

(c) Prepare Miss Take's balance sheet at 31 January in *good style*.

Solution

(a)   **Miss Take Cash Account**

	£		£
Cousin Fool	400	Staff wages	
		(£850 less unpaid £100)	750
Cash sales	270	Rent (3 months @ £150)	450
Credit customers	980	Fixtures	200
		Difference on cash account	
		(Assumed to be drawings but	
		could be cash lost/stolen)	100
		Balance c/d	150
	1,650		1,650

Note to the cash account

The question paper gives no indication of the reason for the difference on the cash account; hence the examinee must make an assumption; the most likely reasons are cash drawings by Miss Take and cash lost. From an examination point of view, choose the most likely reason and treat it consistently through the accounts: that is, if you choose drawings charge it to the proprietor of the business or if you choose cash lost/stolen charge it to the profit and loss account.

(b)   **Miss Take Profit & Loss Account for January Year 11**

	£	£
Cash sales		270
Credit sales		1,180
		1,450
Wages[1]	850	
Rent[1]	150	
Depreciation[2]	2	
Stationery[3]	21	
		1,023
Net profit		427

Notes to the accounts

1   Re wages and rent. Miss Take has inserted in her cash account for these two items the amount incurred during January; hence in correcting the cash account the amount actually paid has been substituted, but in preparing the profit and loss account, the amount incurred is used.

2   Depreciation is calculated: cost of the fixtures £200 less residual value £8 divided by 8 years divided by 12 months, ie (£200 − 81) ÷ 8 ÷ 12 = £2 as depreciation for one month.

3   Re stationery. Miss Take bought £93 stationery but had left £72 worth at the end of the month, therefore she must have used the difference in the month, namely £93 − 72 = £21. The amount unpaid will appear as a liability in the balance sheet.

(c)   **Miss Take Balance Sheet at 31 January Year 11**

	£ Cost	£ Depn	£
Fixed assets			
Fixtures	200	2	198
Current assets			
Stationery	72		
Debtors	200		
Cash	150		
Prepaid rent	300	722	
Liabilities payable within one year			
Wages	100		
Stationery	93	193	529
			727
Liability payable more than year			
Cousin Fool[1]			400
			327
Financed by Capital			Nil
Profit			427
			427
Drawings[2]			100
			327

Notes to the balance sheet

1   It has been assumed that the loan from cousin Fool is not repayable within 1 year; it could have been repayable within 1 year.

2   This item has been treated as drawings.

3   In a report to the board of directors of Pin plc, the Finance Director states:

Although the company has a zero balance at bank, its liabilities due within 1 year amount to £20,000; it should issue at par sufficient ordinary shares of £1 each fully paid for cash, to give an acid test ratio of 1.1 : 1 as compared with the present acid test ratio of 0.1 : 1.

Required

(a) Calculate how many ordinary shares Pin plc must issue to achieve an acid test ratio of 1.1 : 1.

Another director asks:

The company has ordinary shares of £55,000 but no balances on reserves; its present ratio of ordinary shares to fixed interest loans is 0.55 : 1. What will it be if we issued the shares proposed by the Finance Director?

Required

(b) Calculate the new ratio of ordinary shares to fixed interest loans if the number of ordinary shares you have calculated in (a) were issued.

The Finance Director proposes to improve the company's financial position by:

1   issuing the number of ordinary shares calculated in (a) above

2   reducing the level of stock held (at present £8,000) from 3 months' consumption to 1½ months'

3   reducing the credit allowed to debtors (at present £2,000) from 4 months to 3 months

4   keeping the liabilities due within 1 year at £20,000

Required

(c) Assuming that *all* the Finance Director's proposals above are carried out, calculate the proposed amounts for each current asset and then the new working capital ratio.

Solution

(a)   **Ordinary Shares to be Issued**

	Acid test ratio being	*Current assets*	÷	*Liabilities due within one year*
		£		£
Present	0.1 : 1.0	2,000	÷	20,000
Required	1.1 : 1.0	22,000	÷	20,000
Therefore issue at par		20,000		

(b)   **New Ratio of Ordinary Shares to Fixed Interest Loans**

	Ratio	*being*	*Ordinary shares*	÷	*Fixed interest loans*
			£		£
Present	0.55 : 1.0		55,000	÷	100,000
Shares issued in (a)			20,000		
New ratio	0.75 : 1.0		75,000	÷	100,000

(c)   **Working Capital Ratio**

	Before	Proposed
	£	£
Stock[1]	8,000	4,000
Debtors[2]	2,000	1,500
Bank[3]		24,500
		30,000

Revised working capital ratio
Current Assets as above   30,000
      Divided by liabilities due within 1 year   ÷ 20,000
                                                                                                     = 1.5 : 1.0

Notes to the ratio

			Proposed consumption	*Present consumption*		
1	Stock	£ 8,000	× 1½	÷ 3	=	4,000

			Proposed credit	*Present credit*		
2	Debtors	2,000	× 3	÷ 4	=	1,500

			Stock	*Debtors*		
3	Bank	20,000	+ (8,000 − 4,000)	+ (2,000 − 1,500)	=	24,500

4 Door and House began trading as partners on 1 January Year 82 selling Omros and Souds only. Door agreed to sell all the Omros and House agreed to sell all the Souds. As they were unsure how to divide their net profits/losses, they agreed at first to divide net profits/losses on the basis of the gross profit earned by the goods each partner sold.

However, as business was very good, Rat became a partner on 1 September Year 82. The partners agreed to share profits/losses Door : House : Rat in the ratio 5 : 4 : 2, respectively from then onwards.

Analysis of the sales of £200,000 for the Year ended 31 December Year 82 showed:

1   55% of the total sales volume related to Omros.

2   The monthly average sales of Omros was the same throughout the year.

3   The monthly average sales of Souds was seasonal, being twice as much in April, May, June, July, August and September as in the remaining months.

4   The cost of goods sold was 70% of the selling price for Omros and 60% of the selling price for Souds.

The general expenses of £30,000 for the year ended 31 December Year 82 accrued evenly throughout the year.

Required

(a) Divide the total sales value for the year between Omros and Souds.

(b) Calculate the sales value of (i) Omros and (ii) Souds:

(A) before Rat became a partner

(B) after Rat became a partner

(c) Making all calculations to the nearest £, prepare for Door, House and Rat, the trading, profit and loss and appropriation account for Year 82. Use columnar form to show the period 1 January to 31 August separately from the period 1 September to 31 December.

(Note that the examiner has split the instructions into 3 sections to lead the candidate into a logical approach and straightforward way of answering the question, namely to begin by dividing the total sales between Omros and Souds, then to calculate the sales value of the two different items sold into the periods before and after the change in profit/loss sharing ratio caused by the introduction of the new partner and finally to prepare the trading, profit and loss and appropriation account. The candidate should follow the suggested approach.)

Solution

(a) Divide the total sales for the year between Omros and Souds

			£
Omros	55% of total sales	55% × 200,000	110,000
Souds	45% of total sales	45% × 200,000	90,000
			200,000

(b) Calculate the sales value of (i) Omros and (ii) Souds before and after Rat became a partner

	Before	£	*After*	£
(i)	Omros $8/12$ × 110,000	73,333	$4/12$ × 110,000	36,667
(ii)	Souds ([3 × 1] + [5 × 2])		([1 × 2] + [3 × 1])	
	÷ 18 × 90,000	65,000	÷ 18 × 90,000	25,000
		138,333		61,667

(c) **Trading Profit & Loss and Appropriation Account Year ended 31.12.82**

		Before		*After*	
		Omros	*Souds*	*Omros*	*Souds*
		£	£	£	£
Sales as in (a)		73,333	65,000	36,667	25,000
Cost of goods sold	Omros 70%	51,333		25,667	
	Souds 60%		39,000		15,000
Gross profit		22,000	26,000	11,000	10,000

	£	£
Gross profit before Rat became a partner	48,000	
Gross profit after Rat became a partner		21,000
General expenses $^8/_{12}$ before	20,000	
$^4/_{12}$ after		10,000
Net profit	28,000	11,000

Divided between partners
Before on basis of gross profit

		£	£
Door	22,000 ÷ (22,000 + 26,000) × 28,000	12,833	
House	26,000 ÷ (22,000 + 26,000) × 28,000	15,167	

After in agreed ratio

		£	£
Door	5 ÷ 11 × 11,000		5,000
House	4 ÷ 11 × 11,000		4,000
Rat	2 ÷ 11 × 11,000		2,000
		28,000	11,000

5   The summarised Balance Sheets of two companies at 31 March Year 26 are as follows:

	Elephant Ltd £'000	Mouse Ltd £'000
Assets *less* liabilities	1,491	243
Financed by:		
Share capital (£1 ordinary shares fully paid)	1,350	180
Share premium	NIL	18
Retained earnings	141	45
	1,491	243

Included in the assets of Elephant Ltd are 120,000 shares in Mouse Ltd purchased on 1 April Year 24 for £162,000. On that date, the balance on Mouse Ltd's share premium account was £18,000 and its only other reserve was retained earnings of £6,000. Elephant Ltd has no other subsidiary companies.

Required

(a) Prepare the summarised consolidated balance sheet of Elephant Ltd and its subsidiary company at 31 March Year 26. The goodwill/capital reserve arising on consolidation should be shown as a separate item.

(b) Redraft your answer to (a) bringing into consideration *both* the following items:

   (i) Mouse Ltd made a bonus (capitalisation) issue of 1 share for 10 on 31 March Year 26 out of retained earnings.

   (ii) Mouse Ltd has in stock at 31 March Year 26 goods sold to it by Elephant Ltd for £10,000. This figure includes a mark-up of 25% on the cost to Elephant Ltd.

Solution

(a) **Summarised Consolidated Balance Sheet at 31 March Year 26**

	£'000
Intangible fixed assets	
Goodwill arising on consolidation[1]	26
Assets *less* liabilities[2]	1,572
	1,598
Financed by:	
Share capital £1 ordinary shares fully paid	1,350
Retained earnings[3]	167
Minority interest[4]	81
	1,598

Notes

1. Goodwill arising on consolidation

	£
Cost of shares purchased	162
Less proportion of assets *less* liabilities of Mouse Ltd	
$120 \div 180 \times (180 + 18 + 6)$	136
	26

2. Assets less liabilities

Assets *less* liabilities of Elephant Ltd	1,491
Less cost of shares in Mouse Ltd	162
	1,329
Assets *less* liabilities of Mouse Ltd	243
	1,572

3. Retained earnings

Retained earnings of Elephant Ltd	141
Add proportion of profits of Mouse Ltd after acquisition	
$120 \div 180 \times (45,000 - 6000)$	26
	167

4. Minority interest

Proportion of assets *less* liabilities of Mouse Ltd	
$60 \div 180 \times 243,000$	81

(b) Redraft of summarised consolidated balance sheet at 31 March Year 26. Please observe that the question asks for a redraft of the consolidated balance sheet of (a) bringing into consideration *both* points (i) and (ii). Therefore one balance sheet only is required for section (b) of the question.

Redraft of the Summarised Consolidated Balance Sheet at 31 March Year 26

	£'000
Intangible fixed assets	
Goodwill arising on consolidation	26
Assets *less* liabilities[1]	1,570
	1,596
Financed by	
Share capital £1 ordinary shares fully paid	1,350
Capital reserve[2]	8
Retained earnings[3]	157
Minority interest	81
	1,596

Notes

1 Assets less liabilities

	£
As originally	1,572,000
Less mark-up on goods received from Elephant Ltd held in stock of Mouse Ltd at 31 March Year 26	
$10,000 \times 25 \div 125$	2,000
	1,570,000

2 Capital reserve

	£
Bonus issue $10\% \times 180,000$	18,000
Less profits prior to acquisition	6,000
	12,000
Proportion to group $12,000 \times 120 \div 180$	8,000

3 Retained earnings

	£	£
As originally		167,000
Less retained earnings absorbed in bonus issue		
as in **(b)**	8,000	
mark-up in stock held by Mouse Ltd		
as in **(a)**	2,000	
		10,000
		157,000

APPENDIX 3
Extracts from Statements of Standard Accounting Practice and Financial Reporting Standards

After carefully studying this appendix you should be able to:

1 *apply good accounting style and give minimum information required for publication;*

2 *apply fundamental accounting concepts and bases;*

3 *ascertain accounting bases used from given accounts;*

4 *understand the main features of significant Statements of Standard Accounting Practice (SSAPs) and Financial Reporting Standards (FRSs) relating to:*

SSAP 2	*: Disclosure of accounting policies*
SSAP 9	*: Stocks and long-term contracts*
SSAP12	*: Depreciation*
FRS 1	*: Cash flow statements*
SSAP 14 and FRS 2	*: Group accounts*

In Third Level Accounting the students must be able to prepare accounting statements and data in accordance with basic accounting conventions and current accounting practice with reference to:

1 disclosure of accounting policies

2 stocks and long-term contracts

3 accounting for depreciation

4 cash flow statements

5 group accounts

Appendix 3 contains summaries and quotations from the Financial Reporting Standards (FRS) and the Statements of Standard Accounting Practice (SSAP) to enable candidates to comply with this element of the syllabus.

Disclosure of accounting policies

If accounts are prepared on the basis of assumptions which differ in material respects from the generally accepted fundamental accounting policies, the facts must be explained.

If no explanation is given it is assumed that the accounts are prepared on the generally accepted concepts, bases and policies which are given below:

Concepts

The four fundamental concepts are:

1   *Going concern* The enterprise will continue in operational existence for the foreseeable future. As a result the final accounts are prepared on the basis that there is no intention to terminate the business or any significant part of it.

2   *Accruals* Revenue and costs are accrued in the period in which they are earned or incurred, not when the money is received or paid.

3   *Consistency* There is consistency of accounting treatment of like items within each accounting period and from one period to the next.

4   *Prudence* Revenue and profits are not anticipated. They are recognised by inclusion in the profit and loss account only when realised in the form of cash or of other assets, the ultimate cash realisation of which can be assessed with reasonable certainty. Provision is made for all known liabilities (expenses and losses), whether the amount of these is known with certainty or is a best estimate available.

Bases

The bases are the methods developed for applying fundamental accounting concepts to financial transactions and items in financial accounting to:

1   determine the accounting periods in which revenue and costs should be recognised in the profit and loss account

2   determine the amounts at which material items should be stated in the balance sheet

Policies

The concepts are the specific accounting bases selected and consistently followed by a business enterprise as being in the opinion of management appropriate to its circumstances and best suited to present fairly its results and financial position.

Stocks and long-term contracts

The terms used here include:

Stocks

The following may arise under the heading of stocks:

1   goods or other assets purchased for resale

2   consumable stores

3   raw materials and components purchased for incorporation into products for sale

4   products and services in intermediate stages of completion

5   long-term contract balances

6   finished goods

Cost

Cost is the expenditure which has been incurred in the normal course of business in bringing the product or service to its present location and condition.

It comprises:

1   cost of purchase (purchase price, import duties, transport, handling costs and other directly attributable costs, less trade discounts etc)

2   cost of conversion, being costs specifically attributable to production and production overheads based on normal level of activity

3   other overheads to bring the product or service to its present location and condition

Stocks are stated in the periodic financial statements at the lower of:

(a)   cost

(b)   net realisable value of the separate items of stock or of groups of similar items

Cost may be calculated on any of the following bases:

1   *Average cost* This is calculated by dividing the total cost of units by the number of units on a continuous, periodic or moving periodic basis.

2   *FIFO* (first in first out) This is calculated on the assumption that the units on hand are the latest purchased or produced.

3   *Replacement cost* This is the cost at which an identical asset could be purchased or manufactured.

4   *Standard cost* This is calculated on the basis of the management's estimates of expected levels of costs and operations and related expenditure.

Note that the following bases are not acceptable:

1   *Base stock* This is calculated on the assumption that a fixed number of units has a predetermined price, and any excess number of units is valued on a different basis.

2   *LIFO* (last in first out) This is calculated on the assumption that the units on hand are the latest purchased or produced.

Net realisable value means the actual or estimated selling price after deducting trade but not settlement discounts, less all further costs to completion and all costs to be incurred in marketing, selling and distributing.

Long-term contract

A long-term contract is one that takes a long time to complete, usually more than 1 year and falling into 2 or more accounting periods. If it is not accounted for as a long-term contract there would be distortion of the turnover and attributable profit in the financial statements.

When the outcome of a long-term contract can be assessed with reasonable accuracy, the total estimated profit, after allowing for all costs, may be prudently apportioned on the basis that the amount of the work completed to the accounting date bears to the total amount of work and taken to profit and loss account. In the balance sheet, there should be shown the difference between the contract price apportioned on the basis that the amount of the work completed to the accounting date bears to the total amount of work, less any payments received on account to the balance sheet date.

However, all foreseeable losses must be written off regardless of the amount of work that has been completed at the accounting date.

The accounting policies used in relation to stocks and long-term contracts must be disclosed and applied consistently.

Accounting for depreciation

Fixed assets are those which are intended for use on a continuing basis in the enterprise's activities. This statement applies to all fixed assets other than: investments, investment properties, goodwill and development costs.

Depreciation is the measure of the wearing out, consumption or other reduction in the economic life of a fixed asset, whether arising from use, effluxion of time, or obsolescence through technological or market changes.

Depreciation should be allocated so as to charge a fair proportion of cost or valuation of the asset to each accounting period expected to benefit from its use.

In order to allocate to the accounting periods, it is necessary to consider the asset's:

1 carrying amount, ie cost or valuation

2 length of expected useful economic life

3 estimated residual value at the end of its expected useful economic life

If there is a permanent diminution in the value of a fixed asset, it should be written down immediately to the estimated recoverable value which will then be allocated to its remaining useful economic life.

If it would give a fairer presentation of the financial results, the enterprise may change its method of depreciation; the new method will be applied to write off, over its remaining useful life, the net book value of the asset at the time of the change.

Freehold land is not usually subject to depreciation but should be written down if the value is diminished due to depletion or change in the desirability of its location. Buildings are subject to depreciation in the same way as other fixed assets, even though they have longer useful economic lives.

It is necessary to disclose, in the financial statements for each major class of depreciable asset, each of the following:

1 depreciation method used

2 useful economic life or depreciation rate used

3 total depreciation charged for the period

4 gross amount of depreciable assets and related accumulated depreciation

Cash flow statements

Cash flow is an increase or decrease in an amount of cash or cash equivalent resulting from a transaction. A cash flow statement includes all the business's inflows and outflows of cash and equivalents except purchases/sales of cash and equivalents.

The format of cash flow statements should list inflows and outflows of cash and equivalents in the financial period, in the following standard format derived from Financial Reporting Standard No 1:

Example Ltd
Cash Flow Statement for the year ended 31 December Year 52

	Note	£'000	£'000
Net cash inflow from operating activities	(1)		3,967
Returns on investments and servicing of finance			
Interest received		3,011	
Interest paid		−12	
Dividends paid		−2,417	
Net cash inflow from returns on investments and servicing of finance			582
Investing activities			
Payments to acquire intangible fixed assets		−71	
Payments to acquire tangible fixed assets		−1,496	
Receipts from sales of tangible fixed assets		42	
Net cash outflow from investing activities			−1,525
Net cash inflow before financing			3,024
Financing			
Issue of ordinary share capital		211	
Repurchase of debenture loan		−149	
Expenses paid in connection with share issues		−5	
Net cash inflow from financing			57
Increase in cash and equivalents	(2)		3,081

Essential Reconciliations Appearing as Notes to the Cash Flow Statement

1 *Net cash inflow from operating activities*

	£
Operating profit	3,100
Depreciation charges	893
Loss on sale of tangible fixed assets	6
Increase in stocks	−194
Increase in debtors	−72
Increase in creditors	234
Net cash inflow from operating activities	3,967

2 *Increase in cash and equivalents*

	Year 52 £	Year 51 £	Change in year £
Cash at bank and in hand	529	681	−152
Short-term investments	23,936	20,700	3,236
Bank overdrafts	−11	−8	−3
Increase in cash and equivalents	24,454	21,373	3,081

Comment

As taxation does not form part of the Third Level Accounting syllabus, all references to it have been omitted from the above.

Group accounts

The following summarises the sections of Financial Reporting Standard No 2, relevant to Third Level Accounting.

1 An undertaking is a parent undertaking if it:

   (a) holds or controls the majority of voting rights of another undertaking or

   (b) has the right to appoint a majority of the voting rights of the board of another undertaking or

   (c) has the right to exercise or in fact does exercise a dominant influence over another undertaking due to provisions in the other undertaking's constitution or a control contract.

   A parent undertaking should usually prepare consolidated financial statements and every subsidiary must usually be included.

2 The total of minority interests must be shown as a separate item in both the consolidated profit and loss account and the consolidated balance sheet of the group.

3 To the extent that they are reflected in the book value of assets included on the consolidation the full amount of any profits or losses arising from transactions between undertakings within a group must be eliminated.

4 All undertakings within the group must usually adopt the same accounting policies and the same accounting period for the purposes of the consolidation.

APPENDIX 4
Outline answers to practice questions

1.1 **(a) (i)** Current assets;

  (ii) Capital and reserves;

  (iii) Earnings per share;

  (iv) Acid test ratio;

  (v) Balance sheet

(b) (i) £545

  (ii) £520

  (iii) £0.1

  (iv) 1 : 1

(c) *Balance Sheet at 31 December Year 18*

	£'000	£'000
Tangible fixed assets		390
Current assets	545	
Liabilities due within 1 year	215	330
		720
Liabilities due after 1 year		200
		520
Financed by Capital and Reserves		520

1.2 Turnover
14 Returns inwards (deducted)

Cost of sales
16 Cost of raw materials
 6 Remuneration production staff
13 Manufacturing overheads
 1 Depreciation of lorries for raw materials

Gross profit

Distributive expenses
 2 Depreciation of delivery vehicles
 3 Salesmen's vehicles
 9 Remuneration of sales staff

Administrative expenses
 4 Depreciation of motor vehicles of non-executive directors
 5 Auditors' remuneration
10 Legal fees re debts
 7 Office salaries
 8 Non-executive directors' fees

Interest payable
11 Bank overdraft interest
12 Loan interest more than 5 years

Profit on ordinary activities

Extraordinary charges
18 Uninsured fire loss

1.3 **(a)** Fees £500,000 Staff salaries £375,000 Expenses £9,825 Profit £115,175
Int on drawings £5,700 Commissions £875 Salary Isi, £4,000
Fixed Capital Interest £20,000 Residual Solis £39,000, Isi £32,000,
Taurus £25,000

(b)

	Solis	Isi	Taurus
	£	£	£
Balance 1 January Year 27	−18,375	−16,600	800
Residual profits	32,000	32,000	25,000
Commission/Salary/Commission	375	4,000	500
Interest on fixed capital	10,000	7,500	2,500
Interest on drawings	−2,000	−1,900	−1,800
Drawings	−20,000	−19,000	−18,000
Balance 31 December	9,000	6,000	9,000

(c)

	Solis	Isi	Taurus
Balance 1 January Year 27	200,000	150,000	50,000
Revaluations in			
210,000 + 60,000 3 : 2 : 1	135,000	90,000	45,000
Revaluations out	−70,000	−70,000	−70,000
Revised balance	265,000	170,000	25,000

1.4 **(a)** $117,450 \div (2,358 + ((25 \times 100 \div 125) - 29)) = £50$.
Subscriptions $117,450 + 1,450 - 1,000 = 117,900$

(b) $117,900 (100,000 + 23,580) =$ Excess E/I £5,680.

(c) $100,000 \div (50 - 10) = 2,500$.

(d) Subscriptions $(2,358 \times 8 \div 9) \times (50 \times 120 \div 100) = 125,760 -$ expenses
$(100,000 + (23,580 \times 8 \div 9)) =$ Excess I/E £4,800.

2.1 **(a)**

	A	B	C	
	£	£	£	£
Net profit				36,000
Loan interest		3,600		3,600
				32,400
Interest on drawings	−950	−900	−250	2,100
				34,500
Interest on capital	3,000	2,500	2,000	7,500
Salary B		6,000		6,000
Commission A	1,800			1,800
				15,300
Residual profits	9,600	6,400	3,200	19,200
	13,450	17,600	4,950	
Minimum guaranteed	−1,050		+1,050	
	12,400	17,600	6,000	

(b)

	A	B	C	
	£	£	£	£
Net profit				36,000
Loan interest		1,500		1,500
				34,500
Interest on drawings				
Interest on capital				
Salary B				
Commission A				
Residual profits	11,500	11,500	11,500	34,500
Minimum guaranteed	11,500	13,000	11,500	

(c) Albert Dr £900; Bill Dr £4,600; Cyril Cr £5,500.

2.2 **(a)** $(-32 + 12 + 45 + 80 + 45) \div (1 + 2 + 3 + 4 + 5) \times 6 = £60$.

(b) Mouse $(20,000 \times 60\%) \div 60,000 = 20\%$;
Eli $(100\% - 20\%) \times 60\% = 48\%$; Funt 32%.

(c) Balance Sheet: Tangible fixed assets £130; Current assets £165;
Liabilities £20.
Capital: Eli $(180 + 15 + 30 - 28.8) = £196,200$;
Funt $(60 + 10 + 20 - 19.2) = £70,800$; Mouse $(20 - 12) = £8,000$.

3.1 **(a)** 1.1 Debenture interest accrued Dr £100,000 Bank Cr £100,000
15.2 Dividend payable Dr £2,000,000 Cr Bank £2,000,000
1.4 Bank Dr £2,500,000 8% debentures £2,500,000
1.7 Interim dividend Dr £1,400,000 P & L or Debenture interest
Dr £150,000 Bank Cr £1,550,000
31.12 P & L Dr £3,200,000 Interim dividend Cr £1,400,000
Final dividend Cr £1,800,000
P & L or Debenture interest expense Dr £200,000
Debenture interest accrued Cr £200,000

(b) Capital and reserves

	£
20,000,000 ordinary shares of £0.5 fully paid	10,000,000
Liabilities due more than 1 year	
50,000 8% debentures of £100 each fully paid	5,000,000
Liabilities due within 1 year	
Debenture interest	200,000
Proposed final dividend	1,800,000

3.2 **(a)** Administration expenses

13,000 + 170,000 + 8,000 ((160,000 − 100,000) × 0.5%)
+ (160,000 − 100,000 × 99.5% × 3%) = £193,091

Distribution expenses

(135,000 × 20%) + (800,000 − 600,000) × 0.5%) = £28,000

Profit & Loss Account (for publication)

Turnover £800,000 − Cost of sales £560,000 = Gross profit £240,000

Administration £193,091 Distribution £28,000

Exceptional losses £110,000   Loss £91,091

Retained loss b/f £100,000 Retained loss c/f £191,091

(b) Balance Sheet

Tangible fixed assets Land and buildings £110,000

Machinery costs £117,000 Motor vehicles £88,000 = £315,000

Current assets Stock £55,000 + Debtors £57,909 +

Investments £96,000 = £208,909

Creditors due in 1 year Debentures £108,000 +

overdraft £66,000 + Other creditors £141,000 = £315,000

Capital and Reserves Ordinary shares £250,000

Preference shares £150,000

P & L Dr Account £191,091 = £208,909

Note

Preference share dividends are 3 years in arrears, amounting to £45,000.

(c) **(1)** Cash Dr £58,000 Land and Buildings Cr £50,000
Cap recons Cr £8,000

(2) Recons Dr £17,000 Prov Depn Machinery costs Dr £53,000
Machinery costs Cr £70,000
Recons Dr £40,000 Prov Depn Vehicle Dr £47,000
Vehicle Cr £87,000

(3) Recons Dr £7,596 Stock Cr £7,596

(4) Recons Dr £2,619 Prov Discounts Dr £81
Prov Bad Debts Cr £2,700

(5) Cash Dr £115,806 Horse shares Cr £96,000 Recons Cr £19,806

(6) Debentures Dr £108,000 Cash Cr £108,000

(7) Recons Dr £15,000 Cash Cr £15,000

(8) Cash Dr £100,000 £1.00 Ordinary shares Dr £250,000
£0.50 Ordinary shares Cr £125,000 Recons £225,000

(9) Recons Dr £191,091 P & L Cr £191,091

(10) Crs Cr £141,000 Cash Cr £70,500 Recons Cr £70,500

4.1 **(a)**

		Goodbye Ltd	Adios Ltd
(i)	Working capital	4.6 : 1	2.2 : 1
(ii)	Acid test	1.7 : 1	1.3 : 1
(iii)	Gross profit	20%	33.3%
(iv)	Return on capital employed	10%	15%
(v)	Sales to fixed assets	10 times	10 times

(b) **(1)** £106,000

(2) £100,000

(c) Fixed assets £720,800 Stock £650,000 Debtors £750,000
Creditors £300,000 Bank £400,000 Ordinary shares £1,000,000
Profit & Loss Account £400,000
Profit on sale of shares in Adios Ltd £20,800.

(d) Tangible fixed assets £708,300 Goodwill £10,000 Stock £810,000
Debtors £830,000 Bank £10,000 Creditors £354,000
Bank overdraft £400,000 10% Debentures £96,000
Ordinary shares £1,000,000 Profit & Loss Account £397,500
Profit on sale of shares £20,800 Minority interest £1,000,000.

(e) Cash Dr £110,000 Application and Allotment Cr £110,000
Application and Allotment Dr £10,000 Cash Cr £10,000
Application and Allotment Dr £240,000
Ordinary shares Cr £200,000 Share premium Cr £40,000
Cash Dr £140,000 Application and Allotment Cr £140,000
First call Dr £100,000 Ordinary shares Cr £100,000
Cash Dr £99,900 First call Cr £99,900
Forfeited shares Dr £100 First call Cr £100
Ordinary shares Dr £300 Share premium Dr £40 Forfeited shares Cr £340
Second call Dr £99,900 Ordinary shares Cr £99,900
Cash Dr £99,900 Ordinary shares Cr £99,900.

5.1 **(a)** Sales £300,000 Opening stock £20,000 Purchases £338,333
To branch £93,333 Closing stock £25,000 Cost of goods sold £240,000
Gross profit £60,000 Expenses
$(50\% \times 52,000 \times 300 \div 400) + (50\% \times 52,000 \times 4 \div (4 + 1)) = 40,300$
Net profit £19,700.

(b) Head Office Trading £93,333 Dr
Goods sent $(112,000 - 18,667) = £93,333$ Cr.

(c) Goods sent £112,000 Dr Sales $(400,000 - 300,000) = £100,000$
Stock £12,000.

(d) Stock $(12,000 \times 20 \div 120) = £2,000$ Dr
Sales $(100,000 \times 20 \div 120) = £16,667$ Dr
Goods sent $(112,000 \times 20 \div 120) = £18,667$.

(e) Expenses $(6,500 + 5,200) = £11,700$ Net profit £4,967
Gross profit £16,667.

5.2 **(a)**

		N £	I £	C £			N £	I £	C £
Mar 1	Cash (90)	50,000	667	44,333	May 1	Cash (90½)	40,000	1,067	35,133
Jun 1	Cash (92)	70,000	−467	64,867	July 1	Cash		400	
					Aug 1	Cash (60)	60,000	400	35,600
					Dec 31	Balance (55)	20,000		11,000
						Acc'd int		800	
Dec 31	P & L		2,467			P & L			27,467
		120,000	2,667	109,200			120,000	2,667	109,200

(b) Exceptional loss in Profit & Loss Account.

5.3 **(a)** **(i)** Purchases Dr £33,000 Rent Dr £600 Selling and delivery Dr £1,900 Jules Dr £6,300 Vernes Dr £4,200 Sales Cr £41,500 Stock Cr £4,500.

(ii) Bank Dr £15,000 Bank Dr £18,000 Profit Dr £6,300 Cash Cr £36,000 Stock Cr £2,700 Bal Cr £600.

(iii) Bank Dr £600 Bank Dr £1,900 Bank Dr £36,000 Bank Dr £4,200 Bal Dr £600 Cash Cr £6,500 Cash Cr £35,000 Stock Cr £1,800.

(b) Jules Stock Cr £2,700 Vernes Cr £600 Goodwill Cr £1,200. Vernes Stock Cr £1,800 Jules Dr £600 Goodwill Cr £800.

5.4 **(a)** **(i)** Jan (Nov £120 + Dec £532) = £652; Feb (Dec £140 + Jan £608) = £748; Mar (Jan £160 + Feb £304) = £464.

(ii) Jan (Oct £400 × 80% × 97%) = £310.4; Feb (Nov £600 × 80% × 97%) = £465.6; Mar (Dec £700 × 80% × 97%) = £543.2.

(b) Jan 1 Bal Dr £100.0 + Feb Dr £341.6 + Mar Dr £282.4 + Int £12.7 − Apr Cr £79.2.

6.1

Faras plc Cash Flow Statement for Year 9	$'000
Net cash inflow from operating activities	40
Servicing of finance	−23
Investing activities	−16
Net cash inflow before financing	1
Net cash outflow from financing	−5
Decrease in cash and cash equivalents	−4

7.1 **(a)** $\dfrac{\text{Fixed expenses}}{\text{Contribution}} = \dfrac{(4,200 + 1,800 + 10\% \,(7,400 - 1,400))}{[50 - (2 + 23 + 15)]} = \dfrac{6,600}{10} = 660 \text{ members}$

(b)

Year	24	25	26	27	28
	$	$	$	$	$
No × cont	600 × 10 = 6,000	800 × 10 = 8,000	950 × 10 = 9,500	1,050 × 10 = 10,500	1,170 × 10 = 11,700
General expenses	1,800	1,854	1,910	1,967	2,026
Salaries	4,200	4,410	4,631	4,862	5,105
Depreciation	600	600	600	600	600
I/E (E/I)	(600)	1,136	2,359	3,071	3,969

(c)

		JFM		AMJ		JAS		OND
		$		$		$		$
Loan		6,000						
Subscriptions (No × 50 annually)	231	11,550	145	7,250	112	5,600	106 + 7	5,650
		17,550		7,250		5,600		5,650
Badges (3,000 × 2)		6,000						
Concert tickets (600 × 23)		13,800						
Fittings		7,400						
Dinners (600 × 15)								9,000
Salaries (4,200 ÷ 12 = 350)	× 2	700	× 3	1,050		1,050		1,050
General expenses (1,800 ÷ 12 = 150)	× 1	150	× 3	450		450		450
		−28,050		−1,500		−1,500		−10,500
B/fwd				−10,500		−4,750		−650
		−28,050		−12,000		−6,250		−11,150
Receipts		17,550		7,250		5,600		5,650
C/fwd		−10,500		−4,750		−650		−5,500

Interest 20% × (3 ÷ 12) × (10,500 + 4,750 + 650 + 5,500) 1,070

(d)

Income & Expenditure Account	$
Contribution (600 × (50 − (2 + 23 + 15)))	6,000
Fixed (4,200 + 1,800 + 600 + 1,070)	7,670
Excess of expenditure over income	1,670

Balance Sheet

Fixed assets $6,800 Current assets $5,100
Liabilities due in 1 year $7,570 Liabilities due after 1 year $6,000
Accumulated fund excess of expenditure over income $1,670

8.1 **(a)**

	Sales	Stock 1 Jan	Goods sent	Stock 31 Dec	Gross profit
	$	$	$	$	$
X	240,000	150,000	193,000	16,000	48,000
Y	120,000	14,000	93,000	17,000	30,000

	Admin Expenses	Selling	Distribution to shops	Distribution from shops	Bad debts	Net profit
	$	$	$	$	$	$
X	3,900	26,400	8,170	18,667	1,363	−10,500
Y	2,600	13,200	3,830	9,333	1,027	10

(b) Average stock turnover: Xmouth 12.4, Yarville 5.8.

8.2 **(a)** Stock £99,000 + Cash (£66,000 × 2) = £132,000 = £231,000
Suppliers (£99,000 ÷ (3½ − 2)) = £66,000

(b) Stock (£99,000 × 180%) = £178,200 +
Cash (£132,000 − £100,000) = £32,000 £210,200
Suppliers (£66,000 + (£99,000 × 80% × ½)) = £105,600

    (c) Cash Dr £42,500 Application and allotment Cr £42,500
        Application and allotment Dr £12,500   Cash Cr £12,500
        Application and allotment Dr £75,000   Debentures Cr £70,000
          Premium Cr £5,000
        Cash Dr £45,000   Application and allotment Cr £45,000
        Call Dr £30,000   Debenture Cr £30,000
        Cash Dr £30,000   Call Cr £30,000

9.1   **(a)** Going concern; Accruals; Consistency; Prudence.

    (b) (1) Accounting period: Assumption that it is possible to break up the continuance of the life of an entity into separate discrete periods, usually one year.

        This necessitates predictions in relation to unfinished transactions. Without this assumption it would be impossible to measure profit until an entity was wound up.

    (2) Entity: Accounting statements are prepared in respect of entities as distinguished from the persons who are associated with those entities.

        Transactions will therefore be recorded from the viewpoint of the entity and can include transactions between owners and entity. It makes possible the distinction between expenses and appropriations of profit.

    (3) Money measurement: Accounting records only those events which can be measured in monetary terms.

        This enables assets and liabilities of an entity to be expressed in terms of a common denominator and therefore capital and profit to be 'measured'. Much relevant information cannot however appear in financial statements as it cannot be measured in money terms.

    (4) Materiality: In the measurement of assets, liabilities and profit, departures from other concepts are permissible in the interests of simplicity when the effect of such departures is immaterial. This prevents accounting statements becoming cluttered with unnecessary detail.

10.1   **(1)** M £27,000

    (2) O 5,000 + 7,200 + 4,000 + 9,100 + 13,400 = £38,700

    (3) N 100 ÷ 125 × £10,000 = £8,000

    (4) D (15,400 ÷ 11 × (7 + 1)) + (1,400 × 7) = £109,200 = £182,900

10.2   **(a) (i)** £17,750 = (1,500 × 7.5) + (1,000 × 6.5), ie 2,500 units.

     (ii) £13,000 = (2,000 × 5.0) + (500 × 6.0), ie 2,500 units.

(b)	$(2,500 + 1,000 + 500 - 2,000) \times 15$	£30,000	£30,000
(i)	$17,750 + 12,250 - 16,000$	14,000 16,000	
(ii)	$13,000 + 12,250 - 10,000$		15,250 14,750
(c) (i)	Unchanged	16,000	
(ii)	$14,750 - 10,000 + 3,000 + 4,000$		11,750

10.3 FIFO **(1)** $310 **(2)** $550 **(3)** $55 **(4)** $90 **(5)** $803 **(6)** 20 kg **(7)** $2 **(8)** $150 **(9)** $900 **(10)** $2,255 **(11)** 410 kg **(12)** $2,255.

LIFO **(1)** $350 **(2)** $550 **(3)** $55 **(4)** $75 **(5)** $924 **(6)** 20 kg **(7)** $9 **(8)** $125 **(9)** $790 **(10)** $2,255 **(11)** 410 kg **(12)** $2,255.

11.1 **(a)** **(1)** 8 years **(2)** £1,500 **(3)** £565 **(4)** £2,353 **(5)** £1,200 **(6)** £40,800 **(7)** Straight line **(8)** 4 years **(9)** £8,500.

(b) Depreciation is the 'measure of wearing out, consumption or other loss of value of a fixed asset, whether arising from use, effluxion of time or obsolescence through technology and market changes'.

11.2 **(a)** **(i)** 1 Apr £74,700 Purchases £53,850 Trade in £28,200 Sales £67,350 31 March £89,400.

(ii) Sales £24,600 31 March £25,200 1 Apr £31,920 P & L £17,880.

(iii) Disposals Q Loss £945 P Profit £570 T Loss £1,050.

(b) It reflects rapid fall in value initially; balances against increasing repairs; greater cost reflects greater reliability.

			£
11.3	**(a)**	**(i)**	4,500
		(ii) $(126,000 \div (20 - 4) \times 0.6) +$ $((592,800 - 126,000 - 108,000) \times 0.10) =$	40,605
		(iii) Cost $(48,250 - 6,000 + 9,600) = 51,850$ Depn $(27,600 - (6,000 \times 12\frac{1}{2}\% \times 5) = 23,850$ $51,850 - 23,850 \times 25\% =$	7,000
	(b)	Non-distributable increase $(570,000 - 270,000 - [175,500 + 4,500]) =$	120,000
		Distributable decrease $((6,000 \times 3 \times 12\frac{1}{2}\%) - 2,000) =$	250

Index